Taming the Search-and-Switch Customer

Earning Customer Loyalty in a Compulsion-to-Compare World

Jill Griffin

JOSSEY-BASS
A Wiley Imprint
www.josseybass.com

Published by Jossey-Bass
A Wiley Imprint
989 Market Street, San Francisco, CA 94103-1741—www.josseybass.com

Readers should be aware that Internet Web sites offered as citations and/or sources for further information may have changed or disappeared between the time this was written and when it is read.

Limit of Liability/Disclaimer of Warranty: While the publisher and author have used their best efforts in preparing this book, they make no representations or warranties with respect to the accuracy or completeness of the contents of this book and specifically disclaim any implied warranties of merchantability or fitness for a particular purpose. No warranty may be created or extended by sales representatives or written sales materials. The advice and strategies contained herein may not be suitable for your situation. You should consult with a professional where appropriate. Neither the publisher nor author shall be liable for any loss of profit or any other commercial damages, including but not limited to special, incidental, consequential, or other damages.

The following are trademarks of the Griffin Group: The Loyalty Maker (registered trademark), Search-and-Switch Customer (trademark pending), Worth-It Test (trademark pending), and Customer Switch-O-Meter (trademark pending).

Jossey-Bass books and products are available through most bookstores. To contact Jossey-Bass directly call our Customer Care Department within the U.S. at 800-956-7739, outside the U.S. at 317-572-3986, or fax 317-572-4002.

Jossey-Bass also publishes its books in a variety of electronic formats. Some content that appears in print may not be available in electronic books.

Library of Congress Cataloging-in-Publication Data

Griffin, Jill.
    Taming the search-and-switch customer : earning customer loyalty in a compulsion-to-compare world / Jill Griffin.—1st ed.
        p. cm.
    Includes bibliographical references and index.
        ISBN 978-0-470-34504-7 (cloth)
        1. Customer relations.   2. Customer loyalty.   3. Customer services.   I. Title.
    HF5415.5.G7533 2009
    658.8'12—dc22
                                                        2008050160

Printed in the United States of America
FIRST EDITION
HB Printing   10 9 8 7 6 5 4 3 2 1

This book is dedicated to Pat McMahan,
who will forever be a shining light in my world.

Contents

Move On Now!

Preface

It seems like just yesterday . . . I was feeding rolls of dimes into copiers at the Austin Public Library, faithfully reproducing page after page of articles from *Inc.*, *Business Week*, *Forbes*, *Fortune*, *Harvard Business Review*, and the like. Copying the pages was the easy part! Poring over tons of extraneous material in scores of periodicals to *identify* what I wanted was far tougher. But it had to be done. It was 1992, and I was in the throes of early research for what became my first book, *Customer Loyalty: How to Earn It, How to Keep It*, and this information would become documentary notes for the manuscript.

What a difference just a few years make! Now I type a subject into a search box, punch a key on my computer, and Eureka! Instant information.

The ease and precision with which information can now be secured is astonishing. Make no mistake about it: this instant information and the search technologies that deliver it are having a huge influence on how, why, and when people buy. Customer loyalty strategies have turned to a brand-new page.

That's what this book is all about.

As I write this early in the morning, sitting at my home office desk (in my well-worn Stein Mart bathrobe), I'll give it to you straight: I weep nostalgically—*not*—for the good ole library research days. Punching a computer key is simply grand.

Glad to have you with me on this loyalty learning journey.

Jill Griffin
Austin, Texas
www.loyaltysolutions.com

Introduction

Does your brand ace the Worth-It Test in the minds of buyers?

In side-by-side comparisons to key competitors, does your brand prevail?

If your firm is like most, very little time gets spent probing these fundamental questions. Yet, ironically, your customers are surely asking them! Using Internet search engines, your customers are relentlessly comparing . . . *What's available? From whom? With what attributes? At what price?* . . . and switching to your competitors because you come up short.

Consider this book your wake-up call about a new breed of buyer: the Search-and-Switch Customer. The Internet and its search engines have created a compulsion-to-compare planet of buyers, with almost unlimited choice and near-perfect customer information. The requirements for earning and keeping loyalty in this new world are shifting dramatically, and this book will help you mobilize.

Make no mistake about it: businesses in every B2B and B2C market are facing profound, game-changing challenges. No firm is immune, including yours. The power of the Internet search has leveled the competitive playing field as never before, and every position in your firm's organization chart is affected. From the C-suite to operations and across sales, marketing, customer call centers, and the rest, all employees have vital roles to play in ensuring that your firm consistently aces its competitors.

This book is organized as a blueprint of sorts, with three inter-related sets of building blocks. Although each part or chapter of the book can be useful as a stand-alone read, the best learning comes from starting with Chapter One and following through to Chapter Nine.

Here's a quick tour of what's in store.

- *Part One: Get a Grip.* Finding it harder and harder to keep customers? The first two chapters examine how and why the Internet has unleashed intense buying scrutiny unlike anything most firms have ever experienced. In Chapter One, "Welcome to the Compulsion-to-Compare Planet," you'll read about four ever-present market factors that together induce the customer's relentless comparison of purchase options. In Chapter Two, "Why Customers Search and Switch," you'll learn what triggers a customer's search to compare. Moreover, you'll learn what makes a customer's search erupt into a switch, and get an overview of proven ways to lessen these risks.

- *Part Two: Get the Credit You're Due.* This part of the book goes deeper into strategies and guidelines for taming your customers' search-and-switch tendencies. Chapter Three, "Ace Your Buyer's Worth-It Test," describes how to analyze your customer's worth-it mentality and get A+ credit for the customer value you deliver. In Chapter Four, "Manage Perception Makers and Takers," you'll get a close-up look at the three participating parties in any customer relationship: (1) the brand, (2) the customer, and (3) prospects, observ-ers, and influencers who "listen in" or "weigh in" about the brand. You'll see how these three parties separately and collectively feed perceptions about your brand in the mar-ketplace, and you'll learn steps to take to ensure that the perceptions are as positive as possible. Chapter Five, "How to Be (and Stay) Damn Different," is the last chapter in this section on the basics of taming search-and-switch behavior.

In a marketplace brimming with customer "informedness" and limitless competitors, achieving differentiation is a necessity, and this chapter examines what it takes to do differentiation "right." But *being* different requires one set of skills, whereas *staying* different requires another. What's considered unique and different today becomes standard fare tomorrow. This chapter provides insights, examples, and practical guidelines on how to infuse your firm with constant, ongoing innovation to enable your brand to stay different.

• *Part Three: Fortify Your Firewall.* There's still more you can do to keep customers from straying. Part Three shows you how to further insulate your brand from search-and-switch behavior. Chapter Six, "Build Customer Trust," outlines why customer trust is a huge competitive advantage in a search-and-switch world. Then you'll find an easy-to-use, six-stage framework around which you can craft your firm's trust-building plan. (Building a trust plan will be a first for most firms.) In Chapter Seven, "Find and Grow Passionate-to-Serve Employees," you will get a refresher on the subtle but powerful connections between employee attitudes and employee behaviors. From there, you will follow the path of a three-stage life-cycle strategy designed to nurture employees' passion to serve. Whether you are working with a job candidate, new recruit, or veteran employee, you will learn proven ways to anchor and build both employee advocacy and customer centricity at critical employee milestones. Chapter Eight, "Look for Tamers That Teach," takes you inside five carefully chosen B2B and B2C firms to learn how each has leveraged important, but different, skill sets for keeping customers from straying in a compulsion-to-compare world.

• *Part Four: Move On Now!* The Ten-Day Taming Plan in Chapter Nine gives you a way to begin putting into practice the hundreds of guidelines and examples you have read. Following the process outlined in this tool will give you a strong foundation for launching more and more search-and-switch prevention initiatives.

You know the familiar fable: the frog swims in the pot of water on the stove and remains unconcerned and complacent while the temperature steadily rises. When the water reaches the boiling point, the frog is still in the pot, and by that time, it's too late to take action.

The competitive waters in which you swim are heating up fast. Don't delay.

Part I

Get a Grip

1

Welcome to the Compulsion-to-Compare Planet

"I Googled it." These three words describe the game-changing customer behavior that is rewriting the rules for winning customer loyalty.

Think about it: your customer's use of Google or other search engines is now a ubiquitous, taken-for-granted behavior. Listen in on any conversation when folks are discussing new discoveries, and chances are you'll hear, "I Googled [fill in the blank] and found it!" The experience of typing a few keywords into a search engine, hitting the Enter key, and in about a second having a wonderland of relevant listings and links pop up on your screen is downright habit forming. The power of search routinely delivers plenty of payoff to both B2C and B2B customers, making its value delivery indisputable. Little wonder that customers' time online devoted to searching continues to grow.

But know this: when it comes to holding on to your best customers, the power of search in itself is not your biggest worry. Your real threat is what the ability to search breeds in your customers and prospects: *the compulsion to compare your offerings against others*. Make no mistake—the compulsion to compare is an ever-present customer behavior. It's like a special type of gravity that can pull your buyers away from you and into the orbits of your competitors. Left unaddressed and unmanaged, this behavior can lead to switched-away customers and the big losses of sales and profit that follow.

Here's why. Search technologies have enabled an unprecedented state of customer "informedness."[1] The average buyer today can quickly garner near-perfect product information: what's available, from whom, with what attributes, and at what price. Routine customer searches can pit your brand against countless competitors at any given moment. What can trigger your customer's urge to compare? A big service mishap or budget cut can do it. But perhaps even more troubling is that simple curiosity or sheer boredom may be all that's required. Many firms are oblivious to these threats.

Consider the small, niche textile manufacturer supplying linens and chefs' clothing to hotels and restaurants. After rapid growth in the East and Midwest, the Pennsylvania-based firm was looking to expand westward. When the CEO was advised to draw on search-term advertising by buying such key terms as "restaurant napkins" to help efficiently and aggressively attract linen buyers across the United States, his "business as usual" perspective kicked in. "I don't have to be on Google," he declared. "Every linen-rental company knows me."[2] But he was ignoring some tough new realities: purchasing managers come and go in companies; these managers are getting increasingly younger, and younger buyers are more apt to go online. The bottom line: his buyers will increasingly tap into the cyber-marketplace with compulsion-to-compare behaviors, and his firm must aggressively compete there too.

This CEO's story is a classic: he's an extremely hard working, resourceful business leader with a track record of success, whose firm is ripe for solutions for taming today's search-and-switch-prone customer. Can you relate? Want to know more? *Welcome to the compulsion-to-compare planet.*

What's Driving the Compulsion: Four Forces

Human beings have an innate hunger for information and are designed to be "infovores," according to Dr. Irving Biederman, professor of neuroscience at the University of Southern California, whose studies on brain activity suggest that humans experience real pleasure in acquiring information.[3] This finding alone goes a long way to explain today's customers' compulsion to compare. But other factors are driving the behavior as well.

The never-before convergence of four powerful forces is making your customers' already natural compulsion to compare more potent than ever:

1. **Underserved customers**
2. **Unprecedented choice**
3. **Spot-on Web search listings and links**
4. **Bottom-up, social media activism**

For each of these four forces, there are specific underlying factors that feed your customers' insatiable desire to compare. Let's examine these four forces in detail.

Force 1: The Underserved Customer

Two types of underserved customers—service seekers and newness seekers—have deeply rooted compulsion-to-compare tendencies.

Service Seekers

Today's buyers span four generations: the Silent or GI Generation (born 1901–1945), baby boomers (born 1946–1964), Gen X (born 1965–1977), and Gen Y (born 1978–2000). Some three-quarters of these customers have earned the real-world equivalent of a "PhD in Buying" through the twenty to sixty-plus years of consumption experience they have under their belts. These buyers know exactly what real service looks like, and when they don't get it, they move on. Sadly, despite all the talk about improving the customer experience over the past decade, a majority of customers still feel underserved due to subpar service across many industries. A recent worldwide consumer survey by Accenture found that 88 percent of respondents reported suboptimal experiences, 47 percent saying that their expectations were met only sometimes and 41 percent rating service quality fair, poor, or terrible; 59 percent of respondents reported switching service providers during the past year due to bad service experiences. Accenture found that the number of consumers switching due to bad service had increased in relation to the prior year.[4]

Newness Seekers

Another large contingent of underserved customers feeds the compulsion-to-compare threat. Look no further than the seventy million members of Gen Y in the United States, sometimes referred to as millennials. This group is now 26 percent of the overall population; they not only make many of their own purchasing decisions but also heavily influence purchasing decisions in their households. Gen Y consumers feel underserved, but not for reasons related to service. Compared to prior generations, this group cares far less about a quality, personalized shopping experience and far more about keeping up with what their friends and colleagues have and having the newest product of its kind. Having come of age as consumers during a period of rapid, unprecedented advances in technology and connectivity (Internet, e-mail, cell phones, instant messages, MP3 players, camera phones, and so on), members of Gen Y have a preconditioned ravenous appetite for what's new, and feel underserved by firms that don't deliver it. How do they soothe their frustration? By constantly looking out for who's offering what's new and different.[5]

Recognize these newness seekers for the big threat they are! This group with arguably the strongest propensity to compare is seventy million buyers strong and, of all the generations of buyers, has the most lifetime spending value still to come! Now or sometime soon, your brand is likely to need Gen Y buyers.

"I think we'll need a bigger boat" is the oft-repeated line from *Jaws* uttered by the Amityville Island chief of police when he first sees the huge shark with his own eyes. As you start thinking about Gen Y buyers' compulsion to compare and how you will be mobilizing your brand to defend against it, a bigger boat may well be in order.

Force 2: Unprecedented Choice

What motivates underserved buyers to invest time comparing your brand to others? Their belief that plenty of other choices await.

Choice helps drive the compulsion to compare, and today's buyers have a wide number of options from which to select across nearly every industry and brand category. Three factors contribute to this flood of choice.

Fewer Buying Boundaries

For a quick glimpse into the array of choices available to today's customers, walk in the shoes of brides-to-be planning their dream weddings. "I see brides who are inundated with extra choices and options and ideas," reports Rebecca Ginnals, owner of Engaging Concepts, a Florida-based wedding industry consulting firm. "Before the Internet, you were limited to what you found in a bridal magazine or in your hometown. You might have looked at seven candidates for the perfect photographer. Now you might be looking at 70 or 700."[6]

Or ask nursing student Cynthia Zapata, who wanted a designer wedding gown without the designer price. First, she scouted on eBay and connected with a dressmaker able to replicate Zapata's gown of choice—a Casablanca bridal dress that retailed for $1,200. Zapata e-mailed the dressmaker photos of the dress and a few weeks later received the finished gown. Her price: $175 plus a $50 shipping charge. The dressmaker's location? China.[7]

More E-Tailing Choices

Because the Internet offers cost efficiencies unrivaled in any other selling channel, both B2C and B2B vendors are using the Web to provide buyers with wider and deeper product assortments than ever offered before. Little wonder that both B2B and B2C online business continues to skyrocket. During the 2007 holiday season, shoppers spent a whopping $28 billion online, an impressive 19 percent increase from just the year before.[8] Facing fierce online competition, e-tailers are, generally speaking, delivering value for customers. The University of Michigan reports that online retailers are one of the highest-rated industry groups tracked by its American Customer Satisfaction Index.[9]

Private Label Picks Up

If the words *private label* conjure up an image of products wrapped in white packaging with black letters, you'd better push the Delete key on that unit of your memory bank. That's because retailers in Europe and, increasingly, the United States are launching their own powerful brands, further expanding choice availability for today's customers.

Savvy retailers, such as the retail club Costco, have trained their shoppers to expect high quality from private-label products. Through its highly popular private-label line, Kirkland Signature, Costco has applied cobranding strategies to increase shopper appeal. Observed Neal Stern, analyst with McMillan/Doolittle, "the idea with Costco was: Do you really trust Kirkland to make good tires? Well, maybe. But you do trust Kirkland *and* Michelin? It's a way to work with manufacturers such as Whirlpool with refrigerators and Paul Newman with juice where you need some legitimacy and credibility. It allows Costco to go to a top-tier supplier and co-brand with someone who has respect. It's an unbeatable combination."[10]

Look for more expansion of retailers' own brands both in-store and online. Why? Because retailers are using insights from their own loyalty programs and research to out-innovate branded consumer goods manufacturers. After all, retailers, not manufacturers, control the necessary tools—sales data and in-store and online test-drive capability—to adapt and innovate quickly.

Force 3: Spot-on Search Listings and Links

No doubt, the world is brimming with brand choices. But in reality, for choice to succeed in stimulating a customer's compulsion to compare, it must be accessible. The Internet and the search engines that probe it empower customers with accessible choices and, as a result, play powerful, pivotal roles in driving buyers' compulsion to compare.

Internet use has become the norm in America. A recent Pew survey on Internet behaviors found that 73 percent of American adults[11] and 87 percent of American teens use the Internet.[12] The Pew study found that 49 percent of American adult Internet users use a search engine *daily* to find information.[13]

The survey found that the spread of higher-speed, always-on, broadband connections has amplified and intensified Internet use—with people spending more time logged on and increasingly considering the online world as a desirable destination to simply "while away" some time. A recent BurstMedia survey of thirteen thousand Web users (ages eighteen to over sixty-five) found that three out of five respondents visited more Web sites in a typical week than they did one year earlier. Two-thirds of respondents said that their daily routine would be disrupted if their Internet access was taken away and not available for one week, and 43 percent said "significantly" so.[14]

U.S. workers are avid Internet users. The average employee spends roughly eighty-one hours each month online.[15] Search is a valued on-the-job activity, as indicated by these sky-high usage statistics:

- 85 percent of business executives use search,[16] and nearly every member of a purchasing committee uses a search engine sometime in the buying process.

- 80 percent of business executives turn to search to learn more about a product or service, compare it against alternatives, or read reviews about products and services.[17]

- 96 percent of B2B buyers report either finding everything they were looking for online through a search engine or discovering some information online, which they supplemented with offline information. Less than 1 percent said that the search experience was unsuccessful.[18]

Vertical search engines are out to further enhance the shopper's search experience. Web studies find that typical buyers' initial searches are done on a general engine (usually Google) and then as participants move through the research phase, they tend to interact more and more with vertical engines specific to their industry. Consider the B2B vertical search engine Business.com. To assist the seven million business buyers who come to its site each month, Business.com provides drill-down search categories, such as "Construction" (building materials, software, interior design, and so on), "Human Resources" (company policies, employee evaluation, benefits, and so on), and "Transportation & Logistics" (trucking, warehouse management, containers, air freight and cargo, and so on).[19] Such B2B search sites are out to save business buyers significant click time and win their site loyalty in the process. The site's search algorithms are designed to ensure, for example, that the engineer searching with the keyword *pump* for an industrial installation does not get a listings page populated with site links for women's shoes.

B2B marketers understand the targeting potency of search and its ability to position a company's message smack dab in front of a prospect actively searching for the very thing the B2B firm sells. Little wonder that nearly two-thirds of B2B marketers now earmark resources for search engine optimization and other search marketing when formalizing their firms' annual marketing budgets.[20]

Force 4: Social Media Activism

Our picture of compulsion-to-compare forces is almost complete— so far, we've seen how *underserved customers* are empowered with *unprecedented choice* garnered through *spot-on Web search listings and links*. What remaining force helps drive customers' relentless comparison? The opinions of their fellow buyers and shoppers. To fully appreciate the importance of buyers' sharing with buyers, let's take a quick look back in time. Before the Internet, buyer information was mainly a tightly controlled, one-way communication from the enterprise to the customer—think golf outings with reference accounts, creatively edited customer testimonial letters, and firm-hosted trade show dinners with carefully drawn seating charts. Firms largely controlled brand perceptions by making sure that buyers were exposed only to carefully selected information about other customers and their user experiences. Any customer information shared was typically screened and sanitized to ensure that the firm looked good. Even Web 1.0 was dominated by corporate sites overflowing with customer recommendation letters, Web site testimonials, and other corporation-sponsored content.

But Web 2.0's onslaught of social media tools changed these dynamics forever. The advent of blogs, wikis, social networking sites, message boards, RSS alerts, and the like have provided a platform for buyers to share their opinions as customers, without company oversight. This empowerment and authenticity has strongly resonated with shoppers, creating a sea change in how customers now make purchase assessments. In fact, customers now trust each other more than they trust marketing. A recent Nielsen worldwide study in forty-seven markets across the globe found that over three-quarters of respondents (78 percent) rated recommendations from other consumers as the most trusted form of advertising, compared to 63 percent for newspapers and 56 percent for TV and magazines.[21]

Today's bottom-up social media put the opinions of fellow customers front and center. Here's how.

It's a Jungle out There

In the old Tarzan movies filmed in the 1930s and 1940s (featuring Johnny Weissmuller as Tarzan and Maureen O'Sullivan as Jane), tribal drumbeats kept everyone in the jungle alert and informed about what was happening. From telegraphing the invasion of greedy diamond merchants and animal captors to announcing the arrival of helpful do-gooders, a drum language of sorts helped Tarzan, Jane, and the jungle community stay in the know. Think of the Internet's surging flow of blogs, message boards, and other social media as online drumbeats, signaling a cyberbuzz ranging from hard-core factual news, product information, and how-tos to assertion and rumor and, occasionally, downright falsehoods.

Customers' participation in social media will only grow stronger, according to the longitudinal survey work of Roper Starch Worldwide. This firm's fascinating research shows that as more information sources infiltrate people's worlds and they have more and more means of creating and sharing information, people will become even more attached to word-of-mouth sources.[22]

It's a phenomenon that the social networking site Facebook knows well. Its open platform has encouraged programmers worldwide to create innovative new ways for members to share information on the site. Consider ShareThis, a free feature offered by hosted social commerce provider Bazaarvoice. The feature enables, for example, a college student who is psyched about the Hewlett-Packard laptop he just purchased to share the news by posting on his Facebook profile a link to a review that he or someone else wrote. The post, which can also include an HP logo or an image of the laptop alongside a brief comment from the student, will show up on his profile mini feed and in the news feed his Facebook friends see.

Gen Y Lives Online

Gen Y buyers are more heavily influenced by peer groups and word of mouth in the form of text messaging, e-mail, and blogs than they are by such traditional authorities as brand advertising. A Maritz Research poll of shoppers ages eighteen to thirty found that 69 percent said they text approximately seventeen messages per day and that 67 percent use online reviews as a source when making purchasing decisions; 26 percent have posted an online product review.[23]

Online Reviews Keep Growing

Gen Y buyers are not alone in actively seeking and giving customer advice online. More customers across all demographic groups are following suit. A recent Deloitte consumer group survey found that 62 percent of the respondents to an online poll said they read online product reviews written by other consumers. More than eight in ten (82 percent) of those who read reviews said that their purchasing decisions have been directly influenced by those reviews. People have used the reviews both to confirm initial buying decisions and to change them, the study found. Further, 69 percent of the respondents said they have shared online reviews with friends, family, or colleagues—which indicates a viral word of mouth on the word of mouth itself.[24]

Recognizing the trend toward bottom-up media, firms from all types of industries are responding with online tools that leverage this customer predilection.

Take health care. WellPoint, one of the nation's largest health insurers, has teamed with Zagat to let patients rate their doctors, just as diners rate restaurants in Zagat's burgundy-colored guides. This program is available online to more than a million members. WellPoint joins the ranks of a growing list of doctor review sites, including RateMDs.com, which averages a thousand new reviews a day and has seen an eightfold increase in page views in one year. Likewise, the Web site Yelp, where folks can write a review on anything with an address, reports that queries about doctors routinely rate among the top ten most popular search topics.[25]

Are customers influenced by what they read on doctor review sites? Allergist Michael Reid says yes. His Bay Area allergy practice has doubled its number of new patients thanks to positive reviews and a $500-per-month ad on Yelp. Likewise, Manhattan ob-gyn Natalia Meimaris says that paying close attention to online reviews has helped her understand how to improve her practice, such as by getting test results back to patients more rapidly.[26]

But not all doctors are happy about the proliferation of patient reviews. When San Francisco allergist Jeffrey Davidson went online and looked himself up, he was stunned by what he read. Several patients had written negative reviews; one described him as "patronizing" and another as "unprofessional." A third patient complained that his office staff was "too young." "The things people have written about me and my staff are false and unbelievable," said Davidson, who has no reliable way to measure how many prospective patients these reviews have cost him. For example, a Google search returned an entry that said, "I had a horrible experience here and will never go back."[27] But Davidson gets good reviews too, and he's fighting back by running his own Web site and requesting that patients talk to him offline about complaints rather than posting them.

The Power of Context

The context in which a piece of information is "framed" has everything to do with how people perceive the message. Consider this scenario: you have an experience, you react to it, and then you return to your home or office and start retelling the circumstances. Friends, family, and associates pile on with their opinions and experiences, and soon you start to perceive your original experience in a different light. This new perception may be so powerful that you actually return to the folks you encountered in the original experience, but this time you bring with you a different point of view. That's the awesome power of context in action. In today's wired world, the contexts provided by social media are influencing your buyers and prospects like never before.

Think of social media as offering context on steroids. Look no further than a recent Pew study which found that when it comes to solving common problems, more people turn to the Internet than consult experts or family members to provide information and resources.[28] So, rather than a handful of family or friends, there are literally hundreds, if not thousands, of people who can serve as context makers and takers—feeding off the same original customer experience. This can be perilous perception-making ground for any brand, because product and service gaffes can galvanize customers' reactions, and the news about those mistakes spreads quickly. Referencing a politician's gaffes in the race for public office, Kathleen Hall Jamieson, the director of the University of Pennsylvania's Annenberg Public Policy Center, observes, "The public doesn't usually see something as a gaffe until it's interpreted as one by the press and then passes into popular culture."[29] That may be true in the political world, but today's social media can turn any buyer into a gaffe galvanizer. Want a quick example? Simply type a national brand name into Google, followed by the word "sucks," and you'll see plenty.

The Switch Button Looms Large

Do I stay or do I switch? This moment-of-truth question festers in the back (or front!) of the minds of *all* customers when they check out your competitors. Whether your customer is in aggressive search mode or taking a laid-back, just-for-future-information look, the "Do I switch?" question is always lurking. What makes this situation even more threatening is that the act of switching is often so effortless. At this writing, office supply store chain Staples is running its "Easy Button" campaign with the tagline "Don't stress it. Press it." Those same sentiments are in the minds of your competitors as they flaunt their wares to your customers in cyberspace and elsewhere.

Competitors Help Your Customers Switch

Your competitors are making it easier than ever for your customers to leave you. That's one of the findings from my firm's customer loss study conducted with research firm CustomerSat, in which we surveyed more than five hundred senior executives representing a wide cross section of B2B and B2C industries. Consider this eye-opening finding: 59 percent of sales executives and 43 percent of marketing executives reported using switching tools to reduce the hassles customers encounter when moving their accounts! In many industries, such as retail banking, firms have long relied on what I call the Hook Principle to retain customers. Direct deposits of social security and pension checks and automatic monthly withdrawals for insurance, telephone, and utility bills have long kept customers tied to a bank, for example, when they would just as soon leave. Customers perceive the red tape required to change banks as a big pain in the neck, hardly worth the trouble. But now competitors across many industries are wising up. They are sweetening their new customer offerings with switching assistance.

Executives surveyed in the Griffin Group study reported using a host of switching tools to woo customers away from their current vendors:

- 51 percent reported using incentives for switching (fee waivers or welcome gifts).

- 44 percent reported helping customers fill out paperwork required for switching accounts.

- 30 percent reported the use of switch kits that clarify steps customers can follow to move the account.

Tame the Tendency: Now's the Time!

So there you have it: four formidable forces enticing your customers to compare your brand against competitors. Add to that your customers' infovore inclinations and the likelihood that your competitors are offering switching assistance to your customers (or will be soon), and it's clear that you are operating in a search-and-switch marketplace.

How to cope? For starters, consider this unlikely parallel: your customers' compulsion to compare and those pesky brown patches on your lawn have a lot in common. Each is a lurking threat that can never be completely eliminated. Left unmanaged, both brown patch and compulsion-to-compare proclivities can spread to tipping-point status, with consequences that are hard to reverse. That small circle of brown, unsightly grass spreads outward, overtaking more and more of your green, healthy lawn. In the case of the compulsion to compare, tipping-point status can mean that your customer has stayed on the search task long enough to find at least one viable alternative, compared your brand against that alternative, and deemed your brand inferior or, at best, at parity. These search outcomes place your customer right in the middle of the "switch-prone zone," which in turn puts you at high risk for losing that customer!

But here's the good news: there is plenty you can do *now*—precautions to take and remedies to apply—to stop customer search and switch in its tracks. Like brown patch on your lawn, compulsion-to-compare behaviors can never be totally eliminated. But you *can* apply proven methods to tame the tendencies, minimize their negative effects, and in turn protect and sustain your customer revenue streams.

Your first step is to break the compulsion-to-compare challenge into addressable questions and manageable issues. This book gives you a three-part solution, previewed in the next sections with key queries you must confront for each part. (Part Four is a process for tying them all together.) Brace yourself for some tough, unexpected questions.

Part One: Get a Grip

To thrive on the new compulsion-to-compare planet and tame the search-and-switch tendency, your firm must dig deep and develop a keen understanding of customer behavior dynamics. It is simply impossible to craft mission-critical, results-driven solutions without it. Consider these vital queries:

- What, specifically, in your customers' buyer and user experiences triggers search? Switch?

- What is your firm's working definition of customer loyalty? Disloyalty? What customer behaviors and attitudes must be present or absent?

- When a customer becomes more loyal to your brand, what has shifted in the customer's mind-set? When the customer becomes less loyal, what mind shift has occurred?

- What are the factors in your customer's user experience that, when aligned, will trigger immediate disloyal behavior? How do you blunt the effect?

- Your customers' search intents differ. What intents most characterize your customers, and which carry the highest risks? What is your plan for addressing each search intent?

Part Two: Get the Credit You're Due

To flourish in the brave new world of buyer empowerment, your brand must consistently get the credit it's due. The overriding concern here is to ace your buyer's Worth-It Test with a powerful, differentiated value proposition that repeatedly stands its ground when tested against an assault of alternatives. Doing so involves knowing how your customers form and influence perceptions about your brand in the marketplace and making sure your brand stands out—day in, day out. Consider these key questions:

- In your customer's mind, does your brand's perceived pluses outweigh the minuses?

- How do you crack your customers' worth-it code? How do you most advantageously connect the scorecard dots that are floating around in your customers' heads?

- How does your brand stack up against the next best alternative? What's required in order for your brand to constantly win that comparison?

- In today's cyber-marketplace, there are typically three participating parties in any customer relationship. Can you name these parties? Are all three on your radar screen? Do you have a perception-building plan for each?

- In a marketplace brimming with both instant information and nearly limitless competition, how do you make your brand different? Keep your brand different?

Part Three: Fortify Your Firewall

In a search-and-switch-prone world, several factors can serve as buffers of sorts around your customers to help keep competitors at bay. This book addresses three: customer trust, passionate-to-serve employees, and the continual infusion into your firm of fresh, new customer-keeping best practices. To these ends, consider the following questions:

- Does your firm have a specific plan to consistently earn and sustain customer trust in today's low-trust business climate?

- Customer trust is built in stages over time. Is your trust-building plan designed around a multistage strategy?

- The competition for competent employees is rising fast. Does your firm have an up-to-date game plan for attracting and keeping top talent?

- Passionate-to-serve employees need constant nurturing throughout their term of employment with your firm. What best practices does your firm employ to turn prospective employees into new hires? New hires into productive employees? Established employees into fierce company advocates?

- In today's blisteringly competitive, search-and-switch marketplace, every firm needs continual inspiration to help tame customer switching tendencies. Where does your firm look for insight? From whom do you learn?

Moving On

Perhaps you found yourself answering some of the questions in the last section with lots of nos, don't knows, or not sures. If so, don't fret! You're already ahead: just by reading the questions, you zeroed in on key issues you and your firm need to address to prosper in today's compulsion-to-compare marketplace. You've begun the learning journey. The remaining chapters in this book will show you the way.

Next up is the remaining Get a Grip chapter: "Why Customers Search and Switch." Getting a handle on these fundamental principles early is essential to crafting successful strategies later. Read on.

Taming Takeaways

- For the first time in history, your customers can punch a computer key and receive instant buyer information. This puts insights about your competitors' offerings at your customers' fingertips in a few short seconds. Buyers who are even mildly dissatisfied with your product or service can now find alternatives fast.

- The limitless depth and breadth of the Internet, working in concert with the global economy, bring your business into competition with countless businesses and offer your customers a staggering array of buying choices.

- Humans by their very nature are infovores. Comparing product alternatives is one way buyers get their information fix. Expect your customers to compare your brand against others at an increasing rate. The instantaneous results offered by Google and other search engines make search time online feel productive and satisfying.

- Young customers have grown up with the constant onslaught of new technology—and they love it. From their mind-set, the product has to be not only good but also *new*. To retain these buyers, your firm will need to keep its value propositions sharp, fresh, and on the leading edge.

- By offering switching assistance in the form of monetary incentives, paperwork help, switch kits, and so on, your competitors are making it easier than ever for your customers to leave you.

- To stay ahead, you need to act now to secure new customers and keep existing ones from straying—you must make today's search-and-switch marketplace work *for* you rather than *against* you.

2

Why Customers Search and Switch

Customers and geysers: they both are prone to eruption. What can geysers teach us about taming today's customer's search-and-switch-prone tendencies? Plenty, it turns out.

When you think of the word *geyser*, you may associate it with Yellowstone National Park's Old Faithful. I always did. But the name actually originated in Iceland, and dates back to the country's Great Geysir, which first erupted in the fourteenth century. A speaking engagement recently took me to the wonderland of Iceland, where I visited the famous Strokkur geyser, which erupts every five to ten minutes. What a sight! Awaiting the eruption, I intently watched the geyser's water pool. First it was perfectly still; then there was an occasional small bubble and then bigger bubbles breaking the surface with more frequency and some steam; finally, a ferocious stream of steam and hot water shot straight up twenty meters (sixty-five feet) into the air. Like all geysers, Strokkur's power originates deep underground, where volcanic rock heats surface water that has seeped through ground fissures, and sends the boiling water skyward. After a few seconds, the fountain subsides and the surrounding waters calm . . . and Strokkur again appears placid, a sheet of clear water surrounded by wisps of steam.

Customer relationships are a lot like geysers. On the surface, they appear smooth and calm, but underneath, trouble may be brewing. "I thought everything was fine and then—bam!—I lose the account," is the sad refrain heard all too often in corporate hallways. The combination of heat, water, and mounting pressure drives a geyser eruption; what causes a change in your customer's loyalty? A big part of the answer can be found in the geyser analogy. Just as underground water grows increasingly hot and eventually flashes into steam as a geyser, the heat in a customer's "attitude pool" can build to a certain critical level, triggering a decision to switch. A *Forbes* reader, responding to the magazine's feature story on Detroit automakers and their struggles, illustrates this switch-eruption concept and the gradual, rather than sudden, development of geyser-like fury. In his letter to the magazine, the eighty-year-old reader writes,

> I've owned ten Cadillacs, half of them driven right off showroom floors, and I have never received one piece of literature from GM for my loyalty. Instead, I am asked to give a credit card number so they can charge me $5 for a complaint call on my '98 Eldorado. No thanks, GM. My next car will be a Lexus![1]

This customer didn't suddenly get annoyed with GM. The frustration had been building for years, just as the water propelling a geyser takes a while to heat. In today's Googlized, search-obsessed marketplace, what prompts your customer to search for alternatives? To switch? How can you lessen these risks? These are critical questions that deserve careful thought. Let's begin by examining four states of customer loyalty.

Stay or Switch? How Customers Move in and out of Loyalty

Generally speaking, the deeper the customer's loyalty, the less likely it is that he or she will switch. In her doctoral dissertation for the Swedish School of Economics, Christina Nordman provides fresh insights on understanding customer loyalty.[2]

What Makes Up "Loyalty"?

Dr. Nordman persuasively argues (supported by loads of scholarly research and pure common sense) that "overall" customer loyalty consists of both **behavior** (repeat purchasing) and **attitudes.** She considers the full range of customer attitudes: *positive, neutral,* and *negative.* A positive attitude suggests that the customer feels good about being involved in the relationship, and a negative attitude suggests that the customer perceives some problems in being involved in it. A neutral attitude suggests indifference—the customer perceives the relationship neither positively nor negatively.

By defining "overall" loyalty as the product of both behaviors and attitudes, Dr. Nordman examines four states: (1) true loyalty, (2) spurious loyalty, (3) spurious disloyalty, and (4) true disloyalty (Figure 2.1).

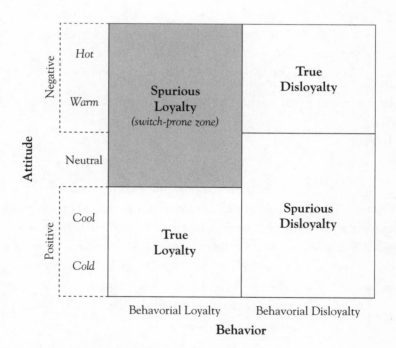

Figure 2.1.   The Four States of Customer Loyalty
Source: Adapted from Christina Nordman's diagram "Customer Loyalty Status," in *Understanding Customer Loyalty and Disloyalty,* Swedish School of Economics, 2004, p. 27.

- **True loyalty.** In the state of true loyalty, the customer has a positive attitude toward the relationship with the brand and shows behavioral loyalty. Behavioral loyalty is the customer's repeat patronage, purchases, or continued relationship (as in the case of a banking customer who maintains an account with a bank).

- **Spurious loyalty.** Random House defines *spurious* as "of doubtful genuineness." In the case of spurious loyalty, the customer shows behavioral loyalty but has a neutral to negative attitude about the relationship with the brand. Despite their attitude, such customers remain behaviorally loyal because, for whatever reason, they are unwilling at present to go through the trouble of switching. For example, a customer may keep an account at a bank, but when asked to recommend it will in effect decline by telling of personal disappointments or voicing doubts about the bank's service. Know this: *spurious loyalty is the high-risk switch-prone zone, where customers are ripe for jumping to a competitor.*

It's important to note that a person's inclination to be a loyal customer (his or her loyalty "proneness") is not necessarily the same across all product or service categories. It is possible, counsels Dr. Nordman, for a customer to be highly loyal to a hairdresser but not to a bank, or for a highly loyal bank customer to be an active switcher of telecom services. Some loyalty scholars consider loyalty proneness to be driven by the degree to which the brand choice matters to the person.

Dr. Nordman uses the term *disloyal* to describe a lack of behavioral loyalty (that is, the customer switches away), regardless of the customer's accompanying attitude. She cites two types of disloyalty: true disloyalty and spurious disloyalty.

- **True disloyalty.** The truly disloyal customer has a negative attitude combined with disloyal behavior. In Dr. Nordman's model, behavioral disloyalty includes any form of switch, from partial switching (customer switches away some, but not all monies spent with you) to total switching.

- **Spurious disloyalty.** There's that "spurious" again. In this case, the customer's attitude is positive to neutral about the relationship to the brand, but for some reason, the behavior is disloyal. To illustrate, Dr. Nordman cites the example of customers who would have preferred to stay loyal to their former bank but were forced to switch because they were not granted a loan.

Taming search-and-switch tendencies requires strategies that (1) earn your customers' true loyalty and keep them in that state, (2) get customers out of the switch-prone zone of spurious loyalty and into a true loyalty state, and (3) keep customers out of the true disloyalty space, and if they migrate there, bring them back into the state of true loyalty. This is a tall order, and to devise such strategies we need to look closer at how customer attitudes heat up and erupt into a switch.

Your Customer's Switch-O-Meter

To understand customer attitude changes and their effect on loyalty states, let's return to the geyser analogy. Think about how the combination of underground water, heat, and mounting pressure drives a geyser eruption. Now imagine that when a customer's attitude reaches a certain high "temperature," a series of switching behaviors ensues. Conversely, the lower the attitude temperature, the less likely a switch eruption will occur.* You can even envision these attitude levels and their effect on switching in terms of a device of sorts that I playfully call the Customer Switch-O-Meter. Take a look at Figure 2.2 and visualize your customer's inclination to switch in terms of temperature levels ranging from low (least likely to switch) to high (most likely to switch).

The next question is, "What drives the temperature of your customer's attitude? Answer: *loyalty drips*. Drips? Yep, that's right! Just stick with me through an extension of the geyser analogy for a minute and I'll show you why.

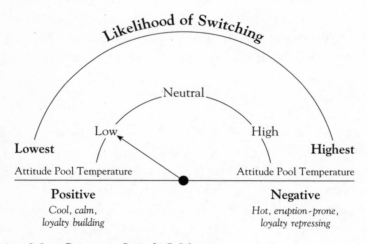

Figure 2.2.   Customer Switch-O-Meter

---

* There are two types of switch that fall outside my Customer Switch-O-Meter analogy. (1) Certain trigger events can cause a customer to switch away even when his or her attitude is very positive about your product or service. The discussion of loyalty-repressing "drips" later in this chapter explains this phenomenon in more detail. (2) Some customers will forever remain in the switch-prone zone of spurious loyalty in a given product or service category. That's because brand choice in that category is naturally unimportant to them. Think of the customer who patronizes a certain hair salon but will occasionally go to other salons as long as their pricing is low and locations are convenient.

Dr. Nordman's research finds that customers are continually influenced by factors with a *positive* effect on customer loyalty status (maintaining or strengthening loyalty) *and* by factors with a *negative* effect on loyalty status (weakening it). To stay with the geyser image, I think of these factors as drips. Imagine that much like the water from rain and snow that works its way underground through rock fractures to eventually bursts into steam as a geyser, certain factors can routinely drip into an "attitude pool" for your brand that resides in the customer's mind.

Drips have various origins and come in two varieties: loyalty-building drips, which have the effect of cooling or calming the attitude pool, and loyalty-repressing ones, which keep the temperature neutral or, in the worst case, raise it to "hot." Both kinds are likely to occur in all relationships. At any given time, a customer's attitude about your brand is the product of the combined effect of these two sets of drips. Here's how they work.

Loyalty-Building Drips: They Strengthen or Maintain Loyalty

There are two kinds of loyalty-building drips: (1) drips that build customer dedication and (2) those that promote customer constraint. Drips that increase customer dedication are things that make customers want to stay in their relationship with your brand. In other words, they have a positive effect on both customer attitude *and* behavior. That earns you true loyalty!

Constraining drips are somewhat different. Although they can have a positive effect on customer behavior (that is, the customer is constrained from switching), they also can produce a neutral to negative effect on customer attitude. Thus constraining drips can produce spurious loyalty, which, as we've discussed, puts your customer smack-dab into the switch-prone zone. Not a good thing! For that reason, this chapter will largely focus on ways to build dedication-based loyalty.

In her research, Dr. Nordman identified five key sources of loyalty-building drips.

1. Environment

Environmental factors relate to the existing surroundings that make a customer inclined to have a positive attitude and exhibit a positive behavior concerning your brand. These positive factors originate entirely outside the customer or the provider and their interaction. (Please note that the term *provider* denotes your firm, its employees, or both.)

Case in Point

Facebook

Harvard student Mark Zuckerberg launched this social networking site in February 2004 with a simple intent: create an interactive, online college student directory for his fellow Harvard students that featured each student's class schedule and social network. Facebook quickly found a following at Harvard, and then throughout Boston and across the Ivy League. Soon schools everywhere were clamoring for access, and the Facebook buzz grew even stronger as students waited their turn until Zuckerberg and team could find the time to add their school. Ultimately, Facebook rolled out beyond universities to high schools and companies; now sign-up is open to anyone. By July 2007, a mind-boggling 150,000 new users were signing up daily! By October 2007, Facebook claimed fifty million active users.[3]

Three types of loyalty-supporting environmental drips help explain Facebook's amazing membership growth and fierce loyalty among college students:

---

1. *Lack of alternatives*. Facebook provided a valuable online information service to college students that was unavailable anywhere else.

2. *Preexisting network*. Facebook was not burdened with the task of creating its user network; instead, the company created a valuable online information and communication platform to support a network of college students that naturally existed (informally) offline. This factor contributed heavily to Facebook's unprecedented popularity.

3. *Peer behavior*. Peer influence among college students is naturally strong, and Facebook's business model leveraged it well. As college students saw their peers sign on, they followed suit. After all, fear of being "out of touch," "not in the know," or "not in the group" are palpable emotions for most young people.

Zuckerberg states, "Our whole theory is that people have real connections in the world. People communicate most naturally and effectively with their friends and the people around them. What we figured is that if we could model what those connections were, [we could] provide that information to a set of applications through which people want to share."[4]

2. Provider

Loyalty-building drips in the provider category stem directly from the product or service provider or the customer's perception of the provider. They are directly related to your business and the efforts you make to produce positive attitudes and behaviors on the part of your customers and potential customers.

Case in Point

United Parcel Service

UPS set out to increase positive provider-category drips in 2005 with the implementation of its $600 million route optimization system. Every evening, the custom-built software program maps out the next day's routing for most of UPS's fifty-six thousand drivers. Whereas just a short time ago, UPS drivers depended on three-by-five note cards and their own memory to optimize their schedules, the new software even minimizes the drivers' number of left turns, thereby lowering wait time and gas spent idling at stoplights.

Before this system was implemented, when a driver left the company, his route efficiency tips left with him. No more. The new "predictive business" system captures that historical, institutional knowledge about customer deliveries into a centralized repository. The result? Burdens on substitute drivers are fewer, the training time for new drivers is shortened, and the chances of customer service lapses are reduced. That's all good news for the UPS customer depending on a driver who, on a given day, routinely delivers four hundred packages.

What's next for the new system's capabilities? Package-flow technology is being developed that will allow a customer to reroute an in-transit package to a different address. Reports Kurt Kuehn, UPS senior VP of worldwide sales and marketing, "We're trying to become a paradox: to be the biggest [delivery] company but also the most flexible."[5]

3. Customer

These loyalty-building factors stem purely from the customer or customer's life situation.

Case in Point

The Hartford

Consider these sobering statistics: the average age of widowhood in the United States is *fifty-five*. Older women are *three times* more likely to be widowed than older men. The bottom line: women live longer and typically earn less than men during their lifetimes. This means that a woman's money must work harder, longer. The Hartford is out to earn and keep the loyalty of the women's market (estimated to be 147 million strong with $6 trillion in buying power) by creating education tools that enlighten financial advisers and clients about the emotional and financial needs of widows and caregivers. For example, "Helping Families Cope with Widowhood" is a training aid that assists brokers in mastering the delicate art of compassionate communication and learning practical ways to help widowed clients understand how their income and expenses are likely to change. Reports Maureen Mohyde, director of the Hartford's gerontology group, "Research has shown that 70% of widows will take their assets to a new financial advisor within three years after the death of their husband. Clearly, this is not good for business or for women who would be better served if they could maintain a sense of financial continuity during this difficult time."[6]

4. Interaction

These are positive drips generated from the interaction between the customer and the provider.

Case in Point

Ritz-Carlton

With the goal to layer on richer, more customized experiences for its guests, Ritz-Carlton Hotel Company secured the services of IDEO, a Palo Alto design firm. Tasked with the role of "scenographer," IDEO went to work to help the luxury hotelier create new guest "scenes" featuring customized service.

First, IDEO created a set of "scenography workbooks" to be used by a handful of staff members from each Ritz property to brainstorm local service scenes. For example, one idea was to send up a champagne toast and samples from the night's menu to guests with reservations in the hotel's restaurant, accompanied by a handwritten note from the executive chef. Accounting for the risk of "too much" interaction between staff and guest, IDEO workbooks also included a section urging staff to come up with ways that such an initiative could get out of hand. Reports Len Wolin, senior director of Ritz-Carlton's program management, "We wanted to bring a little something extra out of each hotel that helps to make the experience personal, unique, and memorable. But most of all, we wanted it to be subtle."[7]

5. Core Services

These are positive drips that originate from the provider's core service or services themselves.

Case in Point

Lexus

Lexus has long been heralded as a superior provider of auto maintenance service. But the automaker continues to look for ways to reinvent its world-class approach. For example, Lexus has begun offering house calls for auto maintenance service and now trains its call center reps to coach customers through installation of their car's cell phone handsets. Says Nancy Fein, VP of customer service at Toyota's Lexus Division, "It's not enough to have cappuccino makers in dealerships anymore; you can get that at Blockbuster. We consider customer service to be an integral part of our brand."[8]

Loyalty-Repressing Drips: They Weaken or Negate Loyalty

Loyalty-repressing drips work against a firm's ability to build and maintain true loyalty. They can be categorized, according to Dr. Nordman's research, into the same five categories as loyalty-building drips. But that's where the similarities end! Loyalty-repressing drips are *not the exact opposites* of loyalty-supporting factors. In other words, the factors that help build loyalty are often very different from those that suppress loyalty. That's why firms must be aware of, and pay attention to, both!

1. Environment

As you learned earlier in this chapter, environmental drips originate outside the relationship. In consumer banking, the market sector on which Dr. Nordman based her research, loyalty-repressing drips of the environmental variety include negative word of mouth, peer behavior, competitors' attraction, press, advertising, and macroeconomic factors (the price of gas, for example).

Case in Point

Harley-Davidson

A steady stream of negative environmental drips is repressing the motorcycle titan's customer loyalty building. Here are four:

1. *U.S. demographic shifts.* After fifteen years of unprecedented growth fueled by baby-boomer customers, the boomer age group, the heart of Harley's buyer demographic, is on the decline as a motorbike market force.

2. *Image issues.* Remember the ad campaign "This is not your father's Oldsmobile"? Harley is facing a similar issue: many boomers' kids want to ride *anything* but their parents' brand of bike.

3. *Tough competitors priced right.* Competitors, such as Honda, Suzuki, and Yamaha, offer sleek, high-performing bikes that Gen X and Y buyers like, at a price point substantially below Harley's price tag.

4. *Big-ticket discretionary challenges.* An uncertain economic environment wreaks havoc on cycle sales. After all, a Harley-Davidson cycle is anything but a household necessity. The subprime mortgage debacle, which began to unfold in 2007, along with rising gas prices, are just two examples of negative economic influences hampering buyer enthusiasm.

2. Provider

These negative factors are linked directly to the service provider or the customer's perception of the provider.

Case in Point

JetBlue

One week after an extraordinary service stumble, JetBlue CEO David Neeleman made an unusual visit to the *Late Show with David Letterman* to try to help repair the damage. Neeleman's unlikely TV appearance in February 2007 was proof positive that the airline had a perception problem that needed addressing—fast. JetBlue had built its image on "bringing humanity back to air travel," but when a devastating ice storm hit JFK Airport, its home base, the airline had a close-to-chaos meltdown of operations—holding passengers for hours on planes and canceling over a thousand flights over a six-day period. Admitted Neeleman, "We should have acted quicker. We should have had contingency plans that were better baked to be able to [unload] customers."[9] JetBlue's average delay (between February 13 and 15), according to travel data firm FlightStats, was 230 minutes, compared to Delta and American at 205 and 202 minutes, respectively. But the event's repercussions for JetBlue's reputation are likely more grave. Observes Valarie Zeithaml, marketing professor at the University of North Carolina, "It runs totally counter to who they are coming out and saying they are and what they live."[10]

3. Customer

These factors stem purely from the customer's life situation or personality.

Case in Point

Kids Getting Older, Younger

KGOY (kids getting older, younger), also known as age compression, is a negative customer drip that has toy makers and toy retailers scrambling. "Tweens," kids ages eight to twelve, are rejecting traditional toys for more sophisticated gadgets, including mobile phones, MP3 players, and video games. Unlike the good old days, when toy makers largely competed with each other, today's toy manufacturers must also compete with the likes of Sony, Nintendo, Apple, and Microsoft for these young, increasingly sophisticated consumers' loyalty and buying power.

4. Interaction

Just like loyalty-building drips, these loyalty-repressing factors occur as an outgrowth of the interaction between the service provider and the customer. Whether you're dealing with positive or negative drips, consider this: it's not uncommon for a drip to fall into two or more of the five categories. The Casey Neistat episode with Apple (described in the next Case in Point) has both interaction and core services drip implications. Read on.

5. Core Services

These negative drips are linked directly to the product or core service itself or its characteristics.

Case in Point

iPod's Dirty Secret

When provoked about a core product or service issue, even customers who otherwise love you will serve up a heaping drip of tough love. But you knew that already. The "new news" is how very, very long those drips can, well, drip!

Look no further than the oft-told account of Casey Neistat, a diehard iPod fan, who in September 2003 set out to solve what he thought was a simple repair problem. His beloved iPod would not hold a charge longer than an hour. Assuming a quick battery replacement was the answer, Casey took his iPod to the Apple store in Manhattan close to where he worked. Imagine his surprise when he learned that no replacement battery existed for the iPod and that his best option was to fork out $257 for a brand-new player for his tunes. Just to be sure, Casey contacted the Apple call center. He even mailed his iPod to the executive offices of Apple CEO Steve Jobs with a note explaining the problem. Their answer? Apple did not repair or replace iPod batteries, and company policy was to recommend purchase of a new iPod when the battery failed.

To Casey and his brother, Van, Apple's battery policy seemed very "un-Apple-like." So what did the brothers do next? Aspiring filmmakers, they made the short film "iPod's Dirty Secret" about the nonreplaceable battery problem, posted it on the Web, and sent the site address to twenty friends. Twenty-four hours later, the site had 300 hits; forty-eight hours later, 40,000 hits. Next, the *Washington Post* picked up the story, followed by the *New York Times, CBS Nightly News,* Fox News, and the BBC. (Soon after, Apple announced a $99 battery replacement option for its next-generation iPod and an extended warranty for $59. The company disavowed any connection between the new policies and "iPod's Dirty Secret".)[11]

Yikes! It's still dripping! At this writing, five years after Casey's online film posting, "iPod's Dirty Secret" ranks an amazing eight on the "iPod battery" Google search list. No doubt, the iconic Apple brand withstands the heat with ease. But what about a smaller, fledging brand? Similar circumstances could cost such a brand a lot of lost business.

Eruption Triggers: Superheated Loyalty-Repressing Drips

Generally speaking, the loyalty-repressing drips examined thus far have a gradual negative effect on your customers' attitudes and behaviors. But not so for eruption triggers! These are a potent subset of loyalty-repressing drips that can superheat your customer's attitude pool and propel switching behaviors in seconds. Left unmanaged, these eruption triggers can lead to immediate disloyal behavior.

Two factors play into the dynamics here. (1) The more *important* a loyalty-repressing drip is in the mind of the customer, the more likely (and the more quickly) the customer will erupt into switch. (2) Likewise, the more *frequently* the drip occurs, the more likely it is that the customer will erupt. In her groundbreaking switching research in the late 1990s, loyalty scholar Dr. Inger Roos coined the term "triggers" and classified them into three categories.[12] (Note that each of these trigger categories has loyalty drip properties that square with Dr. Nordman's research as well.)

> **Reactional triggers.** The customer reacts to some dynamic in the relationship.

> **Case in Point**
>
> Six months ago, my girlfriend Suzanne joined a gym and hired a personal trainer to work with her there. Always time conscious, Suzanne made a point to be at the gym and ready to begin at 7:00 sharp on workout nights. About three months into the relationship, she noticed that her trainer was routinely starting the session five or more minutes late. Suzanne hinted a few times about her displeasure with these late starts, but, alas, her trainer didn't get the message. One night, Suzanne finally had enough. "I looked at the clock.

I decided I would stay on the stationary bike until 7:05, and if she was still socializing with the other trainers, I would simply leave," she recalled. So at 7:06, Suzanne began her protest walk out of the gym. Her trainer caught up with her and asked why she was leaving. Suzanne declared, "Tonight's a wash. Starting next workout, either begin my session on time, or lose me as a client."

Situational triggers. The customer switches because of a shift in the customer's life or work situation.

Case in Point

Nothing triggers a switch more seamlessly in the B2B market than having a client be acquired by a larger firm with suppliers of its own. That's a lesson that Dave Fried, CEO of an employee-leasing company, learned firsthand when he unexpectedly lost two longtime customers, representing almost $7 million in sales, immediately after they were acquired by bigger businesses. Notice came "out of the blue" from his number-one client, a meaty $4.9 million account, the day before the firm's intent-to-acquire announcement. Reports Fried, "The CEO called me and said his company was being bought. It didn't look good for me." Soon after, Fried received the acquiring company's official verdict: his services were no longer needed.[13]

Influential triggers. These triggers originate from the environment, outside the customer-provider relationship.

Case in Point

What can trigger a run on a bank? Northern Rock, Britain's fifth-biggest mortgage lender, found out, when its banking customers became increasingly concerned about the safety of their funds as the U.S. subprime mortgage business worsened and worldwide credit tightened. (Northern Rock found itself particularly vulnerable to the credit squeeze because of its reliance on capital markets, not consumer deposits, to finance its lending.)

At Northern Rock branches across the United Kingdom, customers flocked to the bank to withdraw their money, despite assurances from bank executives that the institution was solvent. Said one depositor, standing in a queue outside the City of London branch, "The website was down and no one was answering the phone this morning. When the shares fell 20 per cent, I decided to come down and take my money out." Reported the *International Herald Tribune*, "A person close to Northern Rock said that account holders withdrew about 1 billion pounds, or more than $2 billion, Friday after Northern Rock turned to the Bank of England for an emergency credit line. This person declined to confirm reports that another 500 million pounds was pulled out Saturday."[14] The result? At this writing, Northern Rock's board has hired investment bank Goldman Sachs to seek bidders for its financially weakened institution.

Taming the Search-and-Switch-Prone Customer: It's All About Drip Management

At any moment in time, each of your customers can fall into one of the four states of loyalty: true loyalty, spurious loyalty, true disloyalty, and spurious disloyalty. (Of course, with either of the disloyalty states, it's time to count these buyers as lapsed customers.) In a perfect world, you could hypothetically grid the two loyalty spaces and closely pinpoint, at all times, the finite position of each of your customers by continually measuring the exact temperature of their "attitude pool." That said, it would be great if all your customers clustered in the true loyalty state, with no customer's attitude temperature registering above "cool." (Recall Figures 2.1 and 2.2 earlier in the chapter.) That's because a neutral to negative customer attitude increases the heat and makes that customer ready to erupt into switching behavior. The eruption can run the gamut from simple window shopping for alternative providers to the customer's moving his or her business completely away from you and buying from a new source.

But even customers with true loyalty and low-temperature, switching-averse attitudes are never a sure thing. The truth is, your customer's attitudes are always in flux. In other words, "drips happen," and at any given time, your customer's attitude about your brand is the combined effect of all the drips into the attitude pool that she carries in her head.

And also know this: your customer's tolerance for service breakdowns or product malfunctions (or any of the other loyalty-repressing drips we've discussed) is narrower than ever! That's because unprecedented choice and ease of search make your buyers more prone to leave you at the first signs of trouble than ever before. Again think in terms of how the customer's negative, heated attitude can quickly move the needle to the high likelihood zone on the Customer Switch-O-Meter. Expect to find negative customer attitudes spiking more quickly, abating more slowly, and lingering longer than in the past. That's why it's crucial to keep customer temperatures as cool (and eruption-proof) as possible.

Here are three basic guidelines, with a couple of examples, to begin. By the time you reach the end of the book, you'll have many, many more to help you tame the search-and-switch customer.

Guideline 1: Check Your Customer's Temperature Early and Often

Take the lead from Automation and Control Solutions (ACS), an $8 billion unit of Honeywell whose forty thousand employees provide environmental sensing and control expertise for corporations. ACS has established a wired alert system tied to customer survey feedback. That means that perceptions of customers are closely monitored. Anthony Pichnarcik, ACS global voice-of-the-customer leader, reports, "When a customer survey score falls below ACS-specified thresholds, or if the customer asks to be contacted, the system does two things: First, a detailed action alert is automatically emailed to the Blackberry, laptop, or desktop PC of people responsible for that customer, including field service leaders, customer care advocates, sales representatives, and regional general managers."[15] Alerts highlight the question response(s) that triggered them and contain links allowing recipients to directly view the entire survey response and associated respondent-describing fields (such as customer name, address, phone, and contract size) for contacting the customer, if appropriate. Second, the system automatically opens cases and, using business rules, assigns them to case managers and teams. Online case management enables team members to share information and coordinate response actions.

Based on internal control group studies, ACS has credited the online action alert system for helping lower account cancellation rates and, in doing so, preserving substantial contract revenue.

Guideline 2: Offset Loyalty-Repressing Drips with Loyalty-Building Drips

There are countless ways to do this. Here's one example. When passenger Bob Emig's Southwest Airlines flight suffered an arduous five-hour delay due to icy weather, the airline unleashed a flow of loyalty-building drips to help offset the repressing ones. The pilot walked the aisles, providing constant updates and answering passenger questions. Flight attendants offered regular updates on connecting flights and, from Emig's vantage point, "really seemed liked they cared."[16] And when Emig returned home, the loyalty-building drips continued. A letter of apology from Southwest arrived within a few days, along with two free round-trip ticket vouchers. Says Emig, "They gave me a gift, for all intents and purposes, to make up for the time spent sitting on the runway."

Beginning in 2001, these loyalty-building drips were hardwired into Southwest protocols. That's when the airline created a new, high-level job tasked with overseeing all proactive customer communication. One of the job's top priorities is the coordination of information dispersed to all frontline reps when major flight disruptions occur. Sending out customer letters, which often include ticket vouchers, is also part of the job. Says Southwest veteran Fred Taylor, who filled the new role, "It's not something we had to do. It's just something we feel our customers deserve."[17]

Guideline 3: Proactively Address Customer Search Intent—It Really Matters

When your customer does a search on your product or on alternatives to your products (or both), what's the intent? That's a critical question to address, for two reasons. (1) Search intents carry different levels of risk for switching. Your goal is always to keep the switch risk from escalating to a higher level. (2) Effectively anticipating the "why" behind your customer's search can help you proactively get the credit you're due or, at minimum, blunt the negativity about your brand that the search may produce.

Consider these three search intents, ordered from lowest switch risk to highest:

1. "I'm in Good Hands . . . Right?" (When Your Customer Searches for Confirmation or Validation)

In my book *Customer Loyalty: How to Earn It, How to Keep It*, I examine buyer post-purchase dissonance and how it arises when there is a disparity between expectations and perceived product performance. The fact is, it's darn hard to manage customer expectations well all the time, and dealing with the disparity between expectation and performance, and the dissonance that follows, is a fact of life for most firms. To self-manage their dissonance, today's customers (like those of yesterday) look for confirmation that they have bought wisely. They seek validation that they are "in good hands."

In fact, the Internet and its ability to deliver countless choices may even have escalated this need for confirmation. Long before the Internet, dissonance research found that (1) the greater the number of alternatives considered before the purchase decision, the more a buyer seeks confirmation after the buy that the purchase was a wise one, and (2) the more attractive a rejected alternative, the more a buyer needs confirmation. The Web and its near-perfect buyer information have likely made these after-the-buy needs more prevalent and intense than ever before. The bottom line: it's highly likely that your buyer will periodically suffer from post-purchase dissonance and will look for relief by searching for information about your product and firm on the Web. That means, of course, that you want the buzz to be as positive as possible.

What you can do:

- *Monitor what is being said about you in cyberspace and take corrective action as needed.*

  For example, within days of a product rollout, a software firm used Web monitoring to spot customer frustration related to certain product features that its own internal research had missed. Soon after, company programmers corrected the bugs and made available a patch for download.

  What's your best monitoring strategy? Develop a list of "must monitor" items and track them closely. Must-haves include your company name, your company URL, your firm's product names, and your products' URLs. Your must monitor these same items relative to your competitors as well. Equally important, know where your buyers and prospects spend their Web time—which message boards, forums, blogs, consumer review sites, industry influencers, and so on do your buyers follow? This list will change over time, and your monitoring strategy must change with it. You may want to consider the services of a Web monitoring company such as CyberAlert to monitor your buzz.

- *Help keep the buzz positive and accurate.*

  For example, Web monitoring enabled a pharmaceutical firm to determine that specialist MDs were inappropriately recommending some of the firm's products. In response, a pharmaceutical staffer published corrective information both whenever and wherever incorrect postings by doctors appeared. (See Chapter Four for more ways to build positive Web buzz.)

2. "I Just Want to Know What Else Is out There" (When Your Customer Searches for Curiosity Relief)

Simple curiosity (and even boredom) often jump-starts your customer's search. Although you cannot control your customer's curiosity, you can work to educate your customer so that he or she favorably compares your brand against others.

What you can do:

- *As the incumbent brand, you need to use your everyday touch points to keep your "scorecard" benefits fresh in your buyer's mind.* (See Chapter Three for ideas.)

- *Help your customers discover you!* The saddest situation is to lose a customer to a competitor over a service that your customer doesn't even know you provide! (See Chapter Four for a discussion of discovery software.)

- *Prepare for the fact that your customers will routinely window-shop your competitors.* It's a reality in today's Googlized world.

You're very likely to come out even stronger if, during this "curiosity" type of search, your buyer receives validation about your brand's merits via positive blog postings, ratings, articles, and so on about your brand. That's a lesson I learned when a high-tech giant contacted my firm for a potential consulting assignment around customer winback strategies. Several members of a corporate committee were tasked with identifying consultant candidates. I was contacted early in the search and ultimately won the job. A committee member told me later that as he continued his Web search for other possible candidates, "All roads led back to you and your Customer Winback book."

3. "Gotta Make a Change—Now!" (When Your Customer Searches to Switch)

In this situation, your customer is in full eruption mode. A trigger event has likely occurred, and your customer intends to switch. A superheated attitude pool now has your customer fully engaged in the first stages of the switching process. This is the toughest of the three search scenarios to defend against.

What you can do:

Your first line of defense is to know as early as possible that an incident has occurred so that you can address it (see guideline 1). Conventional wisdom recommends putting "barriers to switching" into your product or service offering to lessen the risk that the customer will defect. Some say that this approach helps you "save" a customer from switching. True, but as I mentioned earlier, even though these tactics can have a positive effect on customer behavior, they may also have a negative effect on customer attitudes, which can poison perceptions about your brand with potential prospects. (Imagine blogs and customer chat boards full of "I hate [your brand name here], and as soon as my contract is up, I'm gone.")

The ideal strategy here is one that not only acts as a constraint on switching but also has a positive attitudinal effect. Verizon Wireless's partnership with Wachovia to promote online bill pay is one example. When Verizon Wireless customers signed up through Wachovia's online banking to receive and pay their monthly cell phone bills online (through prearranged checking account draft, for example), the feature was considered a convenience by customers and could contribute to positive attitudes about the Verizon Wireless and Wachovia brands. Moreover, this same convenience served as a switching barrier, too. Verizon Wireless customers, for example, became accustomed to the ease of this bill pay and naturally resisted switching to another cell provider because of the cancellation and prepay reset arrangements required. (See Chapter Eight for more details about the Verizon Wireless–Wachovia joint marketing partnership.)

In addition to trigger alerts and carefully designed switching barriers, your best defense against the "Gotta make a change—now" search mode is your brand's scorecard of benefits. The best you can hope for is that as your customer goes deeper into a search for alternatives, your brand exceeds or, at minimum, matches the benefits offered by your customer's next best alternative. (Refer to the discussions in Chapter Three on your customer scorecard and your buyer's next best alternative.)

Sad as it may be, sometimes the switch momentum is so strong that defection is inevitable. When that's the case, your best bet may be to let the customer be and await signals about his or her next steps. If the customer indeed leaves, remain gracious. Send a letter of regret and apologize for the loss. At a point in the not-so-distant future, confirm whether the account is winback worthy. If the answer is yes, begin winback steps. (The winback guidelines in Chapter Six can help.)

Moving On

This chapter took a close look at the whats and whys behind your customer's disposition toward your brand. We explored the loyalty drips that can pacify your customers and the drips that cause frustration and even provoke immediate defection. This understanding lays an important foundation for Part Two: Get the Credit You're Due, where you'll find three essential loyalty-building strategies. The first, the topic of Chapter Three, is to ace your buyer's Worth-It Test. Knowing how to continually score big on this recurring customer test is a fundamental requirement for taming your customers' search-and-switch tendencies.

Taming Takeaways

- Customer dissatisfaction can build slowly and erupt quickly. To prevent customers from switching, your business must monitor customers' attitudes constantly and take proactive measures early.

- Each of your customers falls into one of four loyalty states: true loyalty, spurious loyalty, true disloyalty, or spurious disloyalty. Which state your customer is in depends on that customer's specific combination of behaviors and attitudes about your brand at the given time.

- Your goal is to earn true customer loyalty. This can be accomplished by employing loyalty drip factors that reinforce and nurture loyalty.

- Although you cannot control some loyalty-repressing drips, you can take proactive steps that blunt their negative effect on your customers when they occur. One example is Southwest Airlines' preplanned passenger messaging that is immediately sent out after major flight delays.

- Whether you like it or not, your customer will routinely check out your competitors online (and off) and compare your offering against theirs. To lessen the risk that your customer will actually switch, create strategies to directly address the possible intent of your customer's search. Devise proactive measures to help ensure that your brand comes out on top in these searches.

Part II

Get the Credit You're Due

3

Ace Your Buyer's Worth-It Test

All customers are human calculators of sorts, consciously and unconsciously evaluating the worth-it value of the brands they use. Increasingly, it's a preoccupation for many. Need convincing? A Google search of the term *worth-it* (searched as [worth it]), reveals 30.3 million listings spouting the worth-it (or not!) status of every conceivable product and service, from handbag insurance to a Harvard education to an HD radio. A Yahoo *worth-it* search (searched as [worth it]) found 1.2 billion listings. From user blogs to online chat and community sites to online rating systems, this glut of customer commentary focuses around one overriding theme: whether or not the brand passes muster—alone or in comparison to other buying options.

Can your brand ace this Worth-It Test? Are your brand's benefits so clear that your customers can easily articulate them to others? In your customer's head, does your brand's perceived pluses outweigh the minuses, so that a buyer will choose your brand, again and again, over a host of competitors? In today's search-and-switch world, acing the worth-it test is mandatory. Your ability to get and keep customers depends on it.

Here's the good news: your customers' compulsion to compare can be a powerful ally in earning and keeping their loyalty! But making it so requires that you communicate rich, differentiated benefits that repeatedly prove your product or service superior to the competition's. If your firm is like most, you are still failing to effectively communicate your brand's worth to key decision makers. At best, you are likely preoccupied with creating and delivering value, and greatly negligent about communicating that value. Even if you communicate with your customers about your value delivery, you may still be making mistakes that hinder rather than encourage customer loyalty. Has your firm fallen into any of these communication traps?

- You flood your customers with a ton of benefits rhetoric (from brochures to e-mail to Web site verbiage), expecting them to sort through the rubble and connect with what most matters to them.

- You operate on the flawed notion that your customers are rational beings who cannot resist a sensible selling proposition.

- You depend on your customers to simply "read between the lines" to identify your worth-it benefits.

- You complicate your worth-it message, making it tough for customers to articulate it to others.

- You think you know the benefits your customers truly care about, when in fact you do not.

If you're making any of these mistakes, know this: lackluster worth-it communication makes your buyers easy prey for competitors and ripe for search-and-switch behavior.

Compile a Worth-It Scorecard That Wins

So how do you ace your buyer's worth-it test? By zeroing in on key customer benefits and communicating them effectively. This requires that you crack your customers' worth-it code and connect the dots on the scorecard they already have in their heads. Here are six guidelines to help you.

1. Think *Context* First, *Content* Second

I had a high school friend with the uncanny ability to anticipate test questions before big exams. He could zero in on what our

teachers would test us on and ignore the rest. This meant he opti-
mized his brief but effective study time by focusing on just those
critical areas, while I labored over the books much longer, preparing for questions that were never asked. When I asked him how
he did it, he told me he filtered his test question search by thinking about the style of the particular teacher and how that teacher
approached the material. For example, our science teacher, Mrs.
Williams, taught her course with a "big picture" mentality. So
when my friend studied for Williams's exams, he put less emphasis
on memorizing glossary terms, for example, and more on preparing for "why" questions, such as why one gas when mixed with
another reacted in a certain way. Somehow my friend was able
to deduce these frames of reference and correctly anticipate test
questions with them.

This same strategy applies to your customers' worth-it tests.
Before jumping into the specific questions that might be on your
customer's worth-it scorecard, consider your customer's context or
frames of reference. This is an important first step in identifying
the right worth-it parameters.

The first step in understanding the customer's frame of reference is to recognize the difference between consumer and business market customers. Simply put, the context for buyers in
consumer markets is quite different from that for buyers in business markets.

Consider a Toyota car buyer. This consumer is purchasing a
mass-produced product, and much of the buyer's perception of
value is shaped by brand image plus the buyer's direct usage experience (that is, driving) and preferences. Moreover, the selling
process is relatively quick.

Contrast this to business markets, where, for example, a procurement manager purchases a fleet of Toyota cars for the firm's
sales force. The procurement manager requires a tightly customized fleet of cars and accompanying service maintenance program;
the buyer will not be the fleet's end user; and the purchase process
is relatively long and complex.

Table 3.1.   Consumer vs. Business Market Contexts

Context Parameters	Consumer	Business Buyer
Transaction value	Small	Large
Customization	Less	More
Perceived value	Image-driven	Usage-driven
Selling process	Brief	Long, complex
Decision makers	One or few	Multiple
User	Buyer	Not the buyer

As you contemplate your customer's worth-it scorecard, carefully consider the context in which your brand is being used. Table 3.1 can help jog your thinking.

Your turn: On a sheet of paper, list the six context parameters shown in Table 3.1 and beside each item, describe your specific consumer or business buyer. Are there other relevant parameters that come to mind? Focusing on these parameters is a great way to start the all-important process of thinking like your buyer!

2. Identify (and Name) Your Scorecard Holder(s)

Who is your buyer? In consumer markets, your actual decision maker is typically one person or, at most, a household. Not so in business markets, where buying decisions are often made by a committee that, in addition to the decision maker, can include buyers, gatekeepers, influencers, users, and others. (In a recent Miller Heiman Sales Best Practices Study, more than a third of B2B sales professionals said they needed to persuade six or more people; 82 percent reporting the number to be at least four, and 10 percent of sellers said they needed to persuade more than ten people to close the deal.)[1] Each of these players mentally holds an individual scorecard and calculates a worth-it score for your brand. In today's compulsion-to-compare world, the closer you can get to each scorecard holder, the better.

Your turn: List your scorecard holder(s). For example, if your product is a consumer brand—say, a hotel—you may have multiple scorecard holders: the young family on vacation (with mom as key decision maker), the retired couple (joint decision makers), the business traveler.

If you have a business market product and the buying is done by committee, list each of the stakeholder roles. They may include buyer, gatekeeper, influencer, user, CEO, CFO, and others. If you know specific names and titles for each of these roles, record them (for example, Terry Davis, senior VP of purchasing).

3. Know Each Scorecard Holder's Biggest Worth-It Benefits

The worth-it definition. In consumer markets, where there is generally one buyer (or family) per purchase, a buyer's biggest worth-it benefits are relatively easy to identify. (For instance, McDonald's knows that fast, friendly, efficient service is a biggie on their customers' worth-it scorecard.) Business markets are typically more complex to define because purchases are often driven by committee, with each member typically having a distinctly different benefit interest. For example, when debating a purchase, the plant manager wants to know about factory installation and training time, the maintenance supervisor is concerned about the vendor's service contract, and the purchasing manager is focused on price and delivery schedule. To win in a compulsion-to-compare world, you must identify how each stakeholder defines "worth-it."*

To do that, consider Professor Bob Lauterborn's prescription: identify the specific beliefs each "receiver" must hold in order to behave as you want him to behave. In the case of taming

---

* Two additional points deserve mention. (1) Identifying your brand's worth-it benefits may require more sophisticated techniques than covered here. (2) When identifying your customers' worth-it benefits, always be wary of research bias. For example, customers may tell you they love the latest gizmo on their cell phone, yet testing reveals they never use it and, even worse, get frustrated by the fact that it complicates their use of more basic features. To help eliminate such problems and get purer customer insights, some brands are looking to cognitive psychologists for help. Check **www.loyaltysolutions.com/Resources** for ongoing recommendations on books and other tools addressing these points.

search-and-switch tendencies, the behaviors you want are for the buyer to resist the temptation of a replacement brand and remain your loyal customer.[2]

Note Dr. Lauterborn's use of the word "receiver." To pass the Worth-It Test, your communication must be *received*, not simply *relayed*. That's why it's important to communicate benefits in language the buyer truly understands.

The bottom line: acing the worth-it test means identifying what will most motivate your customers to resist competitive alternatives and stick with you. Here are five proven questions to ask your customers that help uncover each receiver's most important worth-it benefit(s):[3]

- What do you like about buying from us?
- Why did you buy from us in the first place?
- What problems did you have before you bought from us?
- How have we helped you solve those problems?
- How are things better for you now?

The last question is the most important because it tells you, in the language of the customer, what a positive result looks like to that customer.[4]

Case in Point

Magnatag Visible Systems

One company with no problems articulating its worth-it benefits is erasable whiteboard maker Magnatag Visible Systems. Ask Wally Krapf, founder of this twenty-year-old company, what a positive result looks like for customers, and he'll passionately reply, "Our boards are problem solving devices—they are aspirin for people's headaches."[5] Krapf understands that his firm's success is dependent on its continued ability to "raise the perceived value of a product so people think of it as a unique item that they can't compare anything else to," and he leads his team accordingly.

The company's shop, nestled on the shores of the Erie Canal in Macedon, New York, sells whiteboards carefully customized for literally hundreds of different applications, from hospitals and mortgage companies to athletic and church groups. Unlike mass-produced generic whiteboards, Magnatag's boards are printed with graphics and grids customized for the user's specific tasks. Each board also comes with an array of specially designed features and supplies, such as magnets, colored lettering, card holders, and graphic symbols to further enhance user utility. For example, a field service company with a large fleet of repair trucks could choose the "Vehicle Service Monitor" board to track each vehicle's inspection status across multiple predefined and user-defined columns; or the manufacturing plant looking to lower on-the-job injuries might choose the "Safety Cross Safety Motivation System" and its accompanying red, green, and yellow magnets to track accident-free days. Reports Thomas MacNamara, First Horizons Home Loans branch manager, who purchased the popular "Loan Tracker" board, "I've had 80 people on the board at one time and I can look at it and then walk into my assistant's office and go bam, bam, bam, here's what's missing on this application."

Magnatag boards command respectable prices. Individual boards range from $100 to $1,500; multiple-board systems can run $10,000 and more. Due to the requirements of customizing the kits, Magnatag boards are sold exclusively through the company's Web site and catalog. Turnaround time is typically three business days, owing to the firm's careful inventory management system. Annual revenues average "in excess of $10 million and quite a bit above," says Krapf, who reports that to date, he's sold more than half a million boards.

Will the technological revolution make Magnatag boards obsolete? Not likely, says Krapf, who is already talking up the worth-it attributes of his real boards versus the cyberspace kind. He explains, "Stuff on the wall is believable and carries authority. If you get something in email, you wonder if it has changed or when it was sent. The wall can't be a lie."

Your turn: Refer to the names of the scorecard holders you listed in response to guideline 2. Beside each name, list the key worth-it benefit(s) each buyer (or buyer role) is most concerned about. Make sure you are listing the benefits that are truly in your customer's mind and not simply what you believe them to be. Not sure? Find out! Use the five questions listed earlier to jump-start your customer research. (We'll cover more about benefits in Chapter Four.)

If your firm sells B2B, this exercise illustrates the importance of team selling. Simply put, your firm needs a selling team that matches the prospect's buying team. By definition, multiple scorecard holders create discovery and response complexities that a lone salesperson can have trouble addressing effectively, so staff accordingly.

4. Expand Your Scorecard Holder's Benefits List

Consistently acing your customer's Worth-It Test demands vigilance. You must work hard to communicate *all* benefits that truly matter to your customer. That way you lessen the risk that a competitive brand ambushes you on a benefit you provide but that your customer is unaware of! Also, know this: what's at the top of your customer's benefit list today can easily shift to something else tomorrow. So articulating (and delivering!) a rich list of benefits that your customer truly cares about is your best loyalty insurance.

But many firms have real trouble seeing their customer benefits. That's why it often helps to contemplate benefits through a category lens, routinely asking yourself what benefits you can or do offer in each. Here are five key categories to consider. Chances are, right now, your brand is heavily entrenched in hard currency benefits and less so in the remaining four.[6] That spells opportunity.

Hard currency benefits. Every industry has its own "hard currency–speak" to communicate benefits. (Today, in the microchip world it's "performance per watt"; in the health care industry it's "cost per patient day.") No vendor should ignore its industry's conventional view of benefits. Because these calculations are typically easy to verify, buyers rely on them for vendor comparison. But therein lies the problem. As a vendor, when you limit your benefits communication *only* to this category, price war vulnerability often follows. That's because your competitors can often match you toe to toe in this category of benefits.

Tip: Strive for parity or better in the category of hard currency benefits, but differentiate your brand on other benefits. Read on.

Prospector benefits. These benefits are dubbed "prospector" because of the initiative and effort it often takes for you to uncover and substantiate them for the buyer. In the early 1990s, for example, software maker Siebel Systems pushed hard to get pilot projects installed with prospective buyers. Giving prospects actual experience with the software allowed them to estimate cost savings more easily—which in turn paved Siebel's way to a large sale and steady incremental revenue. Think about it. Siebel competitors lacked such data, putting them at a keen disadvantage in a Worth-It Test.

Peace-of-mind benefits. Although difficult for sellers to quantify, peace-of-mind benefits are very real. Just ask the office manager who bypasses two less expensive shipping options and reaches for the FedEx envelope whenever a critically important document must travel cross-country to be on a client's desk the next morning for a nine o'clock meeting. That's the FedEx peace-of-mind benefit at work.

Every firm has peace-of-mind benefits to leverage. Even I do. In my promotional video for my keynote speaker work, I "sell" peace of mind to meeting planners. Early in my video, I describe to viewers how twenty years of platform experience has taught me to deal with the unexpected: from dead microphones and non-responsive audiovisual equipment to malfunctioning fire alarms—hey, I've even had a heckler! Corporate meeting planners know that these perils are very real, and selling them peace-of-mind benefits helps me pass their Worth-It Test.

What peace-of-mind benefits can you leverage? Corporate reputation, innovation acumen, global offices worldwide? Such benefits don't manifest overnight and require the investment of time and money. But peace-of-mind benefits can help command premium pricing. Just ask FedEx.

Extra-mile benefits. Like peace-of-mind benefits, this category is difficult to measure, but unlike peace of mind, extra-mile benefits cannot be "sold"; they must be experienced by the customer to be fully appreciated. You can tell a prospect how you go the extra mile for customers, but until that prospect experiences it firsthand, it's only talk. (But please note that if that "talk" comes from someone outside your company who has experienced the extra miles you go, believability is often higher. That's why word of mouth is such a valuable asset to your business. Chapter Four will examine the critically important topic of word of mouth in more detail.)

Many vendors deliver extra-mile benefits routinely. The East Coast firm's mechanic who flies all night to repair a West Coast client's machine malfunction early the next morning, even though the maintenance contract calls for a seventy-two-hour turnaround, is but one example. The trick is to get word of mouth going about it.

Community benefits. Here's a customer benefit category you may be overlooking: providing your customers access to each other through a customer community. Why is this a benefit? Because today's customers see opportunities for peer learning and experience sharing as extremely valuable but difficult to access. Savvy firms have built customer communities for that very purpose. For example, Harley-Davidson's annual HOG (Harley Owners Group) gatherings are eagerly anticipated social events for many Harley owners. Likewise, Microsoft's Channel 9 is a discussion forum site that helps connect the tens of thousands of developers around the globe who use Microsoft software. For both Harley and Microsoft customers, the benefits of these communities are substantive and real. But building community can be as simple as introducing your clients to each other! Just ask my hairdresser, Mark. Rarely do I go for an appointment in which he doesn't introduce me to another client in the salon. I recently met the wife of a business book author, who had just moved to Austin. Through our connection, her husband soon joined an Austin authors group to which I belong.

Think strategically about customer community benefits and how to leverage them for your brand. The truth is, no other brand will have customers quite like yours, and that distinction can constitute real value in the eyes of your current and prospective buyers.

Your turn: For each of your scorecard holders, list the benefits you now deliver, thinking in terms of the five categories we've discussed. What untapped benefits can help differentiate your brand from the competition? What are you delivering now and not getting credit for? Use Figure 3.1 as a template.

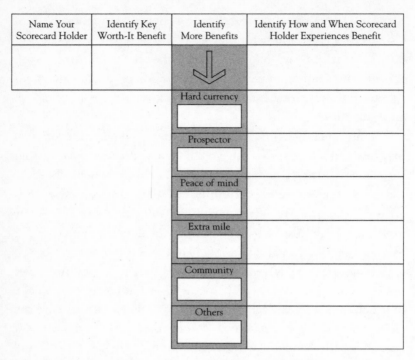

Name Your Scorecard Holder	Identify Key Worth-It Benefit	Identify More Benefits	Identify How and When Scorecard Holder Experiences Benefit
		⬇	
		Hard currency	
		Prospector	
		Peace of mind	
		Extra mile	
		Community	
		Others	

Figure 3.1.   Expand Your Scorecard Holder's Benefits List

5. Help Scorecard Holders "Experience" Your Benefits

Most firms (and even people) are far more focused on delivering benefits than on communicating about their delivery of those benefits. That's a big mistake. Just ask my husband, Mack.

A few days after I returned from a two-week business trip in Europe, Mack and I were taking a walk around our neighborhood. Seemingly out of the blue, he surprised me by saying, "I fixed three things around the house while you were gone, things you'd been after me to fix. But you haven't mentioned one of them since you've been home." With a tiny grin, he continued, "You've got twenty-four hours to identify them, or I'm going to turn into an unhappy camper." I love my husband very much, and of course, as soon as we returned home from our walk, I made it my business to identify his good deeds and praise him for them. In his way, Mack was shrewdly applying an often overlooked worth-it principle: it's not enough to deliver great value; it counts only when your customer notices it.

Consumer market tell. In the consumer space, it's the practice of this worth-it principle that prompts airline pilots to announce the flight's on-time arrival in their "Welcome to Austin [or whatever the city]" greeting at landing, and my Office Depot receipt for desk supplies to read "You saved $7.46," and Westin Hotels' "Do Not Disturb" door hanger to read "I cannot come to the door now. I'm still in heaven," referencing the comfort of Westin's signature Heavenly Bed. These businesses not only provide good service or products but also remind you how good they are.

Business market tell. How can you routinely communicate with your business market clients? It's often a tougher "tell." As we've seen, the business market buyer is often a committee of stakeholders with different benefit interests. How do you routinely get the word out about your good deeds? One way is to follow the lead of a global oil company's specialty chemical division, which provides a monthly letter to inform its customers about the services it has delivered over and above its contractual obligations. The letter is carefully written and designed so as not to come off as boastful or like a sales solicitation. Instead, it is a matter-of-fact report on the additional benefits the supplier provided and the efforts taken to deliver them. In it, the buyer's executives who asked for extra services are identified. These executives often emerge as the vendor's internal champions.

Your turn: List all the ways you currently communicate your worth-it benefits to your individual scorecard holders. How frequent are these communications? Do your communications speak directly to each scorecard holder's biggest worth-it benefits? Evaluate carefully. Where are the holes? How can you fill them? See Figure 3.2 for a way to record your results.

Scorecard Holder (B2B Example)	Worth-It Communication		
	Vehicle/Media	Frequency per year	Benefit Message
Decision maker			
Buyer			
User			
Influencer			
Gatekeeper			
Other			

Figure 3.2.   Showcase Your Worth

6. Devise Your Communications Plan

Attention, B2B readers: the communication process in business markets is complex. And, as a result, most firms do not monitor the needs and concerns of *each* scorecard holder on the buying team. This means they don't communicate their worth-it benefits to key stakeholders either. *It's this lack of communication that makes business buyers especially easy prey for competitors and ripe for search and switch!*

How do you help your firm understand this communication complexity and, in turn, create a game plan that makes this critical communication happen? Consider Harvard professor Das Narayandas's "Stack" exercise.[7] It's a great start.

Your turn: Narayandas recommends these steps. First, using a deck of index cards, list all the benefits your brand offers, one to a card, and then sort the cards into a pile, placing the most important at the bottom of this Benefits stack. Next, create a list of all purchase team members in a Decision Makers stack of cards. Now place the two stacks side by side. (If possible, also identify the key concerns, motivations, and power bases of each member of the purchase committee.) For each decision maker card, go through the Benefits stack and note which cards apply.

As Narayandas counsels, the coupling of the information in these two stacks enables your firm to begin systematically managing each purchase team member's worth-it concerns and, in turn, designing the tactics for getting the right messages to the right receivers. Don't be surprised by the need to customize—for example, by creating six or more separate and different sets of product literature, one for each purchase team member. It's critical that your communication content is tailored for each set of needs and interests.

But know this: it's also critical to brief each of your selling team members about the needs and concerns of all the people in the stack and how these needs will be (or are being) addressed. This way, your entire team has access to the total worth-it picture and can better prevent competitors from winning over purchase committee allies one by one. You want to lock all purchase committee members in with your firm's worth-it reporting as much as possible. It's insurance against your client's compulsion to compare!

Know Your Customer's NBA and Keep That Competitor Close

If ever you think your brand is in a category of one and your customer has no other alternative but to buy your brand, think again. There's no such thing as a sure thing. In the eyes of your customer, there is always a *next best alternative* (NBA). For example, rather than buy your brand, the customer may decide to source the service or product in-house or may even opt simply to do nothing for now. The more common situation, however, is that your customer sees one or more of your competitors as the NBA. The scorecard guidelines in the previous section addressed competition in an implicit way, but now let's get explicit. Why? Because to pass the Worth-It Test consistently, you must be able to trump your NBA. Period. Here are three questions to keep you armed and ready:

> *Question 1: In the eyes of your customer, what is the next best alternative (NBA) to your brand?*

Being perfectly clear on who your buyers consider to be the NBA is crucial. Just ask Nick Swinmurn, founder of online shoe seller Zappos, who launched his company in 2000 thinking that his customer's NBA was other online shoe sellers. Wrong. Swinmurn soon realized that the online shoe market was too small, that he needed to woo bricks-and-mortar store customers—and that Zappos customers' NBA was a real shoe store! Now Swinmurn also figured that the bricks-and-mortar customer would never tolerate the Zappos business model, which depends on distributors to drop ship directly to customers. After all, Zappos would not be able to guarantee service—for example, when a Zappos customer tried to buy shoes, 8 percent of the time the desired pair was not in stock. Confesses Swinmurn, "We realized then who our real competition was, and that we had to find a way to make an inventory model work."[8] That's when Zappos went to work to forge deep, strong supplier relationships by sharing sales data with manufacturers about their online shoe sales. "Traditionally, the vendor-retail relationship was adversarial. We thought instead of trying to hide this information from our vendors, we'll open everything up. They can help us build the business." In return, appreciative sales reps worked closely with Zappos on tantalizing sales promotions that helped drive site sales.

And Zappos and its suppliers have thrived. In just five years after the company set its sights on bricks-and-mortar shoe stores as its customers' NBA, sales skyrocketed from $8.6 million to $300 million.

> Question 2: In your customer's eyes, how do you stack up versus the NBA? More specifically, what is the difference in perceived value between the two offerings (your brand versus your customers' NBA) relative to their price difference?

When deciding what to buy, your prospects and customers do not simply focus on your brand's value delivery for the money paid. Instead, they focus on the difference in value **between your offering and the NBA** relative to their *difference in prices*.

Take Southwest Airlines. In recent years, the Dallas-based airline's discount advantage began to fade as new bargain airlines entered the market and older, established airlines lowered prices and cut costs. Meanwhile, the business traveler—often willing to pay higher fares for extra amenities—was boosting the profit margins of Southwest's competitors. Aiming to improve its profitability, Southwest decided to go after more business travelers (at the time, some 40 to 50 percent of its total passengers).[9]

To achieve that goal, Southwest had to improve its value as perceived by sought-after high-end business travelers, in comparison to the perceived value of mainstream carriers, such as Continental and American. But how? The answer was a big, first-ever change in strategy. Southwest created a new ticket class, Business Select, with one-way fares priced $10 to $30 more than regular tickets; customers paying the premium would receive preferential boarding, bonus frequent-flier credits, and a free cocktail. In addition, the airline introduced renovated boarding areas designed with the business traveler in mind—roomier seating, ample power outlets, workstation counters with stools, and flat-screen TVs tuned to CNN. Time will tell whether the response from business travelers will make the new strategy succeed.

But Southwest deserves credit; in today's compulsion-to-compare marketplace, the carrier astutely realized that with close to pricing parity on fares, it must create new favorable points of difference to woo more business travelers away from Continental, American, and the rest. Good for them!

> *Question 3: Why, specifically, should buyers purchase your brand instead of the NBA?*

This is the million-dollar question! Having one or more compelling points of difference distinguishing you from your NBA—differences that customers can appreciate and articulate to others—is how you earn and keep customer loyalty. (Chapter Five, "How to Be (and Stay) Damn Different," examines this issue in more detail.)

Consider the predicament of Tennant Company, a Minneapolis-based industrial floor cleaner manufacturer, whose customers were increasingly jumping ship to the NBA: foreign competitors flaunting lower costs. But rather than compete with the low-cost producers, Tennant took a gutsy gamble and boldly allocated 3 to 4 percent of annual sales to innovation. Two years of internal tug-of-war followed as Tennant survived a bumpy trip through its innovation maze. Recalling the early prototype for ReadySpace, a scrubber that injects cleaning fluid and water onto circular brushes beneath the machine, engineer and innovation chief Pete Swenson reports, "Before we put that machine in the field, four different people told me we should kill this project, including my boss."[10]

But Swenson and his design team fought to keep the project alive, knowing that the prototype's potential appeal was huge. Unlike conventional scrubbers that spray cleaner and water directly onto carpets, ReadySpace's innovative fluid-on-brush system cuts drying time to a short thirty minutes. This was a compelling benefit for casino operators and Tennant's other institutional customers that routinely had to close off areas being cleaned for up to twenty-four hours. Soon after its launch, ReadySpace

Ask Your Customers These Five Questions	
Yes or no?	Versus your next best buying alternative, the brand provides real, substantive differences that you consider important.
Yes or no?	The brand provides you tangible, convincing proof of these differences.
Yes or no?	You can easily articulate the brand's differences.
Yes or no?	You are served by employees who exemplify the brand's differences through word and deed.
Yes or no?	Relative to the price difference, you perceive the brand as delivering substantially more value than your next best buying alternative.

Figure 3.3.   The Customer Worth-It Test—Does Your Brand Ace It?

became the company's best-selling carpet cleaner, and new product innovation continued to fuel Tennant's revenues. Two years later, the firm's profit topped $30 million, more than double its profit the year prior to the launch.

Obviously, a clear, definitive answer to the question "Why your brand?" can catapult loyalty, customer sales, and profits. Does your brand ace the Worth-It Test in the eyes of your customers? Figure 3.3 can help.

Five More Ways to Ace the Worth-It Test

In today's compulsion-to-compare world, you can never have too many ways to ace your buyer's Worth-It Test. So here are five more!

1. Carefully Match Your Price to Your Worth

Acing your buyer's worth-it test means optimally matching your brand's price to its perceived benefits. In other words, it's crucial that you charge what you are worth. But remember, worth is ultimately defined by your customer, not you. To win this game, you must carefully assign the right benefits across your brand portfolio.

Consider the case of office products manufacturer Swingline, which had been experiencing only modest growth and was in danger of losing retail distribution in the electric stapler category, the industry's largest growth sector. Research showed that the category's top segment of customers demanded a premium stapler that could withstand heavy-duty use, and that customers were willing (even eager!) to pay a premium for a product that would not break down under demanding conditions. With this new market intelligence, Swingline now realized its shortcoming: the brand had failed to communicate to customers why Swingline's premium electric stapler, priced as much as ten times higher than the basic manual model, was an excellent value in this price tier.

What did Swingline do next? It reworked its worth-it strategy across the entire product line. Retailers were persuaded to revamp their stapler shelving layout and signage to address customer benefit tiers better: Swingline's least expensive staplers were promoted as providing basic functionality for the lowest price; midprice staplers emphasized durability and reliability; and the brand's deluxe electric models stressed superior performance.

Customers responded. In only a few short months, the brand's electric stapler sales doubled, and premium manual models (whose previous sales were flat) saw double-digit growth. Moreover, Swingline's new worth-it messaging motivated many customers to trade up, which further increased the brand's sales and margins and ultimate market performance turnaround.[11]

2. Make Sure Your Frontliners Are Worth-It Makers

Research conducted by the Quality Circle Institute and international communication services group WPP found that in more than 90 percent of companies, staff who are responsible for talking to customers could not articulate why customers should buy from them.[12]

Yikes! If employees don't understand the firm's worth-it proposition, and perform accordingly, how will customers ever know?

There's no such problem at Elliott's Hardware in Dallas, where employees can easily articulate the two worth-it factors—selection and service—that keep a loyal cadre of customers driving past Home Depot and shopping at the sixty-year-old Dallas-based family owned business.

Although you won't find lumber, drywall, roofing, or high-priced appliances—items over which the big box stores typically engage in price battles—Elliott's depth of selection on other hardware stock runs deep: 100,000 items to the big box's 35,000 items. Reports president and CEO Kyle Walters, "We carry hard-to-find items that you can't find in a big box."[13] For example, the store's fastener section, stocked with more than fifteen thousand contraptions for fastening things together, is legendary. Same goes for cabinet door pulls, sprinkler heads, and kitchen gadgets, and the list goes on.

But Elliott's employees know that depth of selection is only half the worth-it formula. Service matters too. Just ask Brian Hamilton of Carrollton, Texas, who discovered Elliott's when he began restoration of his Katrina-wrecked sailboat. "I walk in with a part in my hand that needs a missing piece, and they take me straight to it." From teakwood acid wash and brass thread to fiberglass parts, Elliott's service-selection combo has not disappointed Brian. "I couldn't even get [parts] at a marine supply store." Perhaps Dallas designer Billy Mulline, an Elliott's customer of eighteen years, best captured the true power of worth-it delivery on the front lines when he said, "One of the main reasons I shop here two or three times a week is so Home Depot won't put them out of business. I don't want them to go away."

3. Routinely Deliver the Unexpected

Teaching customers to expect the unexpected is another way to ace your buyer's worth-it test, when that "unexpected" is a sought-after treasure. This strategy is helping Costco consistently earn worth-it kudos from customers. Costco charges customers a $50 to $100 annual membership fee for access to warehouses brimming with bulk goods attractively priced at 15 percent above whole-sale. To help sweeten the experience, Costco routinely offers unexpected, limited-availability finds, such as designer jeans and handbags or $80,000 diamond rings. These "found" prizes help keep customers coming back for more treasure hunting. Explains Costco CEO Jim Sinegal, "We wound up finding a place where we could get several million pairs of Calvin Klein jeans and we bought them at a great price. Every department store was sell-ing them for $50. . . . We easily could have said, 'Well, we're selling every pair that we get. . . . Why not sell these for $29.00?' but we didn't. We sold them for $22.99 because we made such a great buy."[14] Says Sinegal, "You come in next time and we don't have those jeans but we have some Coach handbags. That's the treasure-hunt aspect."

4. Earn Favorable Product Ratings and Reviews, and Showcase Them

Favorable customer-generated ratings and reviews are prov-ing vital in helping brands continually pass the worth-it test. Research consistently finds that prospects are more apt to be swayed by opinion from other buyers than by the word of the com-pany. How do you consistently earn sky-high customer reviews? By proving your worth over other alternatives and doing so in a way that your customers can and will articulate to others. (We examine customer-generated ratings and reviews in more depth in Chapter Four. The PETCO case in Chapter Eight also addresses user-generated reviews.)

5. Build Your Buyers' Worth-It Case

When MarketingProfs president Roy Young recently e-mailed prospective attendees (including me) about the firm's annual B2B forum, he thought outside the box. Rather than simply listing the benefits of attending (along with testimonials from last year's attendees), he provided a "Forum ROI Worksheet" to help prospects quantify the benefits of forum attendance in terms of driving sales for the coming year. The worksheet's heading read, "Use this worksheet as a fun way to estimate your own ROI based on your cost of attending. . . . Print this sheet and start calculating!"

I imagine more than a few readers, keen on attending the forum but faced with the tough task of justifying the investment to their budget-conscious supervisors, used the worksheet to sharpen their rationale for signing up.

The lesson here is simple: help customers build their worth-it rationale for buying from you! Step into your buyers' shoes and ask yourself, What are my customers' buy-in barriers? How can I truly help them make the worth-it case? What steps can I perform to reduce their time and effort?

Want more help on acing your customer's Worth-It Test? Visit **www.loyaltysolutions.com/WorthItTest.**

Moving On

No longer can you be passive about communicating your brand's worth. You must be deliberate, and that means knowing your buyers, their scorecards, and their decision-making protocols. Equally important is implanting the right perceptions about your brand in the decision makers' minds. After all, customers' perceptions are what truly determine whether (or not) your brand passes the worth-it test. Perception building is more complex today than ever before. The next chapter examines why this is, and what you can do to make and keep customer perceptions riding high. Right this way . . .

Taming Takeaways

- The Internet has unleashed intense buyer scrutiny unlike anything most firms have ever experienced. To withstand this close look-see, you must ensure that customers are convinced that the product or service being sold to them is worth their loyalty.

- Keeping customers in this age of the easy switch means keeping track of the specifics of your customer's basis of evaluation. Developing a scorecard that specifies individual customers' worth-it criteria is essential.

- Marrying the benefits you provide with the benefits your customers seek goes a long way to establishing and sustaining customer loyalty.

- Whether you sell B2B or directly to single consumers, a worth-it communication plan is a must.

- Although you may not want to admit it, your customers do have alternatives. Knowing what those alternatives are, making sure that your performance surpasses them, and then consistently communicating that fact to your customers will keep you ahead in the loyalty race.

- Your product or service must not only be priced right for the benefits delivered but also offer additional value, such as extra service, unexpected convenience, and other advantages which ensure that the brand tops its next best alternative.

4

Manage Perception Makers and Takers

Consider the following discussion posted on an Internet message board forum for sports enthusiasts (and notice that the discussion is not about sports!).

Contributor 1

When I purchased my new car [brand name here] they told me the loaner car policy was just like Lexus, and I'd be given a loaner whenever my car needed service. Well, today, I went to schedule my 5K service, and asked for a loaner, and I got turned down by not just one, but two dealerships! My next call was to the sales guy I bought the car from and he so nonchalantly says, "Oh, yeah, man, loaner cars go out to customers getting major service. You'll get one when you come in for the 25K."

Argh. . . . Why the heck did I even bother to buy the service package? Hey, I'd just as soon go to Jiffy Lube if I've got to wait for service. I never had that problem when I owned a Lexus. As long as you made an appointment for service, they made sure you got a loaner. You can bet I'm going back to Lexus for my next car. This is a bad deal all around!

———

Contributor 2

    I feel your pain. I had an Infiniti and they were always happy to give me a loaner too. But I've always thought these policies were a dealership by dealership thing.

                ————

Contributor 3

    Next time, save yourself some grief and buy an Acura.☺

    This is just one of thousands of message strings that get pushed out into cyberspace every day. Unlike just a few short years ago, when a conversation like this took place around a watercooler with only a few people present, today literally thousands can "hear" and contribute, if they like, and the perceptions articulated are documented and archived!

    In that online discussion about Lexus, Infiniti, Acura, and the unnamed new car brand, Contributor 1 had the actual customer experience and originated the discussion thread. But Contributors 2 and 3, as influencers and observers, are contributing strong perceptions about the brand for all to see as well. These huge changes in marketplace dynamics bring to mind Dorothy Gale's famous line from *The Wizard of Oz:* "Toto, I have a feeling we're not in Kansas anymore."

The Double Dip: Perception Makers Are Also Takers

Chapter Two examined the role attitudes play in driving customer loyalty. Attitudes are formed through perceptions, so it's vital to understand how the marketplace forms perceptions about your brand. In today's digitized marketplace, there are typically three participating parties in any customer relationship:

1. The "brand," which refers to both the product or service sold and the firm from which it originates

2. The customer

3. Prospects, influencers, and observers who "listen in" or "weigh in" (or both) about the brand

Simply put, the brand, the customer, and the third-party prospects, influencers, and observers—all together or in various combinations—drive brand perceptions. (Note that employees who assume the role of official brand spokesperson are considered an extension of the brand; employees who contribute to brand discussions without their firm's sponsorship are considered third-party influencers.)

As a *perception maker*, each of these three participating parties contributes to what's being "said" about the brand. But each is a *perception taker* as well, in that each party's attitude about the other at any given time is colored by what that party takes (or not) from existing marketplace perceptions. Figure 4.1 shows examples of the dual role of perception maker and perception taker for each of the three parties. For instance, take a look at space 1, where I have written "Internal branding program" because this is often how firms build brand perceptions with their employees. Examples given in the other eight spaces are addressed throughout this chapter. (The Nine Space Rule is officially unveiled toward the end of the chapter.)

Sadly, many firms are still in denial about the relevancy of third-party influences. As branding author and pal Karen Post quipped to me, their "customer development plans belong on the History Channel!" These firms hold on to the old assumption that relationship building is primarily a two-way dynamic between customer and brand. Not so.

Today's customer relationships are clearly a three-party dynamic, and your loyalty strategies must address this reality. Let's

When the Brand Perception Maker Is...

	Brand	Customer	3rd Party
Brand	Internal branding program 1	Customer rating or review 2	Parody of brand commercial on YouTube 3
Customer	Brand-sponsored customer e-letter 4	Brand user's complaint posted on customer community site 5	Phishing 6
3rd Party	Brand commercial on YouTube 7	Brand user's complaint posted on sports enthusiast bulletin board 8	Noncustomer blog entry about brand 9

When the Brand Perception Taker Is...

Figure 4.1.   Perception Making: Each Space Counts!

take a closer look at each of the three parties and their "maker" and "taker" contributions to perceptions of your brand in the marketplace.

The Brand

The advent of both customer-generated commentary and third-party influences makes the role of brand-sponsored messaging more important than ever to your brand's perception building. After all, your brand's market acceptance hinges on your firm's ability to get its intended brand messaging seeded in the marketplace. Two questions deserve careful consideration:

- How does your brand build perception and earn "mind share" in your buyer's brain?
- How does your brand communicate with buyers to *motivate* purchase and defend against search and switch?

Understanding how customers think is the first step to building powerful, targeted brand messages for your loyalty strategy.

Brand Messaging: How Customers Think

Perceptions are formed from thoughts. A thought, according to Harvard professor Gerald Zaltman, is an "activation of a set of neurons" in the brain, and although we may be very aware of having a thought, we are unaware of "the bundled sequence of other thoughts that unfold to produce it."[1] Know this: decisions (a type of thought) and other thoughts occur when neutrons in *different places in the brain* are activated. Cautions Dr. Zaltman, "There is no discrete 'buy button' [in the brain] as some suggest."

So how is it that a brand communicates with buyers? When we think, we generate thoughts that were heretofore absent. We bring them forth. Says Zaltman, "The contemplated 'something' may be a new attitude about a brand, a renewed commitment to it, an inclination to it, etc. A television or magazine advertisement thus attempts to generate thoughts or feelings about a product. . . . A point of purchase display attempts to focus attention that would otherwise be diverted (missing) elsewhere."

Here's the thing: a buyer's thoughts are a product of what linguists call *conceptual blending*, referring to the fact that buyers use prior customer experience and existing ideas to make sense of advertising content. "In this way, consumers and advertisers engage in a process I call the co-creation of meaning. It is these co-created meanings that change a consumer's orientation toward a product or service," advises Zaltman.

In the human brain, thoughts are stored in a network of other thoughts. When a buyer brings forth stored information, it is called a *story*, because customers, as do all humans, think in terms of story diagrams. Every customer has thousands of them! Says Zaltman, "When we swap stories with someone else, we are sharing mental models of related events."

People's story diagrams (and mental models) can vary widely from one another. One person can see a set of circumstances very differently than another person would. That's one reason why perception making is so challenging. Take the following story, considered by most to be an urban legend. The narrative is a fun reminder that perception is, indeed, in the eyes of the beholder.

Ellen and Kay had had a great morning shopping at Dillard's. Loaded down with bags full of purchases, they approached the car in a happy mood. Once in the parking lot, however, their mood quickly changed. Right by the car was a cat that had recently been hit and killed. "Poor kitty," said Ellen, an avid feline lover, as she grabbed Kay's shopping bag and quickly transferred her purchases into it. Thinking she'd perform a quick burial later in her backyard, Ellen gently lifted the cat with tissue paper into her own bag.

They put their purchases into the trunk of the car but were afraid that the cat would overheat in the trunk, so they left the bag on top of the trunk and went into Luby's for lunch.

After going through the cafeteria line, the two friends chose a table near a window with a view of Kay's car. Imagine their surprise when a woman in a red gingham shirt strolled by the car and snared the bag without breaking stride. "Did you see that?" Kay gasped. Before Ellen could adequately respond, they saw the same woman enter the Luby's building and make her way down the line.

They watched as the woman took her tray to a nearby table and began preparations to eat her meal.

But, obviously, the woman's curiosity about the bag's contents was too strong. She pulled the Dillard's bag into her lap and looked with anticipation under the top layer of tissue paper. One good look was all that it took. She began to gasp and choke and clutch at her chest. A server hurried over and began the Heimlich maneuver after sending a busboy to call 911. In a few minutes, EMTs arrived and took charge of the woman. They loaded her on a gurney, gathered her belongings together, and took her to the waiting ambulance. Ellen and Kay's last glimpse of the woman was as she was being lifted into the ambulance with the Dillard's bag perched on her stomach.

Whether you classify the Luby's story as tale or true, the lesson is the same: the perceptions that form in the mind originate through a complex maze of thought processes that are by-products of a customer's past and present experiences. That's why telling your brand's story in a way that will resonate with your customers—the way you intend it to—can be complicated and challenging.

Says Zaltman, "An effective ad . . . is one that activates a relevant frame (mental model or system of constructs), and creates an emotional response based on the material difference offered by the product and fosters the creation of personally relevant stories."

It's All About the Story: Your Brand's and Your Customer's

Question: How does your brand engage with buyers to motivate purchase and word of mouth and, in doing so, defend against search and switch?

Answer: Create the "right" brand story—one that resonates with your buyer's existing internal story network. That way, your customer and brand co-create meaning that will keep your brand's perceptions relevant and positive.

Recall the fact that no "purchase button" exists. Your brand's best bet for remaining relevant is to create marketing messages that activate neurons in many, many parts of the brain.

Sadly, a lot of firms still believe that you build brand relevancy by simply *injecting* meaning into the customer's mind through an assault of brand messaging. (Think junk e-mails, mindless radio and TV ads, Web ad pop-ups, and the like.) Instead, brand relevancy is built by creating a brand story that resonates with either your buyers' past cultural reference points or earlier brand experiences—or some combination.

Here are some storytelling examples:

• **The MSN Butterfly Takes Flight.** Michael Thibodeau and Randall Ringer know firsthand how the "right" brand story can uplift a brand, and they've built an agency to help firms do precisely that. Their story-finding expertise is rooted in an interesting past. Under Thibodeau's leadership at another agency, the power of storytelling was masterfully applied to restage Microsoft's MSN. The brand's restaging began in 2000 when Microsoft faced antitrust charges and Bill Gates was logging long hours on the witness stand. Brand research showed that Microsoft's already weak brand story was further diluted by the trial and a very visible Bill Gates. "We recognized the need to create a compelling metaphor for MSN which would make it more identified as 'my brand' in the customer's mind and less a symbol of 'Bill Gates's interest,'" says Thibodeau, who later cofounded branding agency Verse Group with Ringer in 2004.[2]

The strategic process began by breaking down the brand architecture and removing the name "Microsoft" from the brand. MSN's business strategy—to combine the Internet's potential as an entertainment experience with the practical everyday usefulness of e-mail, search, and other functionality—was carefully considered. Thibodeau says, "We wanted to tell the MSN story with a language developed specifically to use the experiential qualities of the Internet—through motion, depth, sound. And we sought a visual metaphor which would engage consumers at a very deep emotional level."

The solution? The MSN butterfly. "The butterfly itself is a universal symbol of beauty that captivates people," says Thibodeau. "It was the perfect metaphor. The depth and movement of the butterfly conveys the entertainment potential of the Internet. Envisioning that movement of the butterfly and its interaction with the world around it was part of the original creative process." Careful consideration was given to preserving Microsoft's already established identity system: the typography and colors remained the same and "the four parts of the butterfly wings were made consistent with the four flags in the Microsoft Windows logo and the four squares in the Microsoft Office logo," reflecting the visual language of Microsoft, reports Thibodeau.

The result? Global research confirmed that customers and prospects developed very strong co-creation associations around the new brand. In twelve short months, top-of-mind awareness jumped fivefold. Today the MSN butterfly is one of the most distinguished and recognizable brands in Microsoft's portfolio.

• **New Ways to Squeeze the Charmin.** Toilet paper. How do you successfully build a personally relevant brand story around *that* product? Just ask the ace marketers at Procter & Gamble, and they'll point you to the twenty free, deluxe Charmin restrooms opened in New York's Times Square for the 2007 holiday season. At the same location a year earlier, the Charmin holiday restrooms served more than 420,000 people from one hundred countries and all fifty states, so a 2007 encore was in order. But as in 2006, free, family-friendly restrooms (admittedly scarce in the Big Apple) and ample toilet tissue were just one part of the unique, memorable brand story crafted by the Charmin team.

First, friendly folks dressed as dancing toilets greeted passersby on the street, inviting them to visit the Charmin holiday restrooms nearby. As in a theme park experience, visitors then took escalators up and wove through a rope line while a legion of smiling hosts wearing Charmin apparel greeted them and upbeat holiday music played in the background. Inside the stalls (serviced by staff after every use), Ultra Strong and Ultra Soft tissue were available, and afterwards, guests were asked to vote for their favorite. Bounty paper towels and Puffs with Vicks for runny noses were also on hand. Next, guests could step into one of several winter wonderland dioramas and have their picture taken with the Charmin bear. Or they could go on stage and do the Charmin dance, while their image was displayed on flat-screen monitors. For holiday-weary guests who simply wanted to rest for a bit, a fireplace and comfortable seating awaited.[3]

In addition to the brand story "told" in person to the nearly half million Charmin holiday restroom visitors during the season, an impressive one hundred traditional media outlets reported on the project and were followed by a strong wave of social media coverage by Flickr, YouTube, marketing blogs and forums, and the like.[4]

Bottom line? As Verse Group's Randall Ringer sums it up, "The process of creating a brand story is not a reductive process—it is not about distilling our brand down to a single idea or a single word. It is about putting together a rich and robust language of engaging metaphors that will be useful in both very limited media…and in deeper and more fluid media, such as the Internet, video podcasts, retail environments, events, or tradeshows."

• **B2B Brands as Storytellers.** There are hugely effective "storyteller" strategies employed with great success by some of the largest B2B global brands; these are designed to build awareness and demand among their customers' customers. Consider consulting firm Accenture and its High Performance Delivered campaign.

Accenture does not sell consulting services to consumers, only to businesses. Yet the highly visible campaign featuring Tiger Woods has created huge positive awareness for Accenture among the hundreds of thousands of staffers employed at the companies for which Accenture consults. And just think of the brand messaging Accenture undoubtedly registers with clients and prospects invited to participate in Tiger Woods golf events!

Brand Targeting: Earn Efficiencies Fast!

The marketplace is dripping with messages, so building powerful brand communication that breaks through the clutter to plant powerful perceptions with customers is no easy task. Creating an engaging brand story and then reaching the *right buyers* with that story are equally critical. So how can today's search tools help you sharpen your brand targeting capabilities? Turns out, a lot.

As you saw in Chapter One, today's search-driven world is an in-bound world, where prospects, buyers, and third-party influencers spend considerable "keyboard time" checking out choices. Your brand needs to be there. In this new environment, search engines can be great sources for prospecting. *Paid search* (the term used for placing ads for your products or services on search engines and on content sites across the Internet) can greatly help a firm weed out high-potential prospects from mediocre suspects with spot-on targeting effectiveness and audience-specific messaging.

Consider the following B2B example. In an effort to generate better sales leads, software maker Citrix Systems, with the help of online marketer Ion Interactive, began in early 2006 to use real-time, post-click analyses to maximize paid search campaign conversion. This campaign was designed to attract hospitals to Citrix's new software product aimed at coordinating easily with the requirements of the Health Insurance Portability and Accountability Act. The campaign's purpose was to generate high-quality leads for follow-up by the Citrix Systems sales force.

By conducting post-click marketing segmentation analysis, Citrix immediately learned that more than 70 percent of search engine respondents were not in the target audience of hospital decision makers. But even with only 30 percent of the respondents in the target audience, conversion rates still soared 525 percent, based largely on the new campaign's use of directed click paths and audience-specific messaging. Within ten days of launch, RTP analyses (analyses of respondents, traffic sources, and paths) enabled Citrix to confirm Google as the best-performing search engine; by week three, all other search engines were eliminated from the budget.

The sales lead campaign launched with two test paths. Immediate real-time analysis revealed that path A was performing significantly better than path B. Based on real-time data, path C was crafted and launched, with nearly double the results of the already successful path A. This segmented traffic converted at a sales lead rate of 12 percent, or almost 2,500 percent better than the previous campaign launched in 2005. All in all, this campaign recalibration was impressively achieved within the *first three weeks* of campaign launch.[5]

What can we learn from Citrix and other cyber-savvy practitioners? There are two main lessons, with various ways to apply them.

Lesson 1: Invest in Your Web Property

Just a few short years ago, your Web site was a nice-to-have property in your corporate communications toolbox. No more. Now your firm's Web site serves as the gateway to your company for many buyers and prospects. Your Web site's perception-building influences cannot be overstated. Here's how to make the most of them.

- **Keep your message and layout simple.** Make sure your site quickly answers these two questions: (1) What is it you do? (2) What products or services do you sell?

In making messaging simple, perhaps Virgin founder Richard Branson explained it best when he said, "I think my dyslexia has helped. When I launch a new company, I need to understand the advertising. If I can understand it, then I believe anybody can. Virgin speaks in normal language instead of using phrases nobody understands like 'financial services industry.'"[6]

- **Know your referring sources.** What you want to know is (1) How are people finding you? (2) Where are they coming from? (3) Who's hyperlinking to your site? (4) Which of these referring sources bring you *quality* prospects, not just *quantity*? After all, the goal is to convert prospects into loyal, paying customers. Rating your referring sources by conversion rate can be a very insightful metric.

- **Use click paths and landing pages as perception builders.** When prospects click on your Google ad or your e-mail's hyperlink, where on your Web site are they taken? Sadly, many prospects land on a firm's home page or general product page and are immediately bombarded with information irrelevant to their original click motivation. These visitors feel lost, and many will click away in seconds. Solution? Create unique landing pages with compelling reasons to buy (concise product information, for example) and a clear call to action (click here to receive free white paper, or some such). In the visitor's mind, this landing page must show immediate relevance and build on the interest that compelled him or her to click your ad or hyperlink in the first place.

- **Track your wins and losses.** On your site, what do visitors do? Specifically: (1) What pages are they visiting? (2) On what links are they clicking? (3) How do they navigate through your site? (4) What do they find most compelling? As important, where are your visitors falling off? Web site analysis can give you great insights on what's working (or not), enabling you to build strong brand perceptions that ultimately lead to customer conversions. Zero in on your wins and losses and on the visitors' navigation behaviors that produce them. These insights can help you get better and better at building the right brand perceptions.

• **Provide user ratings and reviews.** To increase the time visitors spend on your product pages (and their likelihood of buying!), consider providing user product ratings and reviews. Here are four reasons:

1. Research finds that online consumers spend more time browsing products on a site when user ratings and reviews are offered than when they are not.[7]

2. U.S. shoppers consider buyer ratings and reviews to be the most useful e-commerce site feature, according to a 2007 joint research study by Bazaarvoice and Vizu.[8]

3. Research by the Kelsey Group on the impact of online consumer-generated reviews on the price consumers are willing to pay for a service delivered offline is telling. Consumers were willing to pay at least 20 percent more for services receiving an "Excellent" or 5-star customer rating than for the same service receiving a "Good" or 4-star rating.[9]

4. Web site tracking has found that products with customer-generated reviews and ratings help stimulate online purchase and lower return rates, as compared to nonrated products.[10] (Please see Chapter Eight's PETCO case for more information on the effect of customer-generated ratings and reviews on shopper buying behaviors.)

• **Consider "discovery" software for your site.** "Discovery" is a computing architecture that harnesses the so-called wisdom of crowds (in this case Internet users) to deliver relevant content and product placement in real time for Web site visitors. Since gift e-tailer Delightful Deliveries started using discovery software to help drive gift suggestions for on-site visitors, conversion rates have jumped to 10 percent for customers choosing gifts through the "discovery" window.

Case in Point

A twenty-something-year-old son wants to buy his dad a Father's Day gift. He goes on the Delightful Deliveries site and clicks around a few moments. Chocolates? No. Flowers? Heck no! Then up pops a discovery list powered by Aggregate Knowledge (a discovery software provider)—and on that list is a beer-of-the-month club. "Done," says the son, and he happily completes his transaction. That's discovery software in action. "We serve up gift recommendations based on real-time shopping trends," says Aggregate Knowledge founder Paul Martino, who explained to me that the recommendation was a by-product of what thousands of other people across the Web who made similar click sequences had ultimately bought. "We boost conversion rates by helping our Web clients fight the 'one and done,'" says Martino, referring to an online shopper's tendency to hit the dreaded Back button and leave a site without buying, after viewing just one page of a Web site.

Lesson 2: Invest in Search

Is your firm investing time and dollars to manage its search engine results? Search optimization involves designing your Web site so that it is more likely to show up in a Web search.

Businesses large and small are upping their search optimization budgets. By 2011, the search marketing industry is expected to grow to $18.6 billion, up from $11.5 billion in 2007.[11] Chances are, your competitors are increasingly spending more of their ad dollars to capture more Web traffic. Don't get left behind. Here are some starter guidelines to help:

• **Learn the lingo.** The world of search has a lingo all its own, and it's important to know, at minimum, the most often used terms. Some examples:

> *Organic positions.* These are search listings that appear down the left side of the return page, rather than in the sidebar or sponsored links. Studies suggest users pay more attention to the organic position.

> *Organic (or natural) search.* This is the process by which Web users find Web sites having unpaid search engine listings, as opposed to using sponsored search listings.

> *Sponsored search.* Companies pay Google (and other search engines) for guaranteed high placement on search results pages based on certain keywords.

> *Pay-for-click.* Advertisers pay the search engine only when users click on their Web sites.

• **Know your real estate value.** When you're building brand perceptions, not all the real estate on the search listings pages is equal. Where do visitors click after they type in their search term and land on the search listings page? Research suggests that the following real estate is prime: (1) the top portion of the page, (2) the left side of the page, (3) above the "fold" (that is, the listings that are viewable on the screen, with no scroll-down required).[12] (Please note: other Web research indicates that top rankings in the paid search listings, typically found on the right-hand side of the listings page, also carry positive perception with visitors.)

Indeed, position in search listings can drive brand perceptions. A research study by iProspect found that 36 percent of search engine users believe that the companies whose Web sites are returned at the top of the search results are the top companies in that field. Another 39 percent feel neutral on the question, and only 25 percent believe that top search engine rankings do not automatically denote an industry leader.[13]

- **Understand how search crawlers operate.** *Question:* How do you get your brand to routinely earn great spots in search listings? *Answer:* Provide tons of "relevant" content on your Web site. Search engine crawlers "crawl" the Web looking for content relevant to search words. But these crawlers read your text differently than human eyes. (They don't see text that has been converted into jpeg files, for example. They can't see text that is embedded in your Web video.) That's why it's important to stay up to speed on strategies for search engine optimization, with a particular eye on how to pick popular keywords.

- **Learn as you go.** Recall how Citrix applied various test paths to optimize its search returns. Smart move. One of the Web's huge benefits is the ability to constantly apply what's known in search optimization circles as "A-B split testing" to discern which ads, click paths, search words, and so on are reaping you the best conversions. Don't just guess, test.

The learn-as-you-go approach is also paying off for All Things Aquarium, which provides complete aquarium care, including custom design, ongoing maintenance, aquarium moving, and emergency care to commercial and residential accounts in the Chicago area. The twenty-year-old firm had not previously used the Internet for lead building. With a small budget in hand, owner Jeff Hintze began working with JumpFly, a search marketer, in 2006 to build a plan. First move? Developing and launching a geographically targeted Google AdWords campaign, catering to Internet users in All Things Aquarium's specific service areas. This meant that people searching for terms like *aquarium maintenance* would only find Jeff's listing if they were in his desired target area. In one short month, the firm received more than two hundred qualified local visitors to the Web site, producing numerous phone calls and several new clients. Months later, with continued positive results, Jeff reduced the firm's Yellow Pages ad budget and earmarked more dollars for pay-per-click advertising results. Moreover, the firm launched keyword campaigns on Yahoo! Search Marketing and Microsoft adCenter. Web traffic and the number of new leads tripled. The result? All Things Aquarium's revenue for the first half of 2007 surpassed the firm's total revenue for 2006.[14]

The Customer

Our customers are constantly watching to see if we practice what we preach about "customer first." What we as service providers perceive as inconsequential service details are often seen through the customer's eyes as BIG moments of truth in forming brand perceptions that have significant impact on future purchase decisions. Consider my recent experience:

> It's 5:30 P.M. on a Friday and I'm standing in line at my neighborhood video chain store. It's been a long work-week. I'm holding an armful of DVDs, quietly contemplating the start of my much-needed chill-out, movie mania weekend. I'm in one of two lines being served by checkout reps. There are several folks in line in front of me. I wait (patiently) for three or four minutes while those ahead of me are served. Finally, my turn comes, and I gladly move to the counter.
>
> That's when the rep informs me that he's "closed" and that I will need to move to the other cashier. I'm surprised and disappointed, but I obediently move to the other line and wait. Now I replace my "customer" eyes with my "loyalty maker" gawkers. I notice that the rep who says he is closed is wearing a "Manager" badge on his shirt. I watch him shuffle through a stack of papers and then carry a piece from the stack to an adjoining desk four steps away. My eyes follow him as he returns

to his post and files the piece of paper in a three-ring binder. I sense the customer behind me getting antsy. I turn to her and she shares in hushed tones that she's feeling slighted and ill-served. We wait. The manager feels our eyes. He looks up. He motions me over and says he can help me now—he "just needed to tidy-up some things." He takes me through my transaction. He takes my cash. He asks me if I'd like to try the chain's online service. I say no. He says, "It's free, for a month." I say no again, as I silently ponder . . . if a customer can't come first when she's literally standing in front of you and you are the *manager,* what would service online be like when I'm a lowly e-mail awaiting a response, or stuck in a phone queue on a call center line awaiting a rep? Thanks, but no thanks!

Most everyone has a story like mine. Sadly, the customer experience provided by many firms continues to disappoint. Fortunately, business bookshelves are blessed with a host of insightful how-to books about building competitive, compelling customer experiences. Dive in! (First, you might take a look at some of the titles I recommend on my Web site, **www .loyaltysolutions.com.**) But for now, here are six guidelines to consider to boost your customers' experiences and drive favorable brand perceptions:

1. Prioritize Process Improvements from the Customer's Perspective

When firms make operational improvement decisions, customer intelligence data (customer complaints, for example) closely drive those choices. Right? Wrong.

My company (with the help of research firm CustomerSat) recently asked more than five hundred corporate executives in B2B and B2C firms across various industries how they made operational improvement decisions. Over half (57 percent) of marketing executives and 50 percent of sales executives reported using internal factors or no formal process at all to identify problem areas and prioritize improvement efforts.

Translation? In half or more of the firms surveyed, what's right for the customer took a backseat to other decision-making influences, such as departmental lobbying, squeaky-wheel dynamics, and management "gut feel." Bottom line? If customer insights are not driving your process improvement priorities, your customer experiences are suffering, and so are your brand perceptions!

2. Personalize the Experience to Help Forge an Emotional Connection

When author Colin Shaw, author of *Customer Experience*, and his team signed on to help a U.S. bank redesign its branch loan experience, they found that a reduction in wait time was in order for all loan customers, and the bank streamlined its appointment system accordingly. But observation of customers also revealed some key differences among them and the need to personalize the customer experience by customer type.[15] Here are two examples:

- **"Principal's Office."** That's the name Shaw and his team assigned to one segment of bank customers: younger people who felt nervous applying for a loan. Although this customer group endeavored to do as much online as possible, the loan process required an on-site interview and paper signing. One such customer aptly described the experience as feeling "like I was going to see the principal, and I had done something wrong." Shaw's group observed these customers in the bank's waiting area: they fidgeted and tended to sit on the edge of their chairs, and, not surprising, they seemed increasingly concerned and uncomfortable the longer the wait time.

Personalization solution: Shaw's team recommended putting these customers at ease by having branch employees get out from behind the desk during meetings. Employees were coached on using small talk with the customers and threading into the conversation reassurances about the application process and what would happen next.

- **"Dignity."** Also identified was an older segment of customers who were raised to "pay their own way." The prospect of borrowing money made these people feel embarrassed. In the waiting area, these customers exhibited a tendency to "hide" by sitting with their backs to other customers; in one of the branches, these customers preferred seats tucked away behind a large plant.

Personalization solution: Shaw's team recommended that bank employees allocate ample time in meetings to allow the customer to "confess" why the money was needed, and to hold this discussion in a place with plenty of privacy. Shaw's research found that this private discussion time helped alleviate the burden this segment of customers felt about the whole act of borrowing money.

3. Help the Customer Feel in Control

Each time a firm has an encounter with a customer, within that encounter is at least one interaction known as a "moment of truth" because of its ability to disproportionately affect—positively or negatively—the customer's experience. When comparing customers' moments of truth across industries, an important clue emerges: the driving factor determining whether or not the customer perceives the outcome as positive is often tied to whether the customer experiences feelings of loss of control. The more informed the customer feels, the more the customer feels in control, and good perceptions follow.

Case in Point

With many retailers and manufacturers practicing "just-in-time" inventory management, shipping clients are clamoring for constant input and information. "The client wants to know where the blue socks in size medium are that he ordered two weeks ago from China," explains Jean-Philippe Thenoz, VP of CMA-CGM, the world's third-largest container shipping line by volume. Or take such fruit companies as Dole Food and Chiquita Brands International. These companies harvest green bananas, load them on ships in Fort-de-France, Martinique, and depend on a temperature-controlled, seven-day crossing to Northern France to ripen the fruit so that it's ready for sale in Europe upon arrival. CMA-CGM has instated new technology that now allows clients to request en route changes to the container's temperature.

But perhaps there's no greater moment of truth in shipping than early notification regarding shipping delays. That's why shipping giant Maersk Line has spent years developing sophisticated alert systems that notify customers when bad weather or port backups will delay shipments. This information, in turn, helps optimize the customer's production cycle. For example, an automaker that knows that the engine part made in China will arrive a day late can slow down production of other parts of the car assembly and, in turn, avoid the complication and cost associated with an assembly line shut-down or temporary storage of surplus inventory. Reducing uncertainties is paramount to managing moments of truth and keeping client perception positive. Says Piet Jan Ten Thije, Maersk's director of e-commerce, "The shipping period isn't the black hole it used to be for our customers."[16]

4. Address the "Worry" Question

My friend Bob founded and oversees a robust marketing agency. One of his firm's largest accounts, a multinational high-tech client, had made a recent personnel change on its marketing staff. Soon after, friction began to surface between the agency's account team and the client. To Bob's team, it seemed that the client was now micromanaging project work, asking for constant updates and detailed reports that took precious time away from real project advancement. Agency morale was sinking.

Rather than ignore this early discord and assume that the two teams would find their way, Bob worked on the assumption that an ounce of prevention is worth a pound of cure. In a one-on-one meeting with the client's senior team member, Bob acknowledged the friction and the need to remedy it. Not surprisingly, the feedback Bob received traced back to the client's newest team member. Her oversight demands reflected her new job accountability: ensure that the agency project work was "on time" and "right." So what did Bob do next? He and his agency team mapped out the steps by which project worked flowed between the two firms. He then met with the client's team (including their newest member), shared the map, and asked two critical questions: *What signals are we emitting that trigger your worry? Where on the map do they occur?* (He purposely met with the client team alone so they would feel more open to airing concerns and grievances about the agency's team.) Those questions, coupled with the work-flow map, enabled the two firms to zero in on hot spots and build common-ground solutions.

5. Get Customers Interacting: Help Customers Help Other Customers

When Thor Muller, Amy Muller, and Lane Becker operated Valleyschwag, a promotional giveaway company, they didn't set out to establish an online community forum by which their customers could help each other. But that's exactly what happened, and it turned out to be a great addition to the firm's customer service. Before, the three partners logged long hours answering customer questions by e-mail—many of them repetitive. But that quickly changed when they observed a new development: "In the comment section of our blog, customers began to help other customers," shared Muller.[17] At times, the comments referred to the firm's original blog post (for example, a question concerning a recently announced new product feature). In other cases, customers would initiate a completely different topic, posting questions about shipping solutions, T-shirt sizing, and so on.

Over time, the partners saw some real advantages of an online customer forum: (1) customers themselves are a cost-effective means of enhancing the firm's overall customer service, (2) customer-to-customer response is often speedier than service rep response, and (3) customer answers can often be more helpful and insightful than service rep answers simply because the customer has "lived" the same problem firsthand.

Microsoft's general manager of community support services, Sean O'Driscoll, agrees: "How do you get users to want to stay at your site and engage with others? The only way is peer-to-peer discussion, in their own voices, rather than the company's voice."[18] It's important, says O'Driscoll, that customers can quickly identify the most helpful answers to their most pressing questions. This requires those answers to surface first in response to the customer's search or question query. Moreover, it's important to identify and reward the core customer group that consistently provides answers.

But know that what customers say to each other about your product or brand will not always be positive. Take a deep breath and repeat after me: *The biggest mistake I can make is to try to edit or control the conversation.* Says O'Driscoll, "I spent my whole career being told to manage the brand, control the brand. The emergence of citizen markets means I can't control the brand anymore."

So true. But you *can* control your brand's value proposition. Recall the customer loaner car conversation in this chapter's opening? Peer-to-peer and customer-to-customer access and interaction can and will reveal brand shortcomings. For customer-to-customer interaction to work in your favor, you must keep your brand competitive.

6. Follow Your Mom's Advice

Want to take a big step forward in improving customers' perceptions of your brand? Remember what your mom taught you: *actions speak louder than words.*

Many firms profess to listen to customers, but Dell is out to prove it *really* listens and then *acts*. With a take-off on the word *brainstorm,* Dell aptly named its online customer community site IdeaStorm. The brainchild of Michael Dell himself, the site launched in February 2007, with the mission of providing a forum in which site visitors can share, with Dell and each other, input and ideas on how Dell can improve its products and services. Ideas are displayed on the site according to their most recent popularity with the visitor community. Perhaps the site's most customer-friendly feature is the "Ideas in Action" space in which visitors can see how and where IdeaStorm suggestions have been implemented. For example, in response to a visitor's suggestion to sell ink cartridges at local retail outlets (the site even provides a link to the visitor's original suggestion), Dell reported a new alliance with office store chain Staples, which will sell Dell ink and toner supplies. Visitor suggestions frequently center around changes in the style, design, and hardware of Dell products. Dell employees from various departments routinely join the conversation. Dell assigns a logo to Dell employees who provide updates and feedback in an official capacity.

How is the market responding to IdeaStorm? Enthusiastically. Even Dell's harshest critics seem to be giving Dell its due for this ambitious customer initiative.

Bottom line: our moms were right when they told us actions speak louder than words. Customer sites such as IdeaStorm can help demonstrate to customers that listening is all-important and offer proof positive that the sponsoring firm is paying attention *and* taking action on what it has learned.

Prospects, Influencers, and Observers

For many business veterans, social or "new" media can seem like an alien world—full of confusing, mysterious, unpredictable forces that are better left alone. The truth is, ratings sites, online communities, customer-generated content, blogs, message boards, and the like represent an ever-changing ocean of influence that can't be ignored.

Here are some guidelines to help you navigate this new sea of social media and third-party influencers and have confidence doing it.

1. Go Where the Conversation Is

Where are buyers and influencers talking about your offerings and those of your competitors? (Hint: it's *not* on your corporate Web site.) For example, this blog post by CustomerThink editor Gwynn Young offers clues on where a book publisher (and the author) can find the real conversation: "On a recent trip, I got fed up with the tour guidebook I'd bought. When we got home, I went up on the site I'd bought it from and wrote a review, saying all the reasons the book failed me. Now others will be forewarned, and, maybe, the publisher will see it, too, and make changes."[19]

What you can do:

Build a search on your company's name, products, key employee names, and so on. (Google Blog Search and Technorati can help.) This way you will receive routine notification of what's being said about you. Build a search using competitor names, products, competitors' executives, and so on as well. Find popular discussion boards, blogs, and podcasts that are in your space, and subscribe to them. For example, Twitter, the free social networking and micro-blogging site that allows users to send text-based posts (known as tweets) up to 140 characters long, is proving to be an effective customer listening post for Southwest Airlines. When Travis Johnson sent a complaint about the airline's check-in process into the "online ether," a Southwest employee sent him a quick, pub-lic response that read, "So sorry to hear it! What don't you like about the check-in process? Did your flight get off okay?" Reports Southwest spokesperson Christi Day, "We monitor those channels because we know these conversations are taking place there, and we can either watch the conversation or take part in them."[20]

The airline sees the "listening-in" value of social media sites and has mobilized accordingly. Southwest's social media team includes a chief Twitter officer responsible for tracking Twitter comments and monitoring a Facebook group; an online repre-sentative who oversees the airline's presence on such sites as LinkedIn, Flickr, and YouTube; and another who interacts with bloggers.

2. Bring the Conversation Home: Build Your Own Social Network

Facebook and MySpace are acclaimed social networking companies. But some firms are finding that they don't have to *be* a social networking firm or build a community on one to *make use* of social networks. Just ask Hearst-Argyle Television, which launched High School Playbook, the first high school sports pro-gramming venture to combine social networking with high-defini-tion video provided by TV videographers and camcorder-equipped student journalists. "[On High School Playbook], . . . kids can upload video, talk about games, trash talk kids from other schools and more. You go to a participating city like Louisville and go to your school and see all the games and scores," explains Jerry Sheer, whose firm builds social networks for big companies. High School Playbook's social networking elements include personal profile pages, team pages, school pages, cheerleader pages, voting, and other messaging tools that foster byplay among rival schools and fans.

High School Playbook is proving to be a natural brand extension for Hearst-Argyle, which has television stations in twenty-six U.S. markets. For example, the firm's local TV stations can provide game-day weather reports and tie local sports coverage to High School Playbook. "By creating a social network, a company can watch as its customers build their own communities and their own groups. . . . They will be able to mine whatever information is developed on the site, rather than have it outside of their control. [For example], if a new ad gets a negative reaction, [the firm] can make adjustments in their next campaign. Most companies would rather have that information under their own control, as opposed to being in some group bashing in Facebook," advises Sheer.[21]

What you can do:

Rather than putting a small group of people together in a room, as a typical focus group does, do as Sheer suggests and build a social network to allow literally thousands of people—whether customers, prospects, influencers, or observers—to talk about your brand (or not), positioning your firm to make "better business decisions."

3. Know What Ignites Customer Rant

Hint: Monitor customer frustration.

———————

In recent years, consumer behaviorists have isolated customer frustration (think "I was on hold for fifteen minutes and then got disconnected" and "What should have been a five-minute fix turned into an hour") as a highly negative emotion that occurs in the customer's mind when a potentially rewarding act is blocked or a targeted goal is missed.[22] Interestingly, whereas many firms focus on achieving the customer emotion of delight, few strategies address prevention and care of the toxic emotion of frustration.

What you can do:

Learn from customers' rants (both your customers' and your competitors'). Use them to constantly identify and isolate those aspects of your product and service delivery that ignite customer frustration. (Call a staff meeting, bring in the Web "evidence," and compile a frustration list.) Work hard and stay focused on remedying these culprits.

4. Take Customer "Repair Work" Off the Board or Blog

Some customer rants are not individually addressable. For example, a rant that simply says "I hate [firm name goes here]" is probably not a good investment of your firm's time.

But plenty of rants are very addressable—for example, "After four failed attempts at getting the company's help with the product, it now sits unused in its box." The quicker you reach out, the better. When approaching a frustrated customer in cyberspace, the first step is to ask the customer to contact you directly, one-on-one, through e-mail, phone, or even snail mail. That way, you can start the process of finding a solution in a less public forum.

What you can do:

Assign your customer reps popular discussion boards and blogs to monitor (see point 1). Respond to customer rants early! Teach your customer reps how to effectively console frustrated customers who have posted or blogged. One good way to jump-start a mend-the-fences dialogue with a ranting customer is to post a message like this:

My name is Jason, and I am with [your firm's name]. I read your post and wanted to extend my apologies for the frustration this experience has caused you. If you would contact me directly at [Jason's e-mail address here], I will gladly research this further on your behalf. I hope to hear from you soon.

But know this: ranting customers have already demonstrated their affinity for sharing experiences online. Don't even begin the contact if you're not armed with the know-how and capability to find a real solution. Otherwise, all you'll do is further inflame the situation and ignite more online rant.

Once you have resolved the problem to the customer's satisfaction, ask the customer to please post the "end of the story." We hope that enough goodwill has been created that the customer will agree to do it. If not, or if the post doesn't appear in a reasonable amount of time, then you need to post the facts about how the problem was resolved.

5. Know What Ignites Customer Rave

The simple answer: unexpected value. When a series of hurricanes ravaged Florida in 2004, USAA Insurance reached out to its credit card customers in the state with help: interest rates were lowered to 0 percent through January 2005, credit card payments were deferred ninety days, all late fees were waived, and unsecured loans up to $25,000 were offered to hurricane victims. With proactive customer value moves like that, it's little wonder that USAA topped *Business Week*'s 2007 list of customer service champs.[23]

What you can do:

Take the "What you can do" for customer rants outlined earlier and apply it to customer raves. But one note of caution here: customers cannot appreciate unexpected value when basic, expected value is missing. So first get the frustration culprits out of your systems and processes.

6. When You *Misspeak* in Cyberspace, *Apologize* in Cyberspace

Sooner or later, it's going to happen. You (or someone in your firm) will send out an e-mail, blog entry, discussion post, or other message that you afterward regret. That's the very circumstance in which Edelman exec Steve Rubel found himself. The following is a portion of his open letter of apology to the editor in chief of *PC Magazine* and the employees of Ziff-Davis Media. Steve's letter is a good model of how to follow up and begin to "right the wrong."

> Dear Mr. Louderback,
>
> Last Friday, yes Friday the 13th, I put up a post on Twitter that I wish I hadn't. I said that I don't read the hard copy of *PC Magazine* and that my free subscription goes in the trash. In a guest editorial on Strumpette you weighed whether the magazine in response should blacklist all PR pitches from Edelman, my employer, on behalf of our tech clients.
>
> I learned a valuable lesson. Post too fast without providing context and it can elicit an unintended response. . . .
>
> I apologize if you and the editorial team at Ziff-Davis took offense to my post.[24]

What you can do:

(1) Learn to censor yourself. Ask: Could this text have big, unintended consequences? If yes, better to store it in your "draft" file for more thought. (2) When you've misspoken, humbly and sincerely apologize—the quicker and more "loudly," the better. (3) Confess your transgression with rich context so that readers can quickly grasp the entirety of what you wrote previously and why you are apologizing and retracting. (4) Choose your cyberspace apology channels so that both the quality of readership and the number of eyeballs reading your retraction exceed, or at minimum match, the readership of what you wrote in the first place.

7. Follow the "Trust = Transparency" Rule

Hear ye, hear ye: on the Web, *partial* transparency is a big liability. The Sherlock Holmeses of the blogosphere will root out the whole story, and the exposure is not often pretty. That's what

Wal-Mart discovered soon after the folksy blog "Wal-Marting Across America" was launched, which featured a couple, Laura and Jim, making their maiden voyage in a recreational vehicle from Las Vegas to Georgia. The couple began their RV journey in late September 2006, stopping at Wal-Marts along the way, to enjoy the free parking and hobnob with Wal-Mart employees from store checkers to executives—all of whom described their delight working for the mega-retailer. Laura and Jim cheerfully chronicled these outings with posts and pictures on their "Wal-Marting" blog.

But here's the problem: although the Web site carried a "Working Families for Wal-Mart" banner, nowhere on the site was it disclosed or even alluded to that Wal-Mart had paid for the couple's RV, the gas, their flight to Las Vegas to pick up the RV, or the blog entries.

Predictably, the pundits piled on. For example, in a *Business Week* article one short week after the couple's first blog entry, Jonathan Rees, labor historian and associate professor at Colorado State University at Pueblo, stated, "They pay an unspecified sum to these people to say how great Wal-Mart is—I think it is deceptive."[25]

What you can do:

Before launching any social media campaign, test it against this standard: if the true facts are not for public disclosure, go back to the drawing board and design a campaign that can withstand the consequences of full transparency.

8. Learn About Employee Issues from Employees Who Blog

Guideline: don't shoot the messenger; learn from the message. (For those of you who are baby boomers and older, who cut your career teeth in large corporations where command-and-control hierarchies reigned supreme, this guideline may be a tough one to accept, so keep an open mind as you read on.)

What do you do about that employee who blogs anonymously, taking your company to task on issues ranging from cafeteria food quality to employee evaluation systems? Find him and fire him? Or let him be, and use his rants to improve employee value? Faced with that very situation, Microsoft chose the latter, and here's why.

Since 2004, an anonymous Microsoft manager has blogged under the name Mini-Microsoft, ranting about a host of employee issues. The blog embarrassed Microsoft brass, and early on, there were high-level meetings about how to "out" the rogue blogger. But executives quickly decided against it for one key reason: "Everyone knew he was right. The point was to fix the problems he was bringing up," conceded a former Microsoft executive. And that's what the software giant has done; food quality is up, locker-room towels are back, the human resources VP has launched a well-received internal blog to better communicate with employees, and the list goes on.

Meanwhile, in a deep-cover interview with *Wired* magazine, Mini-Microsoft reported being delighted with Microsoft's responses. He still takes care to blog only from home using an anonymous server, and even his wife is unaware of his blogging. But he has no delusions about why his blog continues: "I exist because they [upper management] haven't come after me."[26]

What you can do:

The old adage about an ounce of prevention being worth a pound of cure, mentioned earlier in this chapter, applies here too. Use internal communication tools—open-door policies, internal blogs, bulletin boards, staff engagement surveys, and so on—to show employees you are listening and taking action. These measures can help stem external employee blogging. But if external blogging strikes, think twice before you try to crush it. Otherwise, you can end up creating far more employee rant and disillusionment than what the original situation alone produces.

9. When Ex-Employees Blog, Think Carefully Before Pouncing

When a former Dell Kiosk employee posted a blog titled "22 Confessions of a Former Dell Sales Manager" and then the *Consumerist* (consumerist.com) blogged about it, lots of cyber-eyeballs followed, including Dell's legal department, which sent the *Consumerist* a take-down notice, citing the information as confidential and proprietary. "22 Confessions" offered buyers tips on getting the best deal from Dell, such as where to look on the Dell site for lowest prices and when in the quarter to buy because quarterly sales reports can push pricing down. The buzz got even stronger when the *Consumerist* posted Dell's take-down letter along with a polite but firm refusal. Dell backed off, and soon after conceded that it had handled the situation poorly. Instead of trying to control the already public information, the company stated it should have simply corrected whatever was inaccurate.[27]

But that's not the only lesson. In the same article, storied Dell watcher Jeff Jarvis adds other important insights: "If people are worried that there's a better price in some other ad or section of the site, give them a guarantee that every quote they get is the lowest price available. . . . If you read between the lines of what the ex-sales guy wrote, you simply see his list of the worries he has heard that keep customers from buying Dell products. Hear those problems and solve them openly and you will sell more products and garner more trust and goodwill and customers. Openness is a strategy."

What you can do:

Dell and Jarvis have it right. Don't try to control the information. You can't. Correct inaccurate information. And look for the customer worries and frustrations hidden in the employee's observations. It's valuable input for your next customer strategy session!

10. Humanize Your Company: Company Bloggers Can Help

People don't bond with brands or firms. They bond with *people*. Company bloggers are proving to be great at helping firms become more "humanized." Bloggers can demonstrate that behind your brand are *real* people with *real* passion and *real* customer commitment.

The best blogs aren't one-way monologues; they foster two-way conversation. Moreover, the most successful company blogs and bloggers don't run from tough, hot issues, but face them head-on. And when a crisis arises, customers learn to rely on these bloggers for their calm, authentic voice and the truth. One of my favorite examples is Dell's Direct2Dell site. Although slow to adopt blogging (the site went live in June 2006), Dell came on board with a vengeance and great form.

What you can do:

Many firms remain stuck in a "look, don't touch" cyberspace mode whereby they follow online customer rants and raves but never join the conversation. That's an unwise approach. As more and more brands enter the conversation in cyberspace, those that don't reach out will likely pay increasingly costly perception penalties.

11. Experiment with New Ways to "Bury" Unwanted Search Results

Are there steps you can try to take to help bury a nasty blog posting or a scathing news story deep in your firm's search listing pages? Yes, say Austin-based search experts Lewis Talbert and Abel Alvarado. They offer these guidelines for burying unwanted research results:

- Create and maintain a Wikipedia profile of your firm. Wikipedia sites typically get high search listings placement.

- Create additional Web sites for your firm. For example, try Googling the word *Google*, and you'll see dozens of Google company Web sites near the top of the search results.

- Issue press releases to help trigger positive news coverage.

- Use good old-fashioned customer relations and contact the blogger with the gripe about your firm and attempt to make amends.[28]

The Nine Space Rule

So now you have seen how each of the three parties—(1) the brand, (2) the customer, and (3) the prospects, influencers, and observers who listen in and weigh in about the brand—plays dual roles: each can be a perception maker and a perception taker. Plot these three parties on a three-by-three matrix and Eureka! The outline for an important new taming strategy emerges! (See Figure 4.2.)

There are nine different perception spaces that require your attention—hence the name Nine Space Rule. In its own way, each space is contributing (or not) to your brand's market perceptions. Filling in the diagram can help you spot your firm's strengths and vulnerabilities. Use the perception-making vehicles listed below the matrix to jump-start your thinking. For instance,

- What online tools do you have in place to help monitor industry sites where third parties and other noncustomers engage in dialogue with your customers about your brand (space 6 on the chart)?

- What provisions have you made to encourage customer interaction so that your customers can share insights and learn from fellow users (space 5 on the chart)?

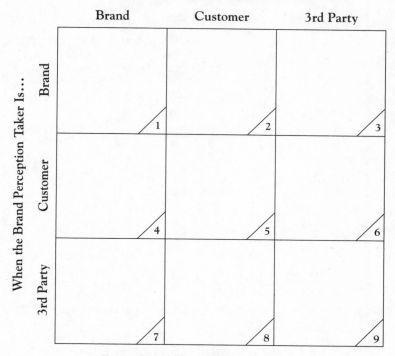

When the Brand Perception Maker Is...

Examples of Perception Making, by Space

1 - Internal branding program
2 - Customer rating or review
3 - Parody of Brand commercial on YouTube
4 - Brand-sponsored customer e-letter
5 - Brand user's complaint posted on customer community site
6 - Phishing
7 - Brand commercial on YouTube
8 - Brand user's complaint posted on sports enthusiast bulletin board
9 - Noncustomer blog entry about brand

Figure 4.2.   Apply the Nine Space Rule

In today's search-and-switch, compulsion-to-compare world, your brand perception-making plan must address the contingencies in each of the nine spaces. That's the rule!

For more information on the Nine Space Rule and how to put it to work for your brand, visit **www.loyaltysolutions.com/ NineSpaceRule.**

Moving On

Although you will never be able to completely control what people say about your brand or your company, you can steer those comments and conversations in the right direction. Your brand, your customers, and other influencers all play critical perception-building roles, and you must devise your loyalty strategies accordingly.

It is essential that you constantly provide these all-important perception makers and takers plenty to crow about regarding your brand. The next chapter can help you do just that!

Taming Takeaways

- In today's wired world, there are typically three parties in any customer relationship: (1) your brand, (2) your customer, and (3) all the other people, online and off, contributing their two cents about your brand and those who observe them. Each of these three parties can participate at any time as brand perception makers and brand perception takers. It is essential that your firm think strategically about how to nurture positive brand perceptions with all three.

- Finding the messaging that truly speaks to why your brand is better than the competition—and getting that story heard correctly and by the right audiences in the marketplace—will go a long way to driving loyalty to your brand.

- The younger your customers, the more they spend time in cyberspace. It's increasingly important that your firm pay close attention to the perceptions your firm is building (intentionally and unintentionally) through its Web site and its search listings.

- More and more of your brand's market perceptions will be driven by new media (user-generated content, including blogs, message boards, forums, community sites, ratings and reviews, and the like). To thrive, your firm cannot ignore this tidal wave of influence and, instead, must equip its employees with the necessary skill sets to leverage new media.

- Practicing the Nine Space Rule and crafting your brand's perception-building plans around it are essential. Leaving any of the nine spaces unattended is a risk to your brand's welfare. Don't make that mistake.

5

How to Be (and Stay) Damn Different

As we learned in Chapter Three, continually acing your buyers' Worth-It Test is how you tame their search-and-switch tendencies. And as we saw in Chapter Four, supplying your brand's all-important perception makers and takers with plenty to crow about is essential to making the worth-it equation work in your favor. Both of these strategies require your brand to be perceived as distinguishably different. Want to know how to *be* different and *stay* different in a marketplace where the compulsion to compare abounds? This chapter is for you!

Being Damn Different

Take these words to heart: differentiate or die. Distinguishing your brand from the competition is more important for attracting and keeping customers than ever before. Here's why.

In today's Googlized, search-driven marketplace, customer knowledge is no longer limited to simple awareness. Instead, in today's networked world, buyers can enjoy deep "informedness"— near-perfect information concerning what's available around the globe, from whom, with what attributes, and for what price. And, in most B2B and B2C categories, the array of product and service choices informed customers can access is staggering—due to big increases in product variety made possible by advancements in manufacturing technology and distribution. The result? Mass-market "fat spots" with high market share now break into portfolios of "sweet spots" with high *margin* share, explains Wharton professor Eric Clemons.[1] From power bars to bottled waters to industrial cleaning services, across almost every product and service category, the array of sweet-spot choices is immense; and more and more often, the "best" product or service in any category is increasingly defined by who is buying and what that customer wants from it.

Thanks to the Internet, your products and services are being "sized up" in record time. Internet-based information tools—comparison shopping sites, blogs, networks, user-generated content—enable buyers to quickly evaluate a brand's differentiation (or lack of it) as never before. Missing the mark on differentiation now carries some stiff customer penalties, including the following:

- **The "me-too" penalty.** Have you ever heard the Stealers Wheel hit tune from the early 1970s, "Stuck in the Middle"? My favorite line is "Clowns to the left of me, jokers to the right / here I am, stuck in the middle with you."[2] In many ways, that's an apt description of your brand's dilemma when it's perceived by customers as an undifferentiated offering, floating in a sea of similar offerings. Under these circumstances, your me-too product or service has a bleak future. Why? Because your brand must compete with other me-too products, and brutal price competition will inevitably ensue. As marketing guru Don Peppers so aptly warns, "You'd better be prepared to match the lowest price of your stupidest competitor."[3] Stuck in the middle, indeed!
- **The compromise penalty.** Clemons coined the phrase "compromise discount" to describe the price penalty that informed customers apply to brands whose "fit" does not match well to their needs. For example, the family planning a Disney World vacation will ascribe a lower value to a hotel that is a significant drive from the theme park than one a short tram ride away. Reports Clemons, "With better information, customers know more about their alternatives, and the compromise discount resulting from poor fit is higher than ever."[4]

Get the picture? Assume that your buyers know as least as much about their buying options as you do and will reward your brand only for the differences they recognize and find compelling. How do you win in this transparent marketplace? By ensuring that your brand is discernibly different.

Doing Differentiation "Right"

So how should your firm approach differentiation? In a marketplace brimming with both customer informedness and limitless competition, what does it take to do differentiation "right"? Here are ten ways successful companies do it.

1. Walk Your Innovation Talk

When it comes to innovation, few firms "walk the talk," according to the recent McKinsey Global Survey on Corporate Innovation. Even though some 70 percent of corporate leaders say innovation is among their top three priorities for driving growth, few firms operate accordingly. "For example, only 36 percent of top managers (and just over a quarter of other executives) say innovation is part of everything the organization does. Further, although more than a third of top managers (those at the senior vice president level and above) say innovation is part of the leadership team's agenda, an equal number say their companies govern innovation in an ad hoc way," reports McKinsey.[5]

What separates firms that do innovation well from those that don't? The study found three key things: (1) performance reviews of C-level executives (CEO, CFO, COO, and so on) include innovation metrics; (2) innovation is a central theme of the organization's annual planning process; and (3) the firms focus as frequently on crucial breakthrough innovations as on innovations pertaining to existing products and processes.

Walking the innovation talk is anything but easy. A firm's ability to innovate is a fragile corporate competency that requires constant nurturing. Even if innovation excellence does manifest for a time, without proper care, the competency fades. Apple's

Steve Jobs describes the predictable downward spiral to which formerly innovative firms often succumb. In the beginning, "Some very good product people invent some very good products and the company achieves a monopoly," explains Jobs. "[But] what's the point of focusing on making the product even better when the only company you can take business from is yourself? So a different group of people starts to move up. And who usually ends up running the show? The sales guy."[6] Over time, according to Jobs, the monopoly runs out, and by then, the best product folks have left or they've lost their influence, and the company goes through a very tough time and either survives or doesn't.

When Jobs returned to Apple in 1997, the company was adrift. "When I got back, Apple had forgotten who we were. Remember that Think Different ad campaign we ran? It was certainly for customers, but it was even more for Apple. That ad was to remind us of who our heroes are and who we are. Companies sometimes do forget. Fortunately, we woke up. And Apple is doing the best work in its history."

2. Move Beyond Customer Data Mining

Question: Name a firm with an unrivaled history for delivering unique, uncompromising product design excellence. *Answer:* Consumer electronics maker Bang & Olufsen (B&O).

Where does this firm find its inspiration and acuity for breakthrough designs? Hint: it's not from incessant mining of customer data or invading customers' privacy about their purchase habits. Instead, B&O looks within.

B&O maintains a strong product-oriented culture of designers and technicians with a passion for design and performance integrity and with keen, instinctive insights into what customers want. "Courage to constantly question the ordinary in search of surprising, long-lasting experiences" is how the Denmark-based firm, founded in 1925, describes its relentless quest for developing innovative and original products that make a noticeable difference.[7]

B&O has been showered with praise from some unlikely design authorities. "No other company has contributed more to modern industrial design than B&O," declares New York's Museum of Modern Art, which in 1972 chose seven B&O products for its permanent design collection. The firm's genius is its ability to deliver brilliant technology housed in stunning aesthetics. And consumers take notice. Reports chief technology officer Peter Peterson, "A few years ago we asked people what they liked most about Bang & Olufsen products. Those who did not own any said, 'the way it looks.' Those who owned our products said, 'The way it works.'"[8]

3. Aim for the Sweet Spots

In plotting your differentiation strategy, fat spots and sweet spots are critical concepts to understand. A fat spot refers to a market's traditional core and the huge concentration of buyers that reside there. Typically, many firms compete for these same fat-spot buyers with products that, in the eyes of the customer, are very similar to one another. In contrast, sweet spots refer to small pockets of buyers residing on the fringes of a category, served by a small contingent of firms providing products highly differentiated from fat-spot offerings. Whereas fat spots typically represent huge share but thin profit margins, sweet spots represent small share but huge margins. That's because customers are willing to pay more for sweet-spot products that precisely match their specific needs than for less differentiated fat-spot products.

Based on nearly a decade of research in B2C markets, Clemons and his colleague Rick Spitler make a convincing case that aiming for the sweet spots is how B2C firms should direct their differentiation endeavors. The rationale is simple and bold: over time, more and more customers who care about a category will find their way to perfect sweet-spot offerings. The fat-spot middle will contains only customers who are largely indifferent, choosing among largely equivalent offerings, and making those choices based almost entirely on price. As more and more competitors introduce highly focused products that delight, it becomes necessary for all products to compete either purely on price or on nearly perfect fit. Clemons and Spitler fiercely drill to this bottom line: it's no longer necessary to focus on getting *most* folks to *like* you, but instead on getting *some* folks to *love* you.[9]

Consider the case of Victory Brewing Company, launched in 1996 in an old Pepperidge Farm factory in Downingtown, Pennsylvania, by beer lovers Ron Barchet and Bill Covaleski. The microbrewery's first two beers were purposely designed to appeal to opposite ends of the beer drinker's taste palate. The first beer, Victory Lager, is a traditional beer, reminiscent of Budweiser and other good, mass-appeal lagers. On the love-like-hate scale, everyone likes it and no one hates it. Yet tellingly, Victory Lager sales represent less than 1 percent of the company's revenues. Now consider the brewery's other launch brand: HopDevil Ale, a bitter brew with a strong taste of orange and pine tar. Owing to its ample use of Northwest Cascades hops, this beer's bitterness scores high: where Budweiser is a 16, HopDevil's is a 68. In fact, its flavor is so intense, many first-time tasters cannot even swallow it. But here's the kicker: even while HopDevil is the *most hated* of Victory beers, it is also the *most loved,* and the beer accounts for almost half of Victory Brewing Company's sales.[10]

4. Focus on Unserved and Underserved Buyers

Jason Lander quickly spotted underserved buyers when he began selling temporary nursing services to understaffed hospitals. His customers' big issue? Tedious, resource-consuming paperwork required for employing nursing temps devoured hospital staff time. So Jason began work on an online system that hospitals could use to book nursing temps and streamline supporting paperwork and documentation. When each of the five Seattle hospitals he met with said they would try the system if he built it, he knew he was on to something. Jason resigned his day job and launched

ShiftWise in 2002. By 2006, with more than 350 customers, annual revenue reached $8.5 million.

ShiftWise client Oakwood Healthcare System illustrates the before-and-after appeal of the ShiftWise system. Located in suburban Detroit, Oakwood contracts with twenty-two nurse employment agencies to help staff its four hospitals and forty-three clinics. Oakwood would issue a steady flow of nursing requests to agencies ad hoc from fax, e-mail, and phone, making the system's paper trail management cumbersome and taxing. Pulling the proper staff certificates for accreditation authorities when they made spot inspections was equally arduous and time consuming. Reported Oakwood's chief nursing officer Barbara Medvec, "We were in a decentralized manual process. It was hours and hours of labor."[11]

ShiftWise helped clear these logjams. Using the online system, Oakwood saved $1.2 million in 2006, due to more efficient nursing scheduling and less use of expensive agency nurses. Moreover, the ShiftWise accounting features helped reduce Oakwood's bookkeeping expenses and lowered staff time requirements related to accreditation spot checks.

ShiftWise sees steady growth and profitability ahead. The U.S. Department of Health and Human Services predicts that the 6 percent shortfall between nursing supply and demand in 2000 will double in 2010. What does that mean for ShiftWise? More business from more hospitals scrambling to fill more open shifts and manage the paperwork that comes with it. No doubt, spotting unserved and underserved buyers, and then serving them, pays.

5. Build Strategy Around Things That Will Not Change

In the world of innovation, a lot of people are preoccupied with efforts to spot the next big thing, constantly scanning the marketplace in search of answers to "What's going to change?" But Amazon founder Jeff Bezos offers contrarian advice: "It helps to base your strategy on things that won't change. . . . At Amazon we're always trying to figure that out, because you can really spin up flywheels around those things. All the energy you invest in them today will still be paying you dividends ten years from now."[12]

How about "unsightly panty lines"? Many women around the world check for them in the mirror every day. And tested against Bezos's "What *won't* change?" standard, there's little chance that this concern will ever go away. (Male readers are possibly shaking their heads now and thinking maybe they should skip this section. Don't you dare!) Can you build a successful product line and a multimillion-dollar company around women's panty-line concerns? You bet!

In 1998, frustrated by the panty-line problem, twenty-seven-year-old Sara Blakely cut the feet off of a pair of panty hose so that she could "look smashing" in a pair of cream-colored slacks worn with strappy sandals. Eureka! Spanx was born.

Blakely, then a national sales manager for an office equipment company, worked nights and weekends to launch her product. She researched and authored her own patent for footless pantyhose. She named her product and penned the slogan "We've got your butt covered."[13] She nabbed hosiery mills for production. She cold-called department store chains. Step-by-step, Blakely shepherded this breakthrough hosiery concept to market. When Oprah Winfrey chose Spanx in 2000 as one of her "favorite things," the product really took off.

In 2007, Blakely's Atlanta-based company generated more than $250 million in annual retail sales.[14] Today, the firm employs a staff of eighty, and offers one hundred different hosiery styles. Major retailers and specialty boutiques nationwide stock her product lines. And Blakely continues to shine her firm's innovation light on timeless women's hosiery issues—with such offerings as Super Spanx (the original footless body-shaping pantyhose with extra tummy control) to Two Timin' Tights (reversible tights, two colors in one pair) to Topless Trouser Socks (no more binding leg band). Blakely's success is proof positive that staying focused on "things that will not change" can fuel innovation and capture devoted customers.[15]

6. Create Your Customer Benefit Ladder

Remember the scene from the *Wizard of Oz* when Dorothy's dog, Toto, tugs at the curtain and reveals the Great Wizard for what he really is—a mere man fumbling with special effects gadgetry to produce smoke and sound? Think of customer informedness that way, as the force pulling back the curtain on brand authenticity. Using information and opinions from countless networked sources, the prospective buyer can quickly answer the question, "Does this brand really provide genuine differences, or is its differentiation based largely on emotion-laden appeals and image?" Take Clemons's caution to heart: "As fact-based, fit-based assessments will begin to override emotive appeals in many categories, the power of emotive appeal [alone] will protect very few companies."[16]

Please note: this does not mean that forging an *emotional connection* between customers and brands is not critical—it is. In fact, equipping the brand with a strong foundation of technical and functional benefits gives the brand credibility and makes the emotional ties that much stronger. So think in terms of creating a bottom-up, three-tier customer benefit ladder: *tier one: technical benefits; tier two: functional benefits; and tier three: emotional benefits*.

Consider Michelin radial tires. The foundation of the brand is its technical benefits: a specially formulated rubber compound. That technical benefit feeds into the brand's functional benefits of shorter stopping distance, better starting grip, and so forth. Then the brand's emotional benefits come into play; in other words, the first two tiers of the benefit ladder are addressed before Michelin engages the buyer emotionally with such benefits as driver and passenger safety, confidence to enjoy the road, feeling like a good parent or protector. These emotional benefits form the basis of Michelin's powerhouse positioning versus competitors; the functional and technical benefits serve as the customer's "reason to believe."

7. "Perry Mason" Your Differences

Will your brand's "reason to believe" defend you successfully against relentless comparison? Could Perry Mason present your "distinguishably different" case to a jury of skeptical buyers and win? Or how about on a blog or online message board: Is your product or service's "Why should I buy?" quickly and easily explainable and defendable?

The differences your brand offers must be able to survive constant scrutiny and attack by customers with a compulsion to compare. That means your differences must, in marketing terms, have credibility and believability. After all, in today's wired world, scores of customers will be weighing in. Your differences must be so strong and clear that they make your story plausible and unique.

Suppose you are one of the fifteen million Americans swimming at least once a week for exercise, and you want music to help keep you pumped when you're doing your laps. What's the product you would trust to give you clear underwater sound?

How about swim-friendly earbuds? Umm, maybe.

Or how about something more radical: a product that bypasses your ears and instead sends sound through the skull by a process called bone conduction?

Now *that's* a Perry Mason difference!

Bone conduction technology is the basis for the waterproof music player SwiMP3, made by swim-gear maker Finis. The device uses cheek pads (which connect to swim goggles) rather than earbuds to send clearer sound underwater. Unlike swim-friendly earbuds, which must compete with water in the ear canal to deliver great sound, bone conduction uses the water in the ear to help seal in the sound.

Two years of product development bore fruit in 2005 when SwiMP3 generated $2 million in retail sales. In 2006, the sales rose to $2.5 million, representing 20 percent of Finis sales.[17] With major retailers now stocking the waterproof tune player, future sales look bright. Perry Mason, no doubt, would agree!

8. Remember, Differences Aren't Just Product Related

Sure, product features drive differences. But what if you sell services? How can you create a meaningful difference? A recent speaking engagement with a Carrier distributor serving southern U.S. dealers brought me in touch with a savvy "difference maker." Meet Wayne Craig, a thirty-year veteran of the wholesale heating and air conditioning business.

Feeling His Customers' Pain

Craig spent the early years of his career as a purchasing agent for a parts distributor. For eight years, Craig heard countless spiels from scores of sales reps and, in the process, experienced firsthand the pain of "being sold." Craig explains, "One of the things that I intensely disliked about salespeople was they would come in and flop down on the chair in my office and sit there and really waste my time. They actually had nothing better to do than to drop in and give me the price sheet. Period."

So, several years later, when Craig himself became an outside sales rep, he was determined to find a better way. "When I got out there and started talking to customers, I saw that my competitors and I, as salespeople, were basically selling the same thing for basically the same price and that if I didn't do something to set myself apart, I was never going to go anywhere."

His early years in the industry had given Craig some important insights. He knew that the contractors who were his customers were preoccupied with selling their systems and making sure that their mechanics got out the door and to their next installation or service call. That meant inventory control often received scant management attention, and this lack of attention often carried significant costs. For example, when a mechanic goes out on a job without the right part on his truck, his drive across town and back for that $6 replacement part typically costs the contractor an hour of billable time. Moreover, this unscheduled delay now means that one whole service call must be scratched from the end of this mechanic's day, causing even further revenue loss for the contractor.

By looking through the eyes of his customers, Craig saw even more inventory control complexities for contractors who buy from multiple wholesalers. Explained Craig, "A mechanic goes out and installs a fan motor that he pulled off the inventory shelf. And three months later, the motor goes bad and it needs to go back for warranty replacement. From which wholesaler did the part originate?"

Customers' Problems = Value-Making Opportunities

Craig embraced these customers' problems by seeing his job in a different context: his job was not about simply making sales; his job was about making value.

He began thinking about developing a *contractor stocking program*, with the vision of making the purchasing and managing of inventory as hassle free for his customers as possible. First, he compiled a recommended list of ten days' worth of inventory for a service truck and parts room, and approached one customer with his new idea: "Let me set up and organize your parts room— complete with bins labeled by part number, shelving to hold the bins, a 'want list' that hangs on the wall for recording additional parts requests, a warranty basket to exchange a bad part, and a pricing book for easy cost reference."

The contractor said yes and was soon experiencing the value of a greatly simplified system for ordering parts, processing warranties, costing out jobs, and reducing pilferage. In the eyes of this customer, Craig had now distinguished himself from the herd of reps trying to simply sell parts. Now this contractor saw Craig as a real problem solver, time saver, and BS detector. And

Craig knew how to leverage this first success. On his next sales call, he reported to the prospect, "I have this stocking program. . . but don't take my word for it—call this guy and see how it's working for him." Craig's reference selling had begun!

What Have You Done for Me Lately?

But Craig understood that in the mind of the customer, it's not the amount of value delivered yesterday that counts. It's the value delivered *today* and *tomorrow* that drives relationship loyalty. Craig keeps a vigilant eye on slow-moving parts, and he's quick to suggest that the contractor send those items back for account credit. Conversely, if there's a part that is moving quickly for the contractor, it's Craig's job to recommend carrying more inventory for that item. But recalling his time as a purchasing agent, Craig is careful not to use such condescending phrases as "You need to do this." Instead, he approaches his accounts with the more consultative approach: "I've got some ideas, and you tell me if you want to do it or not."

Craig has discovered two critical questions for earning customer loyalty and, in turn, making sales: he's constantly listening and watching for clues to "What's on my contractor's worry list?" and "How else can I add value?"

Through this constant probing, Craig spied another problem: the contractor's time-consuming task of costing out a job. He knew that even with just one price list and one price book, it still took close to an hour to cost out a residential air conditioning installation job. And when using multiple wholesaler price books, the costing-out job took even longer. So Craig joined forces with his company's programmer. Using Microsoft FoxPro, they customized job costing software for Craig's customers. The result? The contractor's job costing time went from almost sixty minutes to ten.

In every category—whether product or service related—there exist golden opportunities to be distinguishably different. What's required is a Wayne Craig type of determination to find and leverage them. Craig did it. So can you! To get started, just keep asking those two questions: *What's on my customer's worry list?* and *How else can I add value?*

9. Craft a New Business Model—Don't Just Tweak the Old

"Ours is a much more satisfying purchase experience for the customer than buying 'regular' retail."[18] That's how Austin-based veteran shoe retailer Lalo Castillo describes a shopper's experience at his Designer Clearance House store, where in-the-know women buy hip designer shoes at rock-bottom prices that thrill. (Shoes that normally sell for $300 routinely go for $23 to $50.) How does he deliver his deals? By brilliantly cobbling together a stellar value proposition, working with willing channel partners whose "gets" exceed their "gives." Here's how.

First, the Great Inventory

Approximately twenty designer shoe manufacturers now sell Castillo their end-of-selling-season samples. Why? Besides supplying the immediate cash for the samples, Castillo's store, tucked away in an office park, provides these manufacturers (many of whom are well known in Europe, but not in the United States) an opportunity to build brand awareness among high-end, fashion-conscious shoppers who are candidates for full-price shoe purchases in the future.

What's more, a number of high-end local retailers sell Castillo their end-of-season close-outs for pennies on the dollar. These retailers can sell off merchandise that didn't move after final markdown.

Castillo's message to customers who "love the shoe" but not the size? Visit the regular retailer at the beginning of the season! Castillo will tell you where to shop.

Next, Low Fixed Cost

Castillo keeps his store's operating costs super low by opening his doors only during prime weekend shopping hours a few times a month. He uses e-mail to notify his customers a couple of days in advance of when he will be open. (These openings typically coin-cide with availability of new inventory.) Castillo also offers shop by appointment, whereby a group of girlfriends, for example, can reserve store access and private shopping time

Finally, Word of Mouse

No advertising. Just a Web site where customers can sign up for e-mail notification (there is in-store sign-up too) and learn more about the history of a brand. Castillo sends out e-mails when he has a new shipment, and customers swarm. (Rarely does a first-time customer return without a friend or two with her.)

It's all working: Castillo has expanded twice in less than a year. A third expansion is coming soon. On a recent visit, I watched a departing customer, with new leather boots in tow, call back to Castillo as she walked out the door: "I look forward to your next e-mail!"

What key lesson can we learn from Castillo's success? That busi-ness design plays a crucial role in achieving differentiation. As customer value guru Adrian Slywotzky defines it, "A business design is the totality of how a company (1) selects its customers, (2) defines and differentiates its offerings, (3) defines the task it will perform itself and (4) those it will outsource, (5) configures its resources, (6) goes to market, (7) creates utility for customers, and (8) captures profit."[19]

Castillo resisted conventional wisdom (by renting high-traffic retail store space, for example) and instead brought fresh new thinking to his business design. So can you! Use Slywotzky's eight design fundamentals to jump-start your thinking.

10. Give the IT Department a Seat at the Strategy Table

How important is information technology (IT) to a firm's strate-gic success? Very, says a recent study by Diamond Management &

Technology Consultants.[20] Of business leaders surveyed, 87 percent say they believe that IT is critical to their companies' success. Yet few companies have positioned IT for early, strategic input. Only 33 percent of business leaders say that IT is very involved in strategy development, and only 30 percent say that the business executive responsible for strategy in their company has a close working relationship with IT. These findings offer important clues for firms committed to achieving differentiation and acing the customer Worth-It Test.

The rare firm that puts IT at the strategy table is seeing real benefit. Take the Hartford Financial Services Group (HFSG). For many years, HFSG did not involve the company chief of technology in strategy meetings. Left to its own devices, the IT department treated each of the firm's new insurance products as stand-alone, one-time events instead of a series of steps repeated again and again. As a result, the timetable for product release was painstakingly slow and laborious, averaging three to five years.

When John Chu was recruited as senior VP of e-business and technology in 2003, he reportedly almost didn't take the job fearing that "the role of IT was an order taker."[21] But Hartford officials said otherwise, assuring Chu that IT would be very involved in matters of strategy and that his participation was expected at senior management meetings. Making room for IT at the strategy table paid dividends quickly. Chu and his IT team forged closer working relationships across the company, and they began focusing on tech projects to help streamline new product launches. By 2007, the firm's new product launch cycle had been reduced to just nine short months.

In a marketplace brimming with customer informedness and limitless competition, achieving differentiation is a necessity, and so far we've examined what it takes to do differentiation "right." But *being* different requires one set of skills; *staying* different requires another. Let's now look at how to infuse your firm with constant, ongoing innovation to enable your brand to stay different.

Staying Damn Different

To tame the search-and-switch customer you cannot just *be* different. Your brand must *remain* different, and that's a tall order. Why? Because the competition is working hard every day to earn away your customers. That means you must continue to build fresh competitive advantages that buyers can comprehend, calculate, or measure against their next best alternative. (The NBA is examined closely in Chapter Three.) Here are eight ways to keep your brand different.

1. Manage Commodity Creep

An invisible force is at work in your company. It lurks in your boardroom, your executive suite, in every branch of your org chart, and at your customer sites. Meet *commodity creep*—a powerful dynamic that, left unmanaged, will steadily disintegrate your once sought after, unique, distinguishable brand into a commoditized vanilla offering.

The condition is more widespread than ever. Need convincing? Consider the 2008 Brand Keys Customer Loyalty Engagement Index (CLEI), which found two brands tied for first place in seventeen categories. "Ties between brands used to be the exception, but there are more ties [in 2008] than there have ever been," reports Robert Passikoff, creator of the CLEI system and the annual survey of brands since 1997. The 2008 index ranked 382 brands across fifty-seven categories. "Many brands are now just placeholders. People know the brand names, but they don't know what the brands stand for," says Passikoff.[22]

The Brand Keys research findings are commodity creep personified! And when commoditization strikes your firm, your buyers will no longer comprehend your brand's differences. Instead, they'll see only sameness.

Under these conditions, you'll be left with only one sure way to win buyer favor: underpricing your competition. And that spells real trouble for your brand's profitability, image, and sustainability.

You cannot *eliminate* commodity creep, only *manage* it. That's because globalization, deregulation, and the Internet have turned commoditization into an ever-present force. As a loyalty maker, you must accept the reality that even your most compelling competitive differences will likely fall into commodity status at some point in your brand's life cycle. (Think FedEx's customer system for package tracking and how its key competitors now offer the same feature.)

That's why it's critical to have safeguards against commodity creep in your search-and-switch prevention tool kit. Yet many companies are without this know-how, and their customer loyalty suffers for it. Consider these quick lessons in managing (and triumphing over) commodity creep.

Beware of "Lowest" Pricing

I recently consulted with an international economy lodging brand and spent time in the field interviewing a cross section of their franchisees. I was struck by how these owners fell into two different "branding" camps. One group fervently believed that lowest price was the only way to win customers, and their focus was only on ways to preserve their "lowest price" positioning. Conversely, the second camp of franchisees envisioned their properties as an exceptional lodging value, and although they offered an affordable rate, their focus was on delivering the highest-value experience for the money.

By making lowest price their marketing message, the first group of franchisees unwittingly built a customer base of discount-chasing customers. And these owners were learning the hard way that discount-chasing guests are not loyal customers. The only loyalty these customers have is to the lowest price. Any brand will do as long as the price is right.

Yet this franchisee group seemed unaware of the role they played in driving commoditization. *Through their actions*, they had created a value proposition that attracted discount chasers, but they failed to see that. Instead, these owners held tight to the belief that they were simply responding to customer-related market conditions. "All that today's customers care about is lowest price" was a comment I frequently heard.

Lesson: An overreliance on low pricing is a sure sign that commodity creep has hijacked your brand. Stop the denial. Own your commoditization problem. It's the first critical step to restoring your brand's competitive differences and winning the caliber of customer on which you can build a solid business.

Keep a Careful Eye on Cost Cutting

Ahh . . . corporate cost-cutting and efficiency initiatives. From board meetings to Monday morning staff meetings, executives and managers spend untold hours plotting cost reductions and productivity improvements. Who would think that commodity creep is lurking in these projects? Starbucks chairman Howard Schultz, for one.

The *Wall Street Journal* reported that one Valentine's Day, Schultz sent a blunt memo to Starbucks executives via e-mail with the subject line "The Commoditization of the Starbucks Experience."[23] In it, he wisely questioned whether the chain's aggressive growth and efficiency initiatives were now robbing the customer of the unique experience so pivotal to the brand's storied success. About the chain's switch to automatic espresso machines, he wrote, "We solved a major problem in terms of speed of service and efficiency. At the same time, we overlooked the fact that we would remove much of the romance and theatre." The decision to move to this new machine, he wrote, "became even more damaging" because it "blocked the visual sight line the customer previously had to watch the drink being made, and for the intimate experience with the barista." Regarding the move to "flavor locking packaging," which eliminated the need for fresh coffee to be scooped from bins, he observed, "We achieved fresh roasted bagged coffee, but at what cost? [We suffered] the loss of aroma—perhaps the most powerful non-verbal signal we had in our stores."

Few people understand more about building a memorable, loyalty-building customer experience than Schultz—for many Starbucks customers, it is romance, theatre, engagement with the barista, having a comfortable, familiar third place besides home and work to spend time. And Schultz knows commodity creep when he sees it. At this writing, Starbucks has announced the closing of hundreds of stores. Although overbuilding Starbucks stores was one part of the problem, the dilution of the customer experience within those same stores was a sure contributor to lackluster performance as well.

Lesson: Know your essential customer-experience "hooks" and aggressively preserve them. It's your strongest defense against commodity creep.

Study Firms That Thrive in Commodity-Infested Markets

Every loyalty maker can benefit from an ongoing pipeline of best practices for managing commodity creep. But where should you look? Hint: learn from successful firms whose basic product is a commodity.

For example, Bruce Woolpert, CEO of Graniterock, could write a book on his firm's ability to thrive in a commodity-infested market. His family's business has quarried granite for more than a hundred years, and the company has a dozen locations between San Francisco and Monterey. In an industry where the low bid typically reigns supreme, Graniterock customers have historically paid, on average, 6 percent more than they would with the competition. The firm commands this premium by spotting and leveraging hidden value differentiators.

Citing one of many examples, Woolpert reported, "We thought our job was complete after we had done our mining process and run the rock through the plant and created these beautiful, uniform stockpiles of rock."[24] But research into customer values showed

Woolpert that getting customers' trucks loaded and back on the road was more important to this segment of customers. "And so we developed an automatic loading system called GraniteXpress, available to drivers 24/7. Early on, the truck driver swiped an authorization card and pulled the truck in, and a machine loaded the truck automatically. Now the smart cards have been replaced with radio-frequency tags mounted on the sides of customers' trucks," reports Woolpert. "Before GraniteXpress, it used to take drivers twenty-four minutes from the time they left the public roadway to get loaded, get their sales tag, and be out on the road again. We've got that down to seven minutes now," he says. In business, time is money, and that seventeen-minute savings is something that cities and counties and contractors and individuals who come into Graniterock quarries truly appreciate.

How was Graniterock rewarded? Market share doubled with the implementation of GraniteXpress and other such improvements. And, explained Woolpert, "We did it not by cutting prices, not by stealing our competitors' salespeople, or any of those kinds of things. We did it by changing ourselves."

Lesson: Experience is the best teacher, and commodity-infested markets naturally breed market-tested veterans brimming with commodity creep know-how. Find them and learn!

Need a few questions to help get your learning session rolling? Consider asking these:

- How do you uncover opportunities for new customer benefits?
- What lessons have you learned about formulating strategies that deliver those added benefits?
- How do you ensure effective strategy implementation throughout your firm?

Make no mistake about it: what's considered unique and different in today's market becomes standard fare tomorrow. That's why your firm must have a big arsenal of tools to nurture brand innovation. Read on!

2. Use Your Customers to Shepherd Early Design Decisions

Take the lead from the growing number of companies using Internet-based tools to solicit customer input early in the product's design cycle. Here are two brief examples.

Volvo's "Near Addictive" Input Tool

Before Volvo launched its new C30 model in the United States, the automaker featured a "build your perfect C30" tool on its Web site. The tool enabled American buyers to select the features they most wanted to see on the new model. Equally significant, it gave Volvo important early insights into buyer preferences for various option packages and how to price them. The automaker wisely made using the tool a fun, easy-to-navigate experience, described by some car enthusiasts as almost addictive; the site received ten thousand hits in its first three months. American buyer feedback showed a strong preference for the two-door Volvo to be sportier than the European C-30. In contrast to European customers, who leaned more toward safety-first options, American buyers showed less preference for blind-spot notification systems or antiglare rearview mirrors, for example. Says Art Battaglia, product manager of Volvo's North American cars, "The C30 for us is a different car. We thought we knew what we needed to do, but we needed some proof."[25]

Google's "Innovation, Not Constant Perfection" Strategy

Google's continual flow of new product releases plays squarely into the giant search engine's ability to remain different and "number one" in the minds of customers. In a keynote speech at Stanford University, Marissa Mayer, Google VP for search products, discussed the search giant's "launch and iterate quickly" practice. As a member of the six-person team developing Google News, Mayer and her teammates were deadlocked three to three on whether to program the search feature to sort by date or sort by location. The discussion was heated, and the launch clock was ticking. That's when the team acted on the company's "innovation, not constant perfection" directive and sent the rough product (without either feature) out for user feedback. It didn't take long to get the answer. By the end of day one, 307 Google customers weighed in: 300 wanted it sorted by date. Done.[26]

Although many firms consult with customers on product development issues, you don't have to be a Volvo or a Google to reach out to customers early and, in the case of Google, often.

3. Move in Closer and Observe

"If you want to understand how a lion hunts, you don't go to the zoo, you go to the jungle."[27] That's how Sandy Thompson, global head of strategic planning for advertising agency Saatchi & Saatchi, characterizes his firm's initiatives for staying close to consumers when devising new ad campaigns for some of its clients. Before designing a new ad for JCPenney, for example, the agency staffers shadowed more than fifty women for several days, helping them carpool, cook dinner, shop, and clean their houses. The goal of this research was to develop a deeper understanding of how people in the target market live, by observing, firsthand, the women's behaviors and thereby getting a richer perspective on their emotions. This research laid the foundation for JCPenney's new ad campaign, which earned accolades from Madison Avenue's creative community.

4. Learn from the Market, Not Just Your Customers

In a compulsion-to-compare world, it's imperative to listen and learn from the market—not just your customer. It's not enough to simply survey your customers and their evolving needs. You must keep an ear to your market's changing demands. That's because value gaps between you and competitors are defined by customers of *all* competing organizations, not just *your* customers. Consider the following three sources.

Impartial Frontline Feedback

Market intelligence can be found in unexpected places. When riding on a shuttle bus to the airport after a speaking engagement, noted speaker and sales trainer Patricia Fripp struck up a conversation with the shuttle driver. Realizing that his service was not affiliated with any of the resorts on his pickup route, Fripp asked the driver whether his riders shared their hotel experiences with him. "Yes," he said, "in fact, the general manager of the property where you were staying brings a big box of donuts and has coffee with our drivers once a month. We not only tell him everything we hear about his property, we tell him everything we hear about his competitors."[28]

Just imagine the rich impartial market insights this resourceful GM gathers every month in return for a box of donuts and an hour of time!

Competitive Positioning Mapping

Staying different means continually building fresh competitive advantages that trump the advantages of others. Creating a positioning map that plots your price and your competitors' prices against the brands' primary benefit can help. Such a chart allows you to quickly grasp how the market looks to customers. This insight can help you benchmark against your customers' NBAs, anticipate competitive moves, and preempt rivals.

The creator of this tool, Dartmouth business professor Richard D'Aveni, has applied positioning maps to over thirty industries, from tires to turbines to cellular phones. His straightforward technique for building the chart is particularly applicable to widely distributed consumer brands with product ratings found in such guides as those published by Zagat and Michelin; by independent firms, such as Consumers Union, J. D. Power, and Edmunds; and through government agencies, such as the U.S. National Highway

Traffic Safety Administration. D'Aveni's positioning mapping process uses this unbiased data to uncover a critical piece of competitive insight: which product benefit explains the majority of the difference in products' prices. Armed with this knowledge, firms can plot wiser moves to ace competitors.[29]

Market Panels

Market panels are sweeping, continuing surveys that drill deep for data from a large sample of respondents who model the company's entire customer market. Market panel insights can help companies foresee and react to changing opportunities that they might otherwise miss if they were simply monitoring current customer transactions.

For example, findings from a food and grocery panel indicated that one-third of consumers considered themselves highly engaged in grocery shopping. These customers reported that they were not attracted by sales or promotions; instead, they tended to spend more time shopping and looked for fresh, unique offerings. These shoppers—who were regular customers of Whole Foods and Trader Joe's—spent 47 percent more each week on groceries than the panel's least engaged food and grocery shoppers. Such findings sent a clear directive to the grocery retailer sponsoring the panel: attract more highly engaged shoppers to your store. This strategic insight would have been missed if the retailer had focused only on its own customer data.[30]

5. Think "Value Verbs": Create, Eliminate, Reduce, Raise

To address your customers' changing demands and keep your brand distinguishably different, it pays to focus on four key verbs: *create, eliminate, reduce, raise*.[31]

What Value Elements Should You Create?

Even funeral homes must look for ways to stay compellingly different. Look no further than the nation's largest funeral chain, Service Corporation International. With more than sixteen hundred locations across the United States, the company has faced revenue slowdown due to the growing trend toward cremation, which costs about $2,500 compared to a traditional burial, which runs around $10,000. Service Corporation now offers a number of add-on services to help boost revenue, including Web sites where mourners can go to record memories of the deceased, write online biographies, and create memorial movies featuring video clips, pictures, and voice-overs.

"The Baby Boomers have changed everything they've ever touched. They're also going to change the face of funerals. We have to have products and services that are appealing to that group," says Lee Longino, Service Corporation's managing director of its Florida market.[32]

From NASCAR-themed memorial services to Harley-Davidson motorcycles in the chapel to guests signing basketballs for deceased hoops fans' families, new funeral amenities are constantly in development. Service Corporation has even added a Seattle's Best Coffee kiosk with Wi-Fi Internet access and wide-screen TV for memorial attendees at one of its Orlando funeral homes.

But not everyone wants the extras. Adamant about not having a costly funeral, Ola Jean Lewis of Oklahoma City recalled, "I'd told my husband, if he spent $10,000 on my funeral, I was coming back to haunt him."[33]

What Value Elements Should You Eliminate?

When considering what value elements to eliminate, don't depend on your customers to tell you. That's the lesson Jet Ski maker Kawasaki learned the hard way. As the industry leader in recreational watercraft, Kawasaki asked Jet Ski users for solutions—that is, what they thought could be done to enhance and improve the ride. Customers suggested extra padding on the sides of the Jet Ski so that the standing position was more comfortable. (They never considered the possibility of a seated craft.) So designers worked to add the extra padding, while Kawasaki's savvy competitors took a different direction and developed seated models. This move cost Kawasaki its leadership position in the market.[34]

Next time your customers offer up suggestions in the form of solutions, ask "Why?" and then get them talking about outcomes. That's the kind of input your R&D team can put to work to keep products and services damn different.

What Value Elements Should You Reduce?

Automaker Lexus, legendary for its service delivery, does not rest on its laurels. Recognizing how time-starved today's car owner is, the automaker and its dealers have begun trials to streamline customer service visits so that a complete car maintenance servicing, which used to require two-and-a-half hours, is completed in less than thirty minutes.[35]

Are there ways you can follow Lexus's lead and reduce your customers' time requirements? How about ways to reduce the customer "hassle factor" when using your brand? Think hard about these often-overlooked intangibles as you figure out ways to keep up with your customers' ever-changing needs.

What Value Elements Should You Raise?

In 2000, the Texas-based Luby's Inc. chain of cafeteria-style restaurants was struggling to survive. Luby's stock price had plummeted to $.99, and the firm was swimming in debt, on the verge of bankruptcy. That's when brothers Chris and Harris Pappas, acclaimed restaurant entrepreneurs, came aboard as CEO and COO, respectively, and immediately went to work to aggressively raise an all-important value element: food quality. Where did they start? By upgrading kitchen equipment and restaurant technology to support preparation of "healthy eating" menu items, prepared through small-batch cooking techniques. These "first-things-first" choices were critical to the brand's successful turnaround and its continued success today.

6. Be Data-Driven

In a stark departure from the "gut feel" management dynamics that drive operational improvement decisions in many firms, a new breed of competitor has emerged that is using customer analytics to pinpoint opportunities. At these companies, the debate for resources is increasingly won by those managers using "The data say . . ." approaches rather than simply "I think . . ." appeals.

Consider H&R Block. A constantly changing tax code can make the basics of online tax preparation far from easy for taxpayers and the firms that help them file. In 2006, with tax season looming and stiff competition closing in, H&R Block was in a quandary. Why were some customers willing to recommend the firm's do-it-yourself online tax preparation services and others not? To quickly and accurately answer these concerns and still make course corrections during the busy tax season, H&R Block dove deep into text analytics, employing software that could analyze, overnight, some ten thousand customer contacts (via e-mails, surveys, contact center calls, and so on) and deliver reports early the next morning. The insight helped the firm rapidly uncover accuracy and responsiveness issues. For example, customer intelligence showed that many customers were confused about the 2006 Telephone Excise Tax Refund, and were not factoring it into their returns, although 160 million filers were qualified to receive it. With this insight, H&R Block quickly redesigned its online forms to better explain who was eligible, thereby helping customers maximize their refunds.[36]

7. Constantly Strengthen Your Innovation Model

When Alan Lafley assumed the role of chief executive of Procter & Gamble (P&G) in 2000, he put strengthening the firm's innovation muscle high on his priority list. The longtime P&G veteran was well aware of his company's insular "Proctoids" culture. (It's rumored that the phrase "not invented here" was truly invented at P&G!)

To shake up and reenergize P&G's long-standing innovation model, Lafley launched the Connect + Develop program in 2001, through which seventy-five technology scouts scour the globe looking for new ideas that the consumer products giant might develop. These technology scouts are in addition to P&G's in-house army of nine thousand researchers in eleven research centers around the world. But Lafley didn't stop there. In addition to forging joint ventures with such firms as Clorox, the CEO also championed increased collaboration within the P&G empire. For example, when Crest Whitestrips was in development, three P&G research groups—each with bleach expertise in a different product category (toothpaste, fabric, and home care)—weighed in on development. The company reports that five years after launching Connect + Develop, sales per R&D employee have almost doubled, and half of the company's new innovations now originate from the outside.[37]

8. Be a "Cool-Hunter"

"How do you keep an edge, a crispness, a relevance?" asks Nike chief executive Mark Parker.[38] That burning issue propels him to travel all over the world "cool-hunting" for trends and influences to keep the shoe brand relevant for young consumers. Nike cofounder Phil Knight drove the company to iconic heights by inking endorsements with such sports heroes as Tiger Woods and Michael Jordan. But to keep the brand growing to promised expectations—a 50 percent revenue increase from 2007 levels to $23 billion by 2011—Parker and company must build relevancy among more style-conscious young consumers who are not your typical sports junkies. As Knight reportedly told Parker, "Your job is way more difficult than my job was."

Parker, a veteran Nike employee, came to the CEO post armed with a deep, lifelong interest in popular culture. This natural affinity has helped him to amass, over time, a global network of "influencer's influencers," including designers, DJs, and artists who can offer rich clues into what's hot as well as what's next. Parker is constantly looking for overlap between cultures. For example, since the early 2000s, Nike has fought hard to get traction in the hard-to-crack skateboard market. When a friend in Milan, well connected in the art world, turned Parker on to the Brazilian twins known as Os Gemeos, who paint distinctive street murals featuring skinny, yellow-skinned caricatures, Parker spied an overlap opportunity. Nike promoted the duo's art abroad, and the twins provided designs for a limited line of collectible shoes rationed through a handful of hip independent retailers.

Commenting on how Nike has managed to gain footing in this fickle market, James Jebbia, founder of the well-known New York skate retailer Supreme, reports, "Skateboarding is not corporate and most skaters and true skate shops are anti-establishment. [But Nike has been able to] adjust to the way we do business."

Sure, Parker has cool hunter advantages, such as a corporate jet. But his story offers an important "staying different" lesson nonetheless: go outside your industry and its trade shows for inspiration. Look to seemingly unrelated industries and subject areas for new ideas. That's how you keep an edge.

Moving On

Keeping your brand discernibly different and continually outstanding is a tall order. It requires that you pay attention to countless everyday details as well as remain open to new creative ideas that can come from almost anywhere. Looking at your customer's needs and demands is a good place to start, but watching the competition is important too. So is tapping the insights of employees at all levels in your firm. Finally, looking for innovation ideas outside your industry boosts the probability that your brand can sustain a discernible difference that the market will reward.

Want more ways to do differentiation "right"? Visit **www .loyaltysolutions.com/BeingDifferent.** For now, though, this chapter concludes our tour of "getting due credit" tools. Next up in Part Three is our discussion of firewall fortifiers—initiatives you can take to further insulate your brand from your customers' tendency to have a roving eye toward your competitors. We'll begin with examining how to build customer trust. You need this know-how to succeed in a search-and-switch world, so dig in!

Taming Takeaways

- When your prospects and customers take to the Internet to compare your brand to others, you need to shine. Developing distinctive differences is essential to building customer loyalty.

- It is easy to settle into a mind-set that everything is fine and that you don't have to worry because your product is satisfactory. That's the kiss of death in today's search-and-switch marketplace. Instead, look inside your innovation tool box and divide the know-how into two areas: (1) What tools are helping you be different? (2) What tools are helping you stay different? Then work to keep both areas well stocked with solution finders.

- Constantly questioning your customers and prospects, listening to their complaints and kudos, and always looking for ways to better serve them will keep your brand ahead of the game.

- When considering improvements and changes to make your brand distinctive, don't fish from the same pond as your competitors. If you do, you limit your opportunities to be dramatically different. Instead, seek inspiration from sources well outside your industry.

- Study firms that are thriving in commodity-infested markets. They are likely to be champions at making their brands discernibly different. Soak up their wisdom and experience and learn from their strategies.

- Delighting your customers is job one, and to do that you have to know what they are thinking, what they are hoping for, and what they need. Your employees, your customers, customer data, and the market at large are all important contributors to innovation insight. Failing to tap any of these sources can carry big penalties.

Part III

Fortify Your Firewall

6

Build Customer Trust

"*Because I know I can trust them.*" That's the answer you hope and pray for when your toughest competitors ask your biggest accounts what they like best about buying from your firm. In a search-and-switch-prone world, customer trust is more crucial than ever. It forms a powerful firewall around your customers that helps keep formidable competitors at bay. After all, when you have the trust of your customer, your competitor is at a huge strategic disadvantage.

Building customer trust is a key step in fortifying your firewall against customer attrition. But it has its limitations. Trust alone cannot and will not save you from a switch. If customers perceive your brand as offering less value than the competition, you are in that perilous switch-prone zone, and all bets are off. That's why the strategies for getting the credit you're due, especially the ones in Chapter Five on being and staying damn different, are necessary companions to trust building.

The High Price of Low Trust

When Robert King's home insurance renewal notice arrived in the mail, he did what he'd done for ten previous years—let the policy renew automatically. But when this U.K.-based accountant looked over the renewal more closely a few weeks later, he became uneasy. The renewal amount was 551 pounds. With a quick Web search, he found similar coverage for 200 pounds. When he went to his carrier's own Web site and asked for a quote, he was shocked to receive a quote of 173 pounds—and this was for more coverage than his existing policy!

That's when King phoned his insurance company. "The lady I spoke to was very friendly and polite. She attempted to explain that the difference was down to the discount offered for purchasing the insurance online, plus a discount offered to new customers. I pointed out that, while I could accept that the online quote might be slightly less, we were talking here about the difference between 511 pounds and 173 pounds," reported King.[1] The insurance carrier immediately offered to match the online quote. But for King, the damage was done, and the trust was gone. "It seems likely that I have almost certainly been significantly overcharged for many years," he said.

In today's cynical world, a loss in trust can travel fast. For the insurance company, losing King as a client was only the start of its worries. The firm also had to contend with King's story flashed across the *Guardian* (both the online and hard copy editions) under the biting headline "For the Company, It's as Good as Having a Direct Line into Your Wallet."

Customer distrust carries a big price. Consider the results of the 2008 Chief Marketing Officers (CMO) Council survey of more than a thousand leading B2B technology buyers and IT marketing and customer relationship executives. More than 30 percent of the customer respondents said they would terminate relationships with companies that fail to gain their trust; 62 percent would scale back existing engagements; and 7 percent would no longer consider the vendor for future business.[2]

With customer distrust comes another big problem: customer reluctance to share information. Whether yours is a B2B or a B2C offering, without the continual flow of rich customer information to help tailor solutions, you are forced to keep the relationship in a transactional mode rather than a consultative one. The more your relationship remains in the transactional zone, the more you are prey to commoditization and competitive intrusion.

In today's business climate, customer trust seems harder to earn than ever. Business scandals in the last decade exposed some high-profile firms' apparent greed and lack of concern for employees, stockholders, and customers. This mayhem eroded the public's general trust of business, and, sadly, this sentiment continues. Daniel Yankelovich, considered by many to be the founding father of public opinion research, observes, "[Our] research shows . . . the lack of trust in business has grown. At the peak of the [accounting] scandals—say, in 2002—36% of the public agreed that you could trust business leaders to do what is right most of the time or almost always. Since the scandals now seem to be behind us, you would think that the level of trust would rise. Instead, it fell to 31 percent in 2004 and to 28 percent in 2006. So there's continuing erosion of trust."[3]

Likewise, a recent survey sponsored by public relations and marketing firm Ketchum showed public trust in corporations and CEOs to be at an all-time low among influential consumers. Corporations and their CEOs were perceived as poor stewards of the environment, as not compensating employees fairly, and as not communicating ethically and honestly.[4]

No doubt, customer trust is in short supply in today's marketplace, which makes your need for a trust-building plan that much more critical. Think of it this way: the risk that your customers will compare you against competitors and switch is considerably lower with customer trust than without. The more you have, the better.

Craft Your Trust-Building Plan

When you "grow" a customer's trust, what, exactly, is increasing? "In social psychology, trust is considered to consist of two elements: trust in the partner's *honesty*, and trust in the partner's *benevolence*," reports customer loyalty academician Dr. Christina Nordman. The customer perceives the partner as honest if the "partner stands by his word"; the customer perceives the partner as benevolent if the customer feels that the "partner is interested in the customer's welfare, and will not take actions with negative impact on the customer."[5]

As your customers' belief in your honesty and benevolence grows, their trust grows, too. As trust grows, more and more of the customers' buyer behaviors typically shift away from your competitors and more favorably toward you. For example:

- The breadth of products and services they buy from you may increase.
- Their volume of business with you may increase.
- The number of referrals they send you may increase.

But that's not all. Other increases in benevolent buyer behaviors may manifest as well:

- Approval of your proposals may speed up.
- Your access to upper-level management may increase.
- Your access to their data may increase.
- Their plans for future work with you may become progressively more long term.
- Their defense of your good name may increase.
- Their willingness to help you learn may increase.

All in all, these trust-driven customer behaviors are priceless advantages in a search-and-switch-prone marketplace. Many of these behaviors not only produce sales but also help insulate your prized customers from the pull of competition.

So how can your firm consistently earn and sustain customer trust in today's trust-impaired business climate? By thinking *tactically* about customer trust building. Early on in my customer loyalty work, I devised a customer relationship model centered around customer development stages: suspect, prospect, first-time customer, repeat customer, client,* advocate, and lost customer. (It's called the Profit Generator®. You may know it from my previous book, *Customer Loyalty*, or my **www.loyaltysolutions.com** Web site.) These same customer stages can serve as a template for your trust-focused planning.

Stage 1: Turning Suspects into Qualified Prospects

Trust rule: Target wisely. Carefully evaluate: To whom can you be trustworthy?

Building customer trust doesn't begin with seeding perceptions of trust in the minds of your prospects and buyers. Instead, it begins with your firm's *vision* of its ideal customer and careful consideration of which customers your firm can serve profitably and well in the long term. Targeting matters.

In fact, in today's wired world, mistargeting carries stiff backlash. Steering customers toward purchases they will not find satisfying leads to squandered repurchase opportunities, blistering customer reviews, and little to no new trial and adoptions based on those reviews. And the damage can linger. Commenting on the long life of customers ratings (bad or good) on the Internet, one marketer put it well when he said, "You *are* your Google listings."

Therefore, the question of whom to target is critical. To build and sustain customer trust, you must select your customer targets wisely and then create and deliver unique value to those customers. Consider the following three firms from very different industries, each with unique and effective targeting strategies.

---

* The term *client* is used to describe the customer who spends 100 percent of his or her available budget with you. In contrast, a *repeat customer* may be buying from a competitor as well as from you.

Progressive Auto Insurance

When a potential customer logs on to Progressive's Web site, the prospect can get a quote for Progressive coverage and for similar insurance from all of Progressive's nearest competitors. Progressive quotes are lowest less than half the time, which routinely sends the prospect to a competitor. Bad news for Progressive? Hardly. The firm's "Comparison Quote" (powered by sophisticated, superior data analyses with which competitors are not equipped) sniffs out customer riskiness and assigns a higher rate accordingly. Therefore, Progressive is pleased to have these higher-risk, expensive prospects go elsewhere.[6]

Saber Roofing

For roofers, scoping a prospective project correctly and bidding it accurately are early trust-building tasks. After all, a poorly conceived job estimate is one surefire way to rob the relationship of trust-building potential. That makes the correct targeting and qualification of prospects (and their projects) crucial.

When a landlord contacted Jay Saber about reroofing five apartment buildings located 175 miles away, the Redwood City roofer did a site visit—not by truck, but by computer. Using Google's free Earth software, Saber pulled up aerial views of the buildings, inspecting their condition and measuring the rooflines. He e-mailed his $100,000 bid the next day, saving himself a 350-mile round trip. "Instead of nine hours, I spent 10 minutes on the computer," says Saber.[7] (The accuracy of these aerial views is quite remarkable, reports Saber, who found his measurement was within 50 square feet for a 10,000-square-foot roof when he ultimately measured in person.)

The HealthCentral Network

In today's wired world, a firm often attracts prospects by creating a dedicated Web site and then spending substantial time and money, online and off, pulling visitors to it. But rather than only *pulling* consumers to your site, why not also *push* messaging out through high-traffic, customer-trusted sites to connect with carefully targeted suspects very early in their search process? It's a marketing strategy that The HealthCentral Network (THCN), based in Arlington, Virginia, pursues vigorously for its health care advertising clients. As owner and operator of consumer health Web sites and multimedia affiliate properties, THCN on behalf of its advertising clients, targets, consumers seeking to manage and improve their health. THCN works with nearly all the top ten global pharmaceutical firms and several of the top five medical device manufacturers.

A recent Nielsen research study found that more than 80 percent of Americans use the Internet to search for health information.[8] Recognizing that a consumer's repeated exposure to the same consistent, reliable health information is a trust builder, THCN strives to put its clients' messaging where prospective customers are most apt to search. For example, upon receiving a diagnosis, many patients want to talk to someone else with the same condition to help validate or refute the information they've received. Reports Dennis Upah, THCN's executive VP of broadcast, "Most people in search of accurate health care information begin with the condition, not the brand. . . . These consumers gravitate toward objective online sites in search of unbiased information."[9] At this writing, THCN distributes its content on over thirty of its own health condition Web sites (ranging from osteoarthritis to depression to diabetes), and on upward of 150 different affiliated sites where users actively seek health content.

Notably, social media sites are also an early destination for patients.[10] Says Jeremy Shane, THCN's vice president of business development, "[F]or advertisers trying to reach them during this time, the relevancy of the message really matters."[11] For example, an ad related to postoperative cancer needs to reach a survivor's discussion group, rather than appear on a "just-diagnosed" blog. The more tailored the ad to the health concern, the better.

But reaching patients offline can be important too. Some patients are more apt to begin with another medium, such as television, and then proceed to a recommended site. THCN produces magazine-style television specials called "Medical Breakthroughs

Presented by HealthCentral," and its viewers are urged to seek additional information on the Web. (Unlike infomercials, for which stations are paid, this programming is paid for by television stations through a barter advertising arrangement.) Says Upah, "It's one more way to increase the odds of reaching the right consumer, in the right place, at the right time and with the right blend of objectivity and advertising."

Wise targeting is the first rule of trust building. After all, what's important is not how many target markets you can identify and open; it's how many you can profitably penetrate, market to, and serve admirably. So always be on the alert for new untapped markets you can serve profitably and well. These guidelines can help:

- *Survey the market.* Routinely scan the total market to identify potential new markets of opportunity.
- *Segment your markets.* Break down your list of potential markets into groups with common characteristics.
- *Analyze your markets.* Discover as much as you can about the market groupings you have segmented. Find out what they need, what they want, what they fear. Find out all you can to help evaluate how much potential they offer you and what is required to serve them well. (Your ability to quickly recognize and disqualify markets and prospects with lackluster potential is critical. Analyze your unprofitable customers with an eye toward isolating characteristics that can help you spot insufficient markets early.)
- *Analyze the competition.* Who is succeeding and why?
- *Stratify the market.* Rank various market segments by priority. Your primary market should be the market segment you can reach most easily with the lowest investment and the greatest expectation of return.

- *Test your markets.* In each high-potential market, make contact with some prospects. This can give you insights into which are easiest to sell to, what it takes to reach them, how receptive they are, and what approaches work best. Look for clues on whether or not serving these prospects would be an enjoyable, gratifying experience. Ask why or why not.

- *Stay open minded.* Treat your target market selection as an ongoing, open-ended question. Keep the trust rule "To whom can I be trustworthy?" at the top of your mind.

Stage 2: Turning Qualified Prospects into First-Time Customers

Trust rule: Make only those promises you are able to keep.

Recently, an air conditioning tech climbed down my attic stairs after troubleshooting a problem with an overflow valve—and he taught me a lasting lesson about early trust building. "Who installed your system?" he asked. His company was *not* the installer; I shared that fact, bracing myself for the competitor-bashing comments and sales pitch I was sure would follow. "The company did an excellent job," he said, to my surprise. His six simple words instantly reframed my customer mind-set away from "Can I trust him?" to "How can he help me?" He showed me his willingness to call a spade a spade, and that was an important credibility builder in the critical early moments of the relationship.

Turning qualified prospects into first-time customers is a delicate trust-building process. It's all about building trust through carefully chosen words and actions. Consider these guidelines for growing trust in the minds of fledgling prospects, and earning sales in the process.

Before You Reach Out, Get Informed

The earlier in the selling process a firm can start to build a prospect's trust, the better. Arming sales reps with relevant problem-solving information specific to a prospect's interest really helps. Just ask Stuart Robertson, senior director of marketing for ShareBuilder 401K, a firm whose mission is to provide low-cost retirement solutions for small business. Robertson says, "Our salespeople are ranked very highly because they know what the prospect needs before the prospect says a word."[12] The firm's sales rep conversion rates prove him out.

When the firm's 2007 Web site revamp dramatically boosted sales leads to a whopping ten thousand leads per month per rep, the company needed to get smarter in cherry picking the highest-potential leads for follow-up. That's when the firm implemented a Web analytics program, integrating it with the firm's e-mail marketing. The program detailed visitor click paths, which, in turn, triggered designated e-mail messaging (for example, if the prospect was browsing Web pages regarding program costs, that prospect would receive a cost-related e-mail). Sales reps received a report detailing any activity prospects took with the e-mail (did the message get opened, which links were clicked, and so on), along with a corresponding prospect score estimating the prospect's likelihood for becoming a customer. The program's results were impressive. Sales per rep climbed 17 percent over the program's first six months, and 65 percent of leads closed in the first thirty days after the initial sales contact, up from 51 percent preprogram rates.[13]

The sooner a prospect sees evidence of relevance, the better. Do all you can to get informed before you reach out. It's an opportunity for early trust building that you can't afford to miss.

Approach Browsers Gingerly

When a leading maker of office furniture wanted to generate better sales leads, it looked to the Web to help the generation and qualification process. The strategy was to make virtual salesmanship more proactive. Rather than wait for the Web visitor to click on a Help button, the furniture maker went a step further. When the visitor logged on to the Web site and looked around for several minutes or clicked seven or eight pages deep into content, a service agent detected the visitor and solicited a real-time dialogue through an Instant Messenger–like prompt that read, "May I help you?"

A year later, the company dropped this approach. Although some Web visitors liked the prompt attention, others found it intrusive and in direct conflict with the anonymity of Web browsing. The company listened to customer feedback and wisely dropped the feature, opting instead for customers' making the first move to engage in chat. The lesson here is that just because you *can* doesn't mean you *should* in today's connected marketplace. On the Web, as in person, it's important not to be perceived as too pushy. Both online and off, prospect conversion is a delicate trust-building dance that requires a "lead and follow" balance on both sides of the sales transaction.

Ari Galper understands the need for lead-and-follow balance in closing online sales. So much so that the former sales manager for the analytics firm WebSideStory developed ChatWise®, a sales method that he sells bundled with his chat software.[14] Together, Galper's sales method combined with the software helps online retailers harness the power of instant messaging (IM) to create trust with their site visitors. Just as the office furniture maker discovered, Galper has confirmed that online commerce is the wrong medium for hard sales tactics because shoppers can dismiss you and your overture with one simple keystroke. Galper advises companies to avoid pinging visitors with the overused phrase "How may I help you?" (which years of offline shopping have taught visitors to recognize as a pushy sales tactic), and to use this IM greeting instead: "Hi, my name is Ari, sorry to interrupt . . . just wanted to make sure everything is making sense so far . . . "

Another basic IM sales rule, advises Galper, is never to use periods, and instead to use more conversational ellipses. Also crucial, says Galper, is to resist the temptation to jump in with a sales pitch the moment the visitor expresses interest in a product. Instead, he advises asking a probing question to ferret out the visitor's real need. For example, he says that the line "Can you tell me a little more about your situation?" gives you a better chance of making a highly relevant recommendation and helps gauge how likely the visitor is going to make a purchase.

Use "Seeing Is Believing," but Keep It Real

Blendtec, a small Utah-based maker of high-end home and commercial blenders, needed more business, so executives brainstormed: How do we earn more market awareness on a shoestring budget? Their answer? A series of online "seeing is believing" videos built on a simple, word-of-mouth-friendly premise: viewers watch CEO Tom Dickson, dressed in a white lab coat and goggles, pulverizing a host of everyday objects (baseballs, a tiki torch, a Transformers toy, a video camera) in a lighthearted, don't-try-this-at home demonstration shtick. One spot has Dickson tossing an iPhone into his blender and watching with delight as it morphs into a black puff of smoke. Blendtec's "Yes It Blends" catchphrase then pops onto the screen.

Since posting its first video on YouTube, the company's retail blender sales have soared to $10 million as of early 2008, from $2 million in 2006. Blendtec's original five videos cost the company a mere $50 and have been viewed on YouTube over thirty-five million times.[15]

But George Wright, director of marketing for Blendtec's parent company, K-TEC, counsels caution with brand messaging. "It's critical that you don't stretch the truth. If you exaggerate or try to mislead people, you're running the risk of being exposed in a public or viral way, resulting in overall damage to your brand."[16]

Get CEO Involvement Early and Often

The days of CEOs putting in an "appearance" at important customer sites for the sole purpose of demonstrating that "you and
your business matter to us" are over. Prospects and customers
expect to see the firm's chief executive on board and involved in
the account.

"Ten years ago, a sales executive would have given a pitch, but
today big customers want the CEO's commitment that if they buy
from you, you're forming a partnership with them and will deliver
exactly what you've promised," counsels Ed Peters, CEO of Dallas-
based OpenConnect, a technology innovator in software designed
to ferret out inefficiencies in business processes. "And if you don't,
your failure will be broadcast on the Internet and quash possible
deals with other customers."[17]

From privately held firms such as OpenConnect to large public
companies such as Nike, Microsoft, and Intel, chief executives are
playing increasingly deeper roles in the nitty-gritty of customer
relationship development. Professor Kevin Coyne of Harvard
Business School concurs: "They're getting substantially involved
in the biggest deals, showing up for key parts of a negotiation,"
and following up to ensure that employees are truly delivering
what was promised.[18]

Employ Customer Ratings as Trust Builders

Nurturing trust between buyer and seller is always challenging. But in
the online world, where buyers and sellers may be hemispheres apart,
trust challenges are even more complex. How do you cope? Customer
ratings can help. In a 2007 study on attitudes toward customer ratings and reviews, 80 percent of U.S. shoppers placed more trust
in brands that offer them.[19] It's a trust-building tool that eBay and
Amazon have employed with great success as well.

Getting buyers and sellers to trust each other was paramount
to the early success of online auction giant eBay. In 1995, the
then-fledgling e-commerce company established its now famous

rating mechanism that helps anonymous buyers and sellers trust each other. By October 2007, the eBay auction site had 241 million registered users. The company's rating system has been a fundamental component in the site's successful sales-driven architecture. (One carefully controlled academic experiment showed that eBay buyers bid, on average, 8.1 percent more for an otherwise identical item when it was offered by a reputable, established seller versus a new, unrated seller.)[20]

Many eBay sellers often recognize the "ratings = trust = sales" connection, and when ratings decline, serious sellers take action. For example, when a North Carolina–based DVD and video game seller, offering new and used merchandise, received some bad buyer ratings, he took immediate action: he increased inspection and repair on used discs, added more customer service employees, and offered full refunds to any customer complaining of a defective product. Over time, his sales improved.

Recognizing the importance of seller-buyer trust, eBay has continued to enhance its rating system. In March 2007, the site began displaying more detailed seller ratings, including evaluation factors that address shipping time and how close a seller's product description matched the actual product. Likewise, eBay has added a new feature that lets customers contact other buyers about their experiences with a specific seller. Reported eBay member Pookie Martin, "Being able to network better with people in the buying community made me feel better about buying on eBay."[21]

Another e-commerce site, Amazon, also launched in 1995. Founder Jeff Bezos made the decision early on to put customer ratings on the bookseller site. Publishers were not always pleased when a negative customer review was posted about their books and would send letters to Bezos urging him to show only positive reviews. Says Bezos, "One letter in particular said, 'Maybe you don't understand your business. You make money when you sell things.' But I thought to myself, we don't make money when we sell things; we make money when we help customers make purchase decisions."[22]

Make Your Site Content Trustworthy (and Keep It That Way)

"In the old days (read the 1990s) trust was mostly focused [around] e-commerce [and] how could you trust a website [with] your personal details or credit card numbers. . . . The issue of 'Can I trust this site?' still exists, but the new issue, 'Can I trust the people on it?' is now equally important. The main difference now is that content is being generated by anyone and . . . then rated by anyone," observes Mark McElhaw, head of client services at Webcredible, a London-based Web usability and accessibility consultancy.[23] In this age of user-generated content, what measures can be taken to help ensure that users perceive your site and the information on it as trustworthy? McElhaw offers these guidelines:

- Take measures to ensure that your site users are who they say they are. When users are registering at your site, consider taking such precautions as e-mailing an activation link, sending a test message with an activation code, sending the activation code to a business or home address, or some combination of these.

- To increase trust of your site's user-generated content, make users' profiles publicly available to everyone in the community and allow users to rate a person for his or her content.

- Whenever possible, have real-time, face-to-face interaction with content providers to monitor and substantiate their legitimacy and good faith.

Get Social Responsibility "Right"

Showing social responsibility can be another way to garner customer trust. There's good news and bad news about consumers and social responsibility.

First, the good news. It turns out that telling your social responsibility story can be worth a lot. In 2005, ABC Home Furnishings, a New York retailer, allowed Harvard researchers Nicholas Smyth and Michael Hiscox to test labeling on two lots of towels. One set had no label. The other lot carried a label with the logo "Fair and Square" that read, "These towels have been made under fair labor conditions, in a safe and healthy working environment which is free of discrimination, and where management has committed to respecting the rights and dignity of workers."

Over a five-month observation period, Smyth and Hiscox tested the effect of various changes, including switching the label to the other lot of towels and raising prices. According to the *Economist*, the research findings were striking: "Not only did sales of towels increase when they carried the Fair and Square label, they carried on increasing each time the price was raised."[24]

Little wonder companies around the globe are looking at social responsibility initiatives as a way to strengthen relationships among the ever-growing legions of socially conscious customers.

But here's the bad news. Consumers tend to be suspicious of ethical claims, as shown by a recent study of the labels of more than a thousand products in large stores across North America. The research was conducted by environmental marketing agency TerraChoice, which found that almost all the companies were guilty of some degree of "greenwashing." Highlighting the TerraChoice study, the *Economist* reported, "[The firms responsible for the labeling] did not tell outright lies, but nor did they tell the whole truth."[25]

Be very, very careful when waving a social responsibility banner. Your claims are likely to be scrutinized. Make sure they can stand the heat. Better to make no claim than to make one perceived as less than truthful. As we've seen, bad news travels fast (and has a long shelf life) in the cyberworld.

Stage 3: Turning First-Time Customers into Repeat Customers

Trust rule: First, get the basics right. Early trust building depends on it.

Trust is earned through the constant and consistent delivery of value. Likewise, inconsistency in matters of customer value breeds customer distrust. Consider these factors for nurturing trust in first-time customers.

Score Big and Early on Accuracy and Availability

Loyalty research has long confirmed the importance of a seller's accuracy and availability in establishing trust and confidence with first-time customers.[26] After all, first-time customers are "tryers" who are looking for confirmation clues that they made the right decision to buy from you in the first place. Bottom line: to build trust at this early stage, you must first get the basics right.

Picture yourself as the branch manager of a local bank where Tom, a small business owner, has just opened several business accounts. Tom is now evaluating your banking services through his "new customer" value filter. In this early stage of your relationship, Tom is seeking confirmation that he made the right decision in moving his business to your bank and that your operation is worthy of his trust and confidence. It's a little soon for him to judge your bank on the merits of its cash management consultation, for example, so he will likely grade your bank on the more transactional measures of accuracy (Did my checks arrive when promised? Did my monthly disability insurance premium draft against the right account?) and availability (Was my e-mail answered promptly?).

At this early stage of trust building, it's very important that you stay close to the customer, checking in to make sure all is well. Asking smart questions, such as "Our records indicate that your checks were mailed last week; have you received them?" can help underscore your firm's accuracy and availability without appearing to brag about it.

Telegraph Teamwork

The staff at the Palace Café in New Orleans knows a thing or two about building customer trust early. On my first visit to that storied restaurant many years ago, I had an early dinner alone as I did last-minute prep for an early morning keynote. I came without a reservation and gave the hostess my name. After waiting less than five minutes, the young woman escorted me to a wonderful table upstairs. As we climbed the café's grand staircase, the hostess initiated friendly conversation: *Have you dined at the Palace before? What brings you to New Orleans? Where's home?*

Within a few short minutes of being seated, my waiter appeared and offered his cheerful introduction: "Good evening, Ms. Griffin. My name is Jim. It's a pleasure to have you join us during your convention stay. Since this is your first time dining with us, I'll be sure to point out some of our most popular menu items. And, by the way, I visited your wonderful city of Austin last year and had a ball. Loved the night life on Sixth Street!"

Wow! I think . . . *how in the world would he know all of this about me?* Then it hits me: that seemingly casual banter with the hostess on the way to the table was important guest research that she, in turn, quickly shared with my waiter. It was an early signal to me that Palace Café staff collaborate to make a guest's dining experience as special as possible. That early trust building set the stage for a very memorable meal and has made me a customer for life.

Be Accountable

I launched my firm in 1988. As is true for most new companies, my initial cash flow was tight, and each new project was critical for survival. That same year, I conducted a one-day marketing and selling seminar for a beauty products wholesaler who requested that four key areas be covered in my training program for his sales reps.

A few days after the program, back in my office, I called the decision maker to debrief about the training day. He said he was quite pleased overall, but when I really pressed him, he expressed "some disappointment" with one of the four modules. I thanked him for his feedback, apologized for the disappointment, and concluded the call. I can still remember sitting at my desk, feeling blue, and thinking that I was squarely in the middle of what Jan Carlzon, then CEO of Scandinavian Airlines, referred to as a "moment of truth."

Ever mindful of my lower-than-I-wanted-it-to-be bank balance and the stack of unpaid bills on my desk, I reluctantly reached for my calculator, figured out what 25 percent of the fee represented, and, with a knot in my stomach, wrote the client a check. I mailed it with a note that said something about walking my own talk. I never heard a word from him (but I did notice in my next bank statement that the check had cleared!). About a year later, I landed a major consulting project in his industry. When the new client called me with the good news, she mentioned that while all my references were glowing, one was off the charts. Yep, it was that wholesaler's!

What did this experience teach me? Put yourself in your client's shoes. Be accountable.

Address Your Customer's "Fear of Flying"

Lenn Pryor's intense fear of flying made his air travel traumatic. From preflight nausea to white-knuckle armrest gripping during flights, Pryor suffered real anxiety. To help ease his crash concerns, a United Airlines pilot suggested that Pryor listen in, from his plane seat, to channel nine, the airline's audio feed of pilot communication provided for nervous (or techno-geek) passengers. It helped, said Pryor, to hear real, behind-the-scenes, honest talk, and "the irrational nature of my fear started to fade."[27]

Fast-forward ten years. As platform evangelism director for Microsoft, Pryor recognized a different kind of fear of flying—this time, in the minds of the tens of thousands of software developers writing code and creating programs using the Windows operating system. Reported Pryor, "Those developers must feel like I did on planes—that they're on a fast ride with someone else in control whose thinking they don't understand."[28] What these developers need, reasoned Pryor, was a "window into the Microsoft cockpit."

Pryor lobbied for and won the opportunity to form an in-house team and launch Microsoft's Channel 9, which in essence allows Microsoft code writers to engage in unscripted communication with their outside counterparts. The project's mission: to help lessen "developers' fear of flying Air Microsoft" by combining video, blogging, and a forum-based comments engine to bring Microsoft and its developers together through transparency and dialogue.

By the end of the project's first day in April 2004, an impressive 100,000 visitors had hit the site, driven simply by word of mouth (and mouse). Six months later, traffic climbed to 1.2 million unique visitors per month. By March 2007, Channel 9 enjoyed 4.5 million unique monthly visitors. *Wired* magazine writes that both developers and customers report feeling better about dealing with the company. Says reporter Fred Vogelstein, "While the rest of corporate America is scrambling to figure out whether it wants to allow blogging at all, famously guarded, control freak Microsoft has embraced the idea of transparency with messianic fervor."

Want more customer trust? Build your own "Channel 9" with fledging customers. As Lenn Pryor's instincts so aptly bore out, the more your customers understand how your company thinks, the more opportunity there is for trust to grow.

Stage 4: Turning Repeat Customers into Clients

Trust rule: Learn your customers' unique definition of value and customize your delivery accordingly.

Want to equip your firm with potent trust-building potential? Turn your frontline employees into customer ambassadors armed with unexpected service insights that delight customers.

Show Customers You Know Them

Continental Airlines' first big step in achieving the "show me you know me" outcome for its customers began in the late 1990s.

That's when the company embarked on its arduous four-year journey to consolidate forty-five customer databases into an enterprise-wide customer data depository that would provide nearly every Continental employee some access to customer information. But what *particular* customer information can most help a specific frontline employee achieve the "show me you know me" outcome for a customer? To continually provide fresh answers to that question, the airline's customer relationship management (CRM) department hosts regular think-tank sessions with "ambassadors" from every "vertical" in the company, including flight directors, managers, ticket agents, flight attendants, and baggage handlers. The result? Scores of fresh new ideas for delighting customers. The CRM group then works with the most promising ones, fleshing out logistics, to make them actionable by the airline's front line. For example, the Continental baggage handler who has just been notified that a high-value customer's lost baggage is now safely loaded can board the plane and give the worried passenger the good news before takeoff. Or, notified that a passenger on her flight has recently made Platinum, the flight attendant can offer a personal congratulation.[29]

Acknowledge When Things Go Wrong

This may seem paradoxical, but a product or service mishap is a golden opportunity to earn more customer trust. The key, however, is to acknowledge when things go wrong.

An excellent example is *Consumer Reports* (CR) magazine's quick action in 2007 when its widely read article reporting flaws in some child safety seats during impact tests was found to have serious errors. Suddenly, the highly respected magazine, with well over four million subscribers, faced a serious trust challenge.

Immediately after the National Highway Traffic Safety Administration informed CR of its testing procedure flaws, the magazine checked its own work, confirmed mistakes, and mobilized forces to correct the widespread miscommunication. CR's guiding mission? Ensure that the attention given to the corrected story matched that of the flawed original story.

CR pulled the story from its Web site; issued a press release; notified the national media that the original story had been withdrawn; prepared an extensive follow-up story for the next issue, which included a detailed accounting of the earlier mistakes; sent an apology letter penned by James Guest, the president of Consumers Union, CR's publisher, to the magazine's millions of subscribers; appointed an outside panel to examine what went wrong; and published the panel's findings in the magazine's next issue.

Says Ken Weine, Consumers Union senior director of communication, "Looking back, we had a really responsive leadership . . . who did all the right things by the communications playbook" by acting immediately and with transparency, and then writing a comprehensive story of what went wrong and what was being done about it.[30]

Be Sensitive to Your Customer's Privacy Limits

Staying close to customers by practicing customization strategies can help build client trust. Collaborative filtering (think Amazon's "Those who bought your selections also bought . . ." feature) and other recommendation and discovery Web site functions can help shoppers feel that you know them. But stay sensitive to client privacy boundaries by keeping two key questions top-of-mind:

- From your client's perceptive, what's "too close"?
- Considering your firm's increasing data sophistication and the emerging new ways to customize client messaging, at what point will your client stop feeling served and start feeling watched?

When my technology enthusiast pal Chris heard a National Public Radio program voicing concerns about businesses "listening in" through e-mail scanning, he dismissed the program's thesis as "a little paranoid" and perhaps "too much fuss about nothing." Soon, he wasn't so sure. That's because he noticed that his e-mail content to a fellow consultant was being monitored by his e-mail provider, Gmail. How could he tell? Simple. The ads in the e-mail's right sidebar directly related to the information shared in his e-mails!

But this privacy lesson was not yet over: when I e-mailed Chris to ask his help in fleshing out the details of his story, my message included information about this book project and its working title. Chris replied with a "check this out" e-mail showing me the sidebar ads sent to him alongside my original e-mail. Yep, you guessed it: all the ads related to writing! They included "A Manual for Writers," "Writing Your Own Novel?" "Freelance Writing Job," "You Write and We Publish," and the like. We learned something new: although I don't have a Gmail account, once I got in Chris's e-mail orbit, my e-mail was scanned too!

How is Chris feeling about Gmail and privacy? Has he changed any e-mail habits? Observes Chris, "Yes, I have definitely scaled back the use of Gmail for business purposes. It just doesn't feel right to me to conduct correspondence with or about a client (especially when that client has a certain expectation of confidentiality) and all the while Gmail is pushing ads based on the content of my e-mail."

Stage 5: Turning Clients into Advocates

Trust rule: Graduate value delivery to the level of partnership and advice.

———

What's better than clients who give 100 percent of their business to you? Clients who have such deep trust that they will go out on a limb and be an advocate for you. Here are some ways to earn that level of trust.

When the Going Gets Tough for Clients, Be There

How do you anchor deep-rooted trust? By being there when clients need you most and coming through when challenges are the greatest.

Picture this: nearby wildfires are threatening your family's seven-thousand-square-foot dream home in Idaho. You stand outside, helplessly watching the smoke and flames in the distance, knowing that firefighters' efforts may not be enough to stop the fire's perilous forward march. Suddenly, the wind shifts, and now the wildfire appears closer than ever.

That's the exact moment a guy with a spray gun and a truck full of fire-retardant goop begins spreading the shield all over your roof and house, courtesy of your insurer.

That reportedly happened for homeowner Al LaPeter when wildfires threatened his large house on the Big Wood River and his insurer, AIG, came to help. "They called me. I didn't even know that they did this," reported LaPeter.[31]

It's the first time AIG Private Client Group had sent help from its Wildfire Protection Unit to Idaho to assist high-end clients who, the company reports, are paying on average $10,000 per year for homeowners' insurance. Insurance industry experts report that AIG is the only major insurer providing fire retardant services to some homeowner policyholders.

Translate "Literal" into "Actionable"

At this stage in loyalty development, customers trust you to be able to translate their requests through an experienced "solutions" filter. Acting on a customer's literal request can be a mistake. More interpretation may be required.

For example, when customers say they want one-stop shopping, does that mean that a firm should give a client just one person to talk to? That's the question Diane Schueneman, Merrill Lynch senior VP and head of global operations, and her team asked themselves. Their conclusion? No. Explains Schueneman, "What the customers are really saying is that they want consistency; they want a common way to access all of their information with us. And they want simplification. When they want to open a relationship across five products, they want to be treated like one customer, not five. Can we do paperwork once, instead of five times? In other words, they want the power of all 50,000 people, but organized in such a way that we deliver their service in a simple way."[32]

Reward Client Purchases with Highly Sought Services

Nothing builds trust like creating win-wins between your firm and your client. Consider the following example.

Almost every health care provider on the planet is desperate for more staff training. So that's exactly where one supplier looked to reward its loyal clients for purchases.

When the Coloplast Group, a worldwide provider of medical products and maker of appliances for ostomy, continence, and wound care, looked for a unique new way to reward clients for purchases, staff training was high on the idea list. The company created a B2B loyalty rewards program with staff training as the payoff.

Here's how it works: Coloplast employs a network of skilled nurses whose time can only be "bought" by a client that has earned enough loyalty points in the form of training hours. The point system is transparent and rewards such client purchase behaviors as purchasing products at designated times in the quarter and in the right batch sizes. When a doctor's office, surgery center, or nursing home contacts the call center to place an order, the operator is able to advise the buyer on how to best earn points to secure his or her organization's next round of Coloplast specialist training. Coloplast reports that its clients consider the staff training rewards program as a big win-win.[33]

Tell Client Stories That Showcase Your Worth

How do you continue to nurture trust with a long-time client? By telling stories about other customers that use your expertise as the backdrop, not as the subject.

That's shrewd trust-building advice from fellow loyalty author Chip Bell, and precisely the strategy my girlfriend's longtime jeweler uses to cleverly showcase his expertise. My girlfriend has a deep love of fine jewelry. In a recent telephone visit with her jeweler (he's on the East Coast, she's in Texas), he told her about a first-time client who had purchased a 12-carat pink diamond for $1.2 million. A short twenty-four months later, the rock was valued at a cool $4 million! No doubt, my friend and her jeweler had fun with their "who'd have 'thunk it'!" banter about the purchase. The story's newsworthiness, in turn, prompted my girlfriend to immediately call me to further marvel at the buyer's good fortune.

Knowingly or not, the jeweler was practicing Bell's advice and reinforcing his worth through client storytelling. "Competence should be constantly in the demonstrator mode," advises Bell. He continues, "Proving your proficiency is not about boasting; it is reminding the customer he or she made a smart decision coming to you. It is important the service provider knows how to show off without being a show-off."[34] Bingo.

Stage 6: Keeping Advocates Advocating

Trust rule: Practice client reciprocity; reward "tit for tat."

There's an important difference between a client and an advocate. Advocates do more than simply buy from you. Advocates are *engaged* customers who demonstrate their vendor allegiance through such activities as spreading positive word of mouth, recruiting new prospects, and helping their vendors improve. How can a firm nurture trust to help sustain these important advocate behaviors? Try these suggestions.

Identify Those Customers Who Refer You, and Thank Them!

The truth is, we "train" people in how to treat us.

When a client refers you to another potential client, treat it as the big deal it is! Most firms have gotten far too casual in both identifying and acknowledging referrals. That's bad business for two reasons. When we fail to acknowledge a referral, we reduce the likelihood that the client will repeat the behavior in the future. But that's just one transgression. The other is the violation of the customer's tit-for-tat rule of trust that says, When I do something nice for your business, let me know you know.

Of course, it's not possible to know the source of every referral or acknowledge it every time, but having a referral identification process in place can go a long way! Consider these guidelines for rooting out advocates and thanking them:

- *Query new prospects and buyers to identify advocates.* The question "How did you hear about us?" is key to smoking out advocates. (When you discover customers recommending your brand online, take note of them too!)

  Name that person to your advocate list and keep the list distributed to your front line. At staff meetings, routinely discuss which customers are on the list.

- *Immediately thank the advocate for the referral.* Send a written thank-you note or, at a minimum, acknowledge the referral in a phone call or personal e-mail. It makes no difference whether the particular referral bears fruit or not; the advocacy deserves a thank-you.

- *Personally greet advocates when they visit on-site.* For example, a car dealership "flags" advocates who bring their cars for servicing. A senior dealership staff member greets these advocates while they are at the dealership. This acknowledgment is in addition to their interaction with the service team.

- *Send periodic value-added correspondence.* In the age of seemingly impersonal e-mail newsletters and such, a how-to article along with a handwritten note sent through the mail carries a "specialness factor" that cyberspace cannot match. Of course, the sheer size of your advocate list may dissuade you from this approach. But consider the 80-20 rule. It's likely that 20 percent of your advocates drive 80 percent of your referrals. This group may warrant some kind of special correspondence. Remember, the handwritten, personal touch is what makes this communication special. (A personal e-mail, though not as "standout" as a handwritten note, can sometimes work as well.)

- *Host thank-you events for advocates.* If geographically feasible, occasionally invite your advocates to an informal drop-in. (If your advocate list is long, consider subdividing the list into several mini-events.) Maybe it's happy hour at a local wine room or lunch at a popular café. Whether the advocates attend or not, you're telegraphing an important message: *we recognize and appreciate your actions on our behalf.*

Honor Conscientious Complainers and Learn from Them

Complainers can be advocates too. And when you get a conscientious complainer, they're often worth their weight in learning. Consider Dr. Eric Clemons, Wharton professor of operations and information management, who, more than a decade ago, endured what he described as an "awful" stay at the InterContinental Hotel in London. But Clemons dutifully submitted a detailed review of his stay and all that went wrong. At checkout, the hotel's guest relations manager asked if she could spend more time with him on the specifics of the problems he encountered.

Clemons returned, and from that visit forward, the hotel provided accommodations commensurate with his guest profile. For example, when his young daughter accompanied him on a stay, he was given a room without a balcony so that the child would be safe from a fall. Clemons estimates that he now stays at InterContinental hotels sixty nights a year.[35]

Rosalind Pearson, the hotel's guest relations manager who debriefed Clemons twelve years ago, now heads up the front office of InterContinental's Chicago property. She's seen firsthand the value of this special class of advocates. "If they care enough to bring it to your attention, then it is important to turn things around for them and turn that to strength. I've followed up on quite a few regular guests who have had problems. They can end up being your most loyal customers," explains Pearson.[36]

Always remember: when customers take the time to complain, it's an act of trust. This time, they are trusting that you will take their feedback seriously, make amends to them if warranted, and correct root causes of the performance failure. Customer trust goes up when you do these things on behalf of the customer and down when you don't.

Nurture Customer Community

Cyberspace offers some exciting "engagement" tools that enable customers and clients to more deeply advocate on behalf of your firm. Now you may be thinking, how does this nurture trust? Think Relationship 101. The more positively you interact with a brand and other brand users, the more likely your trust will grow.

Here's one scenario. A group of three hundred to five hundred prospects and customers with desirable demographics agrees to provide feedback, insight, and advice through a facilitated online community for a period of months (or even years). Surveys, discussion threads, brainstorms, chats, and other activities engage community members on a private branded and password-protected Web site, and community members agree to visit the site regularly to participate in the dialogue. Most important, the site supports and encourages interaction between members. These interactions are usually very robust and frequently provide novel, unsolicited insights into the opinions, emotions, and behaviors of community members.

Brokerage giant Charles Schwab uses by-invitation-only, online communities built and hosted by Massachusetts-based Communispace. Reports Jack Hawn, VP of Schwab's retail brokerage, "We can get an idea . . . and within a week, we can get back to the originator and say, "We took your ideas out to 400 clients and here's what they said."[37] Continues Hawn, "[Our customers] know their ideas and suggestions are being listened to, and that what they are saying is being considered by Schwab management up to and including the chairman." The power of that understanding became apparent when the chairman, Charles Schwab, was involved in a set of online customer interactions on his own. In preparation for an upcoming press tour, Mr. Schwab wanted up-to-the-minute information about his clients' investing strategies and views of the market. Working with Mr. Schwab, the site design and facilitation team prepared a questionnaire and wrote a letter addressed to the community. Reports Hawn, "He had the highest response to date. Clients were literally writing essays to him about what they liked and what needed improvement."

Want to keep advocates advocating for your brand and nurture their trust in the process? Consider creating an online community to help foster direct relationships with customers and to help nurture your customers' relationships with one another.

Leverage Your Fansumers' Social Networks

Jeremiah Owyang, social media analyst for Forrester Research, coined the term *fansumer* to describe someone who likes a brand so much that he routinely sings its praises to his social network. The strength and reach of fansumer advocacy can be summed up in Owyang's formula:[38]

Affinity + trusted network + connections = trusted efficient word-of-mouth marketing

---

Southwest Airlines is putting that formula to work via its strong brand presence on the popular social networking site Facebook. With over fifty-six Southwest-related groups on the site, the largest of which boasts more than forty-five thousand members, the brand gets plenty of buzz. On Facebook, Southwest leverages an advocate's social graph (in this case, a Southwest customer's network of Facebook "friends") to help stimulate discussion around brand happenings. For example, when Southwest introduced its new, enhanced boarding procedures, there were lots of posts—mostly positive, but some negative—about changes in the brand's long-held boarding protocols. Southwest's online marketing team describes their focus this way: "What we're trying to do is provide a space for customers to be able to talk to each other as well as to Southwest Airlines. We want to be where our customers are to listen to them and provide an opportunity to interact with us."[39]

Postscript: Winning Back Lost Customers

It's a sad fact that the average company loses 10 to 40 percent of its customers every year. Loss of customer trust is often the culprit.

Mishandled or unattended, customer trust dissipates. And when trust disappears, so do customers. As we've seen in this and other chapters, customer trust breakdowns stem from a host of causes, including unhappiness with product or service performance, improper handling of a complaint, disapproval of a change in price or policy, or just plain feeling disappointed. No trust-building plan is 100 percent foolproof. Therefore, when you lose a high-value customer, it's important that your firm have protocols in place to start the careful rebuilding of trust required to win back that customer. Please refer to my book *Customer Winback: How to Recapture Lost Customers—and Keep Them Loyal*, cowritten with Michael Lowenstein, to get the full prescription for rebuilding trust and winning back lost customers.

But I'm not going to leave you hanging! For now, consider these seven proven steps to regain trust and win back a customer you simply can't afford to lose.

1. Ask the question, "What can we do to win back your business?"
2. Listen closely to what the customer tells you.
3. Meet the customer's requirements; communicate the changes you have made. Ask again for the customer's business.
4. Be patient with the customer. Be open. Remember, some wounds heal slowly.
5. Stay in touch with the lost customer.
6. Make it easy for customers to come back to you. Avoid the "I told you so" stance.
7. When the customer does return, earn his or her trust every day.

Form a Trust Team—Now!

Ready to get *really* serious about building customer trust? Form a cross-functional team of employees and, together, map out the customer development stages as they apply to your firm's products or services, and identify trust builders and trust breakers inherent at each customer stage.

Brainstorm these questions:

- Where are your best trust-building opportunities?
- How can you capitalize on them?
- What are your biggest threats to building and maintaining trust?
- What safeguards can be implanted to protect against potential loss of trust?
- For lost customers, what specific actions can immediately be taken to start the process of rebuilding trust?

Repeat the same exercise, but this time focus on building staff trust. Why? Because you can't expect employees to build customer trust when they themselves don't trust the company. (Chapter Seven, which focuses on staff, can help as well.)

These steps are likely to uncover a surprising truth: a host of trust-building opportunities already exist in your company and are simply waiting to be tapped. Capture the best ideas and create a company-wide implementation plan for senior management review and buy-in. It's time well spent. Trust me.

Want more help on how to create and implement a trust-building plan? Visit **www.loyaltysolutions.com/CustomerTrustPlan**.

Moving On

Customer trust helps form a strong firewall around your buyers. But know this: customer trust is most effective in this buffer role when it is protecting brands that have valuable, discernible, superior differences as compared to your competitors' brands. If your brand doesn't currently have this perception advantage over the competition, keep working to get it. In the meantime, know that customer trust can help you trump a competitive offering when customers perceive your brand at parity with their next best alternative.

The next chapter examines another important piece of your firewall: passionate-to-serve employees. Like customer trust, value-delivering employees can provide vital insulation that fends off competitive attacks and keeps customers from succumbing to switch temptations.

Taming Takeaways

- In today's search-and-switch marketplace, customer trust can serve as a powerful buffer that insulates your customers against competitive poaching.

- The current business climate conspires against the building of customer trust. This fact makes it more important than ever for your firm to think tactically about trust building and to have a plan.

- It's helpful to think of trust building through the lens of customer stages: suspect, prospect, first-time customer, repeat customer, client, advocate, lost customer.

- Each customer stage has its own notable trust triggers, and it's important that your trust-building plan address them.

- Forming a cross-functional team to identify trust builders and trust breakers in the realm of the user experience can help move trust planning ahead in your firm.

- Customer trust can help block customer switching tendencies when it comes to brands perceived by buyers as being at least at parity with their next best alternative. But customers' trust in your brand cannot save you from customer defection if your brand is perceived by customers as offering less value than the competition.

Find and Grow Passionate-to-Serve Employees

Suppose you go out on the street, quiz some folks, and find a handful who are gainfully employed. You then ask each of them to name just one "golden oldie" that best expresses his true feelings about his company's culture, his work experience, and his job satisfaction. *What song would each of them choose? And knowing the choice of song, what employee behaviors would you expect to see?*

Frivolous questions? Hardly. Some theme, in song form or not, already plays in every employee's head *right now*, directly impacting job performance and the ultimate experience delivered to customers. Consider these three very different song possibilities and the employee behaviors that accompany them. (And if these oldies tunes don't ring a bell for you, then check out **www.loyalty solutions.com/Oldies**, where you'll find song titles nominated by fellow readers to characterize employee attitudes and behaviors.)

Johnny Paycheck's "Take This Job and Shove It." No doubt, this ballad has been the anthem for job dissatisfaction since the song's debut in the early 1980s. But this theme spells more risk than ever for today's employer. That's because Internet capability has created a virtual "shove it" tool kit for disillusioned employees, producing company consequences that range from deep embarrassment to heavy financial losses, as illustrated by these three scenarios:

> Four burned-out employees of a Canadian coffee bar walked off the job. To underscore their frustration, they taped a highly visible poster (complete with store name, address, and logo) in the store's front window. A passer-by

photographed the poster and then posted it online. Ben McConnell and Jackie Huba saw the post and linked it to their churchofthecustomer.com blog site, where it got 100,000 hits. The poster read:

Dear [name withheld],

Your staff is tired of your attitude, your inconsideration, your ungratefulness and lack of trust. If you expected more from us, you should have thought more about your staff than your business.

We are good, loyal workers but you always let us down. Be more of a people person, okay? You will see that it pays more. We quit today because this is the end and you didn't do anything to prevent it. Treat your staff better.

Signed, [signatures of all four employees][1]

The following quote is a paraphrase of an entry posted on an Internet chat board where customers exchange tips on how to negotiate cheaper cell phone services with carriers. Note how the ex-employee, bitter from her job as a cellular service rep, willingly shared insider tips: "I have worked for [company name] as an accounts manager in the Saves Team . . . and one thing I would suggest you do is always cancel your contract after twelve months. Just bring your number to your new contract. Here's the low down . . . " She goes on to give detailed insider information about rate plans and what to say to call center reps to manipulate the best deal.

At the end of her post, she rants, "You're [held] worthless as a customer and it's rubbish! It's not the reps' fault, it's higher management setting hard and unreachable targets for the reps, and the reps are forced to choose between feeding their family or giving the customer what they deserve."

On March 4, 2002, UBS Paine Webber analyst Roger Duronio, upset by what he considered to be a meager annual bonus, released a logic bomb virus that disabled two thousand of the firm's Unix servers. Because of this sabotage, UBS financial traders were unable to make trades for up to several weeks in some locations. Four long years later, the company reported that some of the systems had still not been recovered. Although the firm has not released the cost of the lost business, it reported costs of $3 million for getting the systems back up. (Duronio, fifty-nine, was ultimately convicted of computer sabotage and sentenced to ninety-seven months in prison.)[2]

Sly & the Family Stone's "Hot Fun in the Summer Time." A chance discussion with my seatmate on a recent flight provided this example of what a "Hot Fun" company culture can reap:

What would motivate a young husband in his late twenties, with a wife newly diagnosed with a chronic disease that limited her earning capabilities, to stay in an entry-level $31,000 job he took temporarily with Enterprise Rent-A-Car, even after he finally gets the $51,000 offer from the utility company for which he'd interviewed a month before?

His wife says, "When will you start?"

He replies, "We have a problem."

"What kind of problem?"

"I'm having so much fun at Enterprise. For the first time ever, it's like I'm not even working. I put in these long, ridiculous hours, but time flies by. I love the folks I work with. I don't want to quit."

The couple makes a pact, and he stays on with Enterprise. Financial circumstances over the next twelve months test their resolve. They move out of their apartment and in with her parents. They borrow from his mom, juggle credit card debt, and live paycheck-to-paycheck. But despite his long, demanding work schedule, he's engaged and having fun. He locks into Enterprise's brisk advancement path and works closely with his supervisors to set goals, timelines, and compensation targets. One high-performance year later, his first big promotion arrives. More promotions follow in years two and three, further deepening his commitment to his fellow team members and the firm.

John Lennon's "Imagine." Lennon's utopian song, recorded in 1971, challenges listeners to think well beyond today's world and imagine something much more.

Likewise, search giant Google has built a company culture that propels its employees to "disregard the impossible" and relentlessly search for fresh new ways to fulfill the firm's mission: "to collect all the world's information" and make it accessible to everyone.

Charged with protecting this unique culture is Google's twentieth employee, Marissa Mayer, who is keen on making sure the search giant remains an unrivaled idea factory. "A License to Pursue Dreams" is how this VP of search projects refers to the company's "20 Percent Time" policy, by which all employees are allowed to use 20 percent of their work time to focus on their own, self-directed "what if" projects.

At the heart of the policy is the trust that Google places in employees to pursue whatever they want. It's a policy that has paid big returns for Google, reports Mayer. For example, of the company's new product launches and features released in the second half of 2005, a whopping 50 percent of those innovations originated from 20 Percent Time projects.[3]

What's playing in your employee's head? Whatever the "song," it's an amalgam of the thoughts and perceptions residing in your employee's mind at any particular time. Remember the perception maker and taker dynamics discussed early in Chapter Four? That same concept helps explain employees' attitudes about their firms. In this case, three parties—the employee, the firm, and third-party influencers, together or in some combination—create perceptions about the employee experience. Employees are perception takers, and their attitudes about their jobs are driven by what they take (or not) from perception makers.

Among those perceptions are employees' experiences, both with prior employers and in their life in general. These experiences factor into how employees form perceptions about their current employers and their jobs. For each employee, the "songs" may shuffle around a bit, but one key theme usually predominates. And it's critical to your firm that the employee's theme be a positive one! Why? Think back to all the strategies you have read about for taming search-and-switch customers. From acing the Worth-It Test to building customer trust, each of these strategies depends on one irreplaceable point of execution: *customer-driven staff members, at every level in the organization, who are passionate to serve*.

Winning the Talent Tug-of-War

Creating a customer-driven staff is not as simple as it once was. There's a tug-of-war for talent going on worldwide, and most experts predict that the competition for competent employees will continue to be fierce. For example, McKinsey research finds that between the years 2006 and 2012, the number of American jobs that emphasize complex, intricate interactions that require superior levels of judgment will have grown two-and-a-half times as fast as the number of jobs that are easily scripted or automated, and three times as fast as employment in general.[4] As other economies outside the United States lean toward the same requirements, global demand for workers who can do jobs requiring complex skills will continue to escalate.

Intensifying this race for competent employees will be decreased supply. RHR International predicts that by the year 2010 or so, America's five hundred largest companies will lose half their senior managers. Yet the talent pool of potential leaders in these same firms is small due to decades of downsizing and reengineering.[5] The bottom line: every firm will have to fight harder and smarter to attract and keep talent.

So how can a firm find and grow passionate-to-serve employees? By crafting a stage-based employee care strategy. Recall the discussion in Chapter Six on building customer trust and the customer stages around which that plan was crafted. Here I recommend a similar stage-oriented plan for building staff. For simplicity's sake, we'll focus on three key stages:

1. Turning prospective employees into new hires

2. Turning new hires into productive employees

3. Turning employees into fierce company advocates

Many chapters, if not whole books, could be written on each of these stages, so consider the following guidelines as a quick jump-start for your firm's planning.

Stage 1: Turning Prospective Employees into New Hires

The old adage "An ounce of prevention is worth a pound of cure" is an apt descriptor for Stage One measures. In other words, making wise hiring choices now pays big dividends later, and mishandled hiring decisions will require a heavy remedy down the road.

1. Hire People Predisposed to Serve

"Whenever the topic of customer service is broached, people always ask us about our training. We respond by talking about recruitment," reports Barbara Talbott, executive VP of marketing at Four Seasons Hotels. She continues, "There is an aspect of good customer service that's un-teachable. It really comes down to how we select our employees. We believe that there are certain attitudes that some people bring to their job that predispose them to being an effective deliverer of service. [Those include] kindness, helpfulness, a genuine desire to see other people happy and taking pride in doing things well."[6]

So true! Consider my recent customer service experience:

> After days at home nursing a cold, I am running at breakneck speed to get a week's worth of errands completed in one afternoon. For the last two weeks, my hardwood floors had remained unmopped because I was out of the refinisher's recommended cleaner. Several years back, Mack and I paid top dollar for our city's premier refinisher to restore our oak floors. Delighted with the refinisher's work, we'd been treating our hardwoods with meticulous, loving care ever since. Nothing but the refinisher's recommended cleaner would do. So off I go to my refinisher's store to pick up more bottles.
>
> I walk in and request the cleaner from the woman behind the counter. "Here's the last two bottles," she says, adding that they would be ordering more. "How much?" I ask. "Ten dollars," she says, and I silently congratulate myself for having first stopped by at an ATM and gotten the appropriate cash. "Here's a twenty," I say, and her face falls. "I don't have change," she declares. I dig deeper into my purse, and this time I find eight one-dollar bills. "It's all I have," I say. "You don't have a check?" comes the retort. "Nope," I say, "just the cash."
>
> At this point we're deadlocked. We stand, alone, in this quiet store, no supervisor or coworker in sight, and I'm thinking, "Why should I leave and go get change? Aren't I the customer?" She's saying to herself, "Rules are rules. My job is to collect the ten dollars." I take the plunge and ask, "Are you really going to let me walk away for two dollars?" thinking all the time about

the mucho dinero we paid this firm a few years back
for refinishing work and the numerous friends Mack
and I have referred since. Surely we're worth two dollars to this business. But she has different thoughts.
She raises her arms in an I-give-up stance and screams
out in a shrill, disgusted tone, "OKAY, I'LL PAY FOR IT
MYSELF." Startled at the outburst and feeling grateful
that there is a counter separating us, I hand over my
eight dollars, collect my two bottles of cleaner, and
quickly exit.

Kindness? Helpfulness? Genuine desire to see other people
happy? Not likely. This poor soul was anything but a "people person," and it showed. The smart firms put "people people" on their
front line. It's a lesson that career site Monster.com learned quickly.
When the firm launched a twenty-city workshop tour to help clients learn how to use the site, crowds were small. That's when
Monster switched gears and hired a former customer as forum facil-
itator. Suddenly, the once staid event took on the feeling of a big
party. "The man has a huge personality. He throws Monster trin-
kets around, people love him and now 500 to 800 people show up.
You get the right person with the right temperament and clients
will notice," confirms Neal Bruce, VP of innovation for Monster.[7]

2. Hire Up, Not Down

Fact 1: Class A talent wants to work with other A-level talent.

Fact 2: Class B talent feels threatened by A-level talent and therefore recruits equally unremarkable people.

Once B-level talent infiltrates a firm, it's increasingly difficult
(if not impossible) for the firm to attract and keep A-level players.
That's because real winners want to work with other winners, and
they can sniff out B players a mile away.

Google is keenly aware of the dangers of creeping mediocrity, and its grueling hiring process, which includes Mensa-like I.Q. tests and multiple layers of interviews, helps protect against it. Google relentlessly culls out top talent. "Yes, it takes longer, but we believe it's worth it," proclaims the Google recruitment site (google.com/support/jobs). It continues, "If you hire great people and involve them intensively in the hiring process, you'll get more great people. We started building this positive feedback loop when the company was founded, and it has had a huge payoff."

The firm values nonconformity nearly as much as I.Q. The Google site states, "Here at Google, we value talent and intelligence, group spirit and diversity, creativity and idealism. . . . Googlers range from former neurosurgeons and puzzle champions to alligator wrestlers and Lego maniacs. Tell us what makes you unique!"

3. Ace Your Recruit's Worth-It Test

Think about recruitment this way: you have a product called a job that is being sold to a customer called an employee. To win that recruit, you must pass her Worth-It Test—that is, you must present your employee a value proposition in a compelling way that showcases what she'll get out of working for your firm. No doubt, pay and benefits loom large on this scorecard, but so do factors like a congenial culture and the opportunity to develop and sharpen job skills.

Why it pays. Recruitment research suggests that big rewards await firms that manage their employee scorecards well. A recent study by the Corporate Executive Board found that firms which did so enjoyed a potential talent pool 20 percent larger than the norm and a workforce with four times more commitment than the norm. Perhaps the most surprising finding was the payroll savings. Firms that manage their employee scorecards well were found to be able to offer salaries about 10 percent lower than firms that did not.[8]

Defining your recruit's worth-it scorecard. Most firms do a lackluster job nailing down the recruitment value proposition. Human resource departments tend to focus on communicating the company's culture and character. Sure, these are important, but today's recruits first want to know about rewards and opportunities. For example, I recently consulted on staff recruitment with a large global organization in stiff competition for technology talent. What was the number-one item on the scorecard of many of these highly sought after professionals? It was group recruiting, which would enable their already successful collaboration and research with trusted teammates to continue.

What's on your recruits' worth-it scorecard? Go back and reread Chapter Three, "Ace Your Buyer's Worth-It Test," substituting the word *employee* for *buyer*. It's one sure way to start thinking about your recruitment value proposition in a new light.

4. Target Imaginatively

Never has it been more important to think outside the box to identify and connect with talent.

- **Tap passive candidates.** Often the best candidates are passive candidates who are not actively looking for a new position. One proven way to connect with these individuals is to go through a list of people attending a conference and target the stars. For example, the newly recruited dean of a highly ranked business school told me that although he did not realize it at the time, his recruitment began when a university representative "just happened" to sit beside him at a professional conference and informally began the dialogue.

  Another popular way to identify passive candidates is to buy information about competing firms and the employees who work there, or to use Web searches. For example, firms often identify top-notch engineering candidates by searching the Web for new patent holders.

- **Make a recruiting wish list.** Facing a blisteringly competitive market for video game producers, Mark Kern, CEO of the upstart Red 5 Studios, knew his company had to dramatically shift its recruitment tactics away from conventional ad placement and professional recruiting firms. His solution? Research and compile a wish list of video game developers whose animation style or technology was right for Red 5. Kern and his team put together a beginning list of 250 prospects. Four months of tedious research followed, which included renting and playing the developers' games. The research served two purposes: first, it identified those developers whose style best fit Red 5, enabling the firm to trim the list down to a final one hundred prospects; second, it gave the company clues on how to customize the individual pitch for each of the one hundred "dream hire" finalists.[9]

Fast-forward three months later. FedEx packages began arriving on the desks of the "dream hire" developers. Inside were five nested boxes (think Russian dolls, each one inside another). The final box contained an iPod Shuffle music player with the developer's name engraved on it. Hit the Play button, and on came the voice of Mark Kern talking specifically about the developer's past work and why it fit Red 5. "I was blown away," said video game designer Scott Youngblood, who received the package and within two weeks interviewed at Red 5.[10] Just over a month later, Youngblood left Sony Computer Entertainment America, relocating over eight hundred miles away to begin a new job at Red 5 in California.

Four months after the recruitment campaign launch, Red 5 had snagged three candidates, another was interviewing, and the firm was enjoying a much higher industry profile thanks to strong positive buzz about the campaign.

- **Consider online recruitment tools.** Many firms are finding success using a host of new online recruitment tools. The very use of online tools can often send an important signal to recruits about the culture of the firm and its open-ness to cool new techniques of communication. Here are two good examples:

Mindful that millennials (born between 1980 and 1995 or so) spent huge amounts of time online and on social net-working sites, Verizon Communications launched targeted ads on Facebook beginning in late 2007. "Sponsored sto-ries," as Facebook calls the paid advertising, have been dis-tributed in two waves: to college seniors and recent grads with majors in specific fields, and to experienced profession-als with work history in the same areas. Verizon reported that the campaign generated over a million clicks.[11]

Looking for a way to catch the eye of ever-shrinking numbers of accounting and finance majors, Aronson & Company, a top fifty–ranked accounting and consulting firm, launched the "Show Us Your Future" video submission contest. The prize? A $2,500 student-to-professional make-over. The firm asked students to submit a three-minute video that demonstrated where they see themselves after graduation. Videos were posted to YouTube, where people could vote for their favorite. Says Lisa Cines, Aronson's managing officer, "We are very excited about what we feel is a really fun and inventive way to approach recruiting during a time marked by significant competition. Not only does it give us a creative platform for reaching students and prospective employees, but it also gives them a platform to show us what is important to them . . . to be heard."[12]

Aronson's director of marketing and sales, Stephen White, reports that the firm's first-ever contest helped stimu-late recruitment success on a number of fronts. Resume sub-missions jumped 25 percent compared to the previous year, and, most important, the quality of the firm's recruitment class for both full-time hires and interns rose substantially. According to White, the firm will use more online recruit-ment tools in the future. Aronson & Company intends to transform its contest Web site into a clearinghouse of sorts for even more candidate expression, including blogs, news links, and other information to help students better grasp the CPA profession.[13]

5. To Woo Young Recruits, Woo the Parents, Too

One of the biggest shifts in recruiting the twenty-something age group is in the role parents now play in the recruitment process. The bottom line: parents must be wooed too.

Merrill Lynch has embraced this reality and built parent-involving recruitment strategies accordingly. And it's paying off, according to Subha Barry, Merrill's global head of diversity. Barry recalls seeing a colleague lunching with a prospective summer recruit along with someone else Barry did not know. Who was it? The boy's mom! "If someone would have said to me, 'You're interviewing for a job somewhere, and you're going to bring your mother to the closing, decision-making lunch,' I would have said, 'You've got to be crazy,'" she said. "But I tell you, his mother was sold. And that boy will end up at Merrill next summer. I can guarantee that."[14]

6. Think Carefully About the Job Requirements

What exactly is expected of those employees whose jobs are the most essential to your day-to-day business? Do their current job requirements nurture or needle your mission-critical talent?

That's the question United Parcel Service considered with regard to its drivers. Although the package delivery giant worked hard to screen and select its drivers carefully, turnover remained high, for one very big reason: drivers simply hated the tedious, back-breaking chore of loading trucks each morning before beginning their routes. The solution? Big Brown redesigned the driver's job, removing the truck loading tasks and contracting out those duties to part-timers, who were much easier to find than drivers.[15]

Stage 2: Turning New Hires into Productive, Long-Term Employees

Consider these two eye-catching statistics: every single month in America, 4.6 million employees start with a new employer; Corporate Executive Board research finds that 75 percent of new recruits feel that their employers are failing to deliver on their promises, and these same recruits say they are less committed to their work because of it.[16] Obviously, there's plenty of opportunity to better manage this crucial stage of the employee life cycle. Here are eight recommendations.

1. Make the First Day on the Job Memorable

Ask many new hires about their first day on the job, and you are likely to hear about such mediocre activities as getting office key cards or being assigned network ID numbers and passwords. Maybe the new employee had a picture ID card made or received a parking lot pass. Truth is, the new hire's first day on the job is often a missed opportunity for your firm to score big, positive first impressions that can last a lifetime.

For example, consider the engineering firm that wanted to make a new twenty-something's first day on the job unforgettable. The new hire's mom (there's that mom thing again!) was invited to be there when her daughter began her first workday. Imagine the daughter's amazement as her mom walked through the crowd of staff members assembled to welcome the new recruit. Soon afterward, the president took the employee and her mom on a tour of the company, emphasizing why new employees were so important to the firm. The mom then turned to her daughter and said, "You are not allowed to quit this job. Real companies are not like this."[17]

Some may read that last comment and say she's right . . . *real* companies don't do this! But why not? It's one more way to build a worth-it factor into the staff member's scorecard. Remember, employees join and stay with a company on the basis of its differences from other firms, not its similarities.

2. Incubate New Recruits

Think safety nets when considering ways to make the most of the new recruit's first year. For example, twenty-somethings come from a world of support from family, friends, and school, and the closer firms can replicate that cocoon of support on the job, the less the flight risk. That's what IBM has done with a host of online tools that include podcasts, blogs, and online brainstorm sessions called jams, in an effort to blanket new recruits with a virtual network of mentors, peers, and senior staff support from day one.[18]

When American Express discovered that far too many of its new managers were leaving within the first two years, the firm launched aggressive retention initiatives. They included assigning new manager recruits to projects overseen by the CEO and providing new managers with "assimilation coaches" to help point the way.[19]

3. Do Destination Planning

To keep talented workers, it's crucial that your firm consistently send the signal that "there are no dead ends here." Yet employee destination planning—identifying where employees want to go career-wise, and how to help take them there—gets shoved aside in many firms. The same is true of one of the essential tools of destination planning: employee performance reviews. Do you know any manager who doesn't dread preparing and delivering them?

To help remedy this malaise, more and more companies worldwide are adopting some form of talent management technology. For example, Web-based software can track the progress of employees from their initial application through their last day on the job. One aim of such a system is to simplify the performance review process for both employee and employer. In some instances, the software allows a manager to input ratings and notes into employee profiles and then view the data cumulatively and in head-to-head comparisons. Employees can look up information at any time, type in their feedback, and view suggestions on how to achieve a specific goal or to progress to the next level. The Yankee Group estimates that in 2005, more than twenty-three hundred companies worldwide adopted such software and that by 2011, demand will double.[20]

For many firms, talent management software has moved from being a nice-to-have to a must-have. Says John Brenna, VP of human resources for San Francisco–based Advent Software, "Employees now tend to expect this. They find easy access to information in all aspects of their lives and expect the company they work for to provide the same."[21]

4. Make Your Firm a Learning Organization

Talented employees expect to be taught transferable skills. They keenly realize that their only real security in the marketplace is their skill base, and they search out employers that can help them broaden it. Want to improve your staff retention? Find fresh new ways to turn your organization into a learning environment.

Training buddies. The Container Store assigns a training buddy to help each new recruit master the details of everything from modular storage products to sales and stocking skills. But that's not all—new hires are trained extensively through a 241-hour training program over a twelve-month period, which is a huge contrast to the eight hours given the average new retail worker. To further facilitate training, each of the chain's stores (thirty-eight coast-to-coast locations, at this writing) employs a full-time sales trainer. Employee response is overwhelmingly positive. The Texas-based company has landed near the top of *Fortune*'s annual list of 100 Best Companies to Work For for eight consecutive years, and employee turnover remains well below retail industry norms.[22]

Big-picture insight. The day after Best Buy's quarterly conference call, CFO Darren Jackson serves up a similar financial presentation for employees. The ninety-minute presentation not only covers the quarter's financials but also provides employees with a chance to learn some financial basics. "For people who aren't schooled in financial statements, the numbers can be very intimidating," reports

Jackson. He continues, "We spend so much time putting presentations together for investors and outsiders, why not spend the same amount of time on the people who make it all happen?"[23] The "Donuts with Darren" sessions—complete with donuts, crullers, and Bavarian creams—are popular events at Best Buy, with around six hundred employees participating.

On-the-job learning. Formal training is on the rise in many companies through corporate universities and online training programs. But don't think informal learning isn't critical in the minds of employees. It is. Most employees prefer on-the-job training over any other form of learning. That's according to a recent Deloitte survey, which found that 67 percent of respondents said they learned best when working alongside a colleague, as opposed to only 22 percent who preferred doing their own research and 2 percent who were happiest with a textbook or manual.[24]

Life-change learning. Getting married, starting a family—these are huge, life-changing events that can leave professionals feeling overwhelmed in their struggle to manage it all. Some firms are providing support to employees as they confront major events in their lives. For example, PricewaterhouseCoopers offers help in navigating through these changes with an off-site, weeklong class called Turning Point that staffers with four to five years of tenure can attend.[25]

5. Get Recognition Right

Many frontliners fight hard to deliver exceptional customer experiences, day in and day out. And those efforts require amazing fortitude. Key advice? Keep your employee recognition channels in working order. I witnessed firsthand how a national sporting goods chain's broken customer feedback system let down a hardworking, "make-it-happen" frontline customer care warrior, and it broke my heart.

> When I entered the sprawling sporting goods store on a Thursday morning, I was on a critical mission for a dear friend, whose two-year battle with blood cancer had

left her weak and fragile. Days before, her mother had passed away, and on Friday her oldest son would turn thirteen. My friend's fervent wish was to get the collapsed Ping-Pong table in her basement (thankfully covered by a service agreement) removed and replaced by another table within twenty-four hours. Her son was hosting a birthday sleepover, and Ping-Pong would be in high demand. Shaky and fatigued, my friend shuffled into the retail store where she had bought the table a few months back. We found her a chair. I quickly located the manager—we'll call him Dave—and out of earshot of my friend, I laid out the facts and appealed for his help: *please* make this happen. Dave "got it" and pulled out every stop. Within four short hours, a fully assembled new table was standing in my friend's basement. I profusely thanked Dave. His only request? Go to the Web address on the store receipt and take the customer survey.

If only it had been that easy. The retailer's feedback system was a nightmare. Back at my friend's home computer, I typed in the survey's site address to discover the page had expired. Next, I went to the corporate Web site in search of another feedback option, and found nothing. I then searched the corporate site under Contact Us for a corporate snail-mail address. Again, nothing. Next, I searched the site under Investment Information. Surely this public corporation's headquarters address would be posted. Again, nothing! I finally called the store and explained my dilemma, and a different manager on duty gave me a blind e-mail address to send my comments. Fearing my e-mail could funnel into a black hole, I also requested the corporate headquarters mailing address; for that, she had to call me back after looking it up.

Dave's corporation failed him and his team. The chain's sloppy feedback system and poor corporate oversight discouraged customer feedback, to put it mildly. What kept me in the game? The thought that this amazing customer warrior and his team were trapped in such a system. As I saw it, I *owed* it to Dave and my ailing friend to provide the "high five" feedback, and, whatever it took, I would keep prodding the retailer's dysfunctional apparatus to find a way. But, sadly, most customers stop after one feedback attempt. The tragic result? Everybody—corporation, employee, and customer—loses.

What employee recognition lessons can be gleaned from this retailer mishap?

- **Make it simple and easy for customers to provide feedback about employee performance.** (In this case, the delivery team could have at least handed out a paper survey form for mail-in. For a more high-tech solution, the delivery driver could have offered me a handheld electronic device on which I could tap out a survey response and push the Send button while he oversaw the completion of final delivery chores.)

- **Look for employee performance hot spots and give these interactions customer feedback priority.** For example, the sporting goods company could flag for customer feedback priority any home deliveries tied to service agreement contracts. After all, such deliveries typically occur because of a product or service breakdown, and these situations abound with rich learning opportunities about relationship repair. For example, the survey could ask for customer feedback on the store's problem-solving capability, delivery crew performance, and so on.

6. *Reward Thoughtfully*

In many firms, reward structures directly conflict with employees' motivations to serve. For example, the service bays in auto dealerships are both vital profit generators and critical links back to the showroom once customers are ready for another vehicle. In fact, industry research has shown that if car buyers use their dealers' service departments throughout the life cycle of the vehicle, these same customers are as much as seventeen times more likely to repurchase at that dealership.

But pop in to a dealer and inquire about the rewards and recognition that service reps receive, and you'll often get a different picture. At best, many of these service writers, as they are called, are rewarded on service dollars written per customer—in other words, how many service dollars were sold per customer. Period. Does this reward system help drive service excellence? Hardly. What could? Assigning service reps (and teams) to specific customers and rewarding these reps for bringing these customers back, time and again, for service maintenance. Here are a few ideas: a monthly reward for the service rep (or team) with the most returning customers, a monthly reward for the service rep with the most first-time customers who came because of referrals from existing customers, and a monthly reward for the service rep who serviced the most "second vehicles" of existing customers.

The lesson here is simple: reward employees on behaviors that nurture long-term customer relationships. It's one important way to build a passionate-to-serve company culture.

7. Both Listen and Hear

Think Psych 101: people want to work for and with people they believe care about them. How do you demonstrate this caring? Through careful listening. Here's how two leaders do it well:

CEO listening tour. When Jim Schroer assumed the CEO helm at Carlson Marketing in 2005, he spent much of his first hundred days in listening sessions with employees. In these sessions, he primarily asked questions and heard employee concerns. Schroer knew this was time well spent, for two reasons: the sessions helped him learn the business, and they enabled him to begin building trust bonds with employees. Says Schroer, "I don't believe that trust can be created any other way than face-to-face."[26]

Birthday calls. Tom Schmitt, president and CEO of FedEx Global Supply Chain Services, calls each of his 550 employees on his or her birthday. "[W]hen I call them, it's not to sing them 'Happy Birthday,' but to ask what the biggest single thing is they are working on and what their headaches are. It gives me a collective pulse of what's going on, makes them feel I care enough about what is going on. It takes just five minutes to have that conversation."[27]

But as Schroer and Schmitt no doubt recognize (and practice), the art of listening and the ability actually to *hear* the employee feedback are two very different management skills. Employees want to feel heard, not simply listened to—and they know the difference. For example, a *Wall Street Journal* reader recalled his exit interview with the human resources manager of a "too-big software" firm. "When I [told the HR manager] that I was tired of finding out who my new boss was via email, he apologized for that happening once," said the reader. "When I told him the latest email was one of three "Your boss is . . . ." emails, he stuck out his hand and said, "Been nice working with you."[28]

No doubt, this lack of being heard (from the HR manager no less!) left the departing employee feeling totally reinforced about his decision to leave!

Show employees that you are both listening and hearing. That's the winning combination.

8. *Watch Your Words*

Ask Alex Brennan-Martin, co-owner of the storied restaurants Brennan's (Houston) and Commander's Palace (New Orleans and Destin, Florida), about his "blinding flash of the obvious," and he is likely to tell you about a leader's words and the power they have on employees.

"One day, I went into a staff meeting, and all of our folks were arguing with one another. I slammed my hand down on the table, turned to the person sitting next to me, and said, "What's your job?"' As Brennan-Martin listened to all the employees, one by one, describe their jobs, he was struck with insight. "[I] realized that the customer had not been mentioned. But I realized that the common denominator was [the person who] had hired all these people," he said. "Who had given them their job descriptions? Who had told them what success looked like for them? And it was me."[29]

Brennan-Martin says this revelation led him and his team to a simple yet profound truth: customers are coming to their restaurants for great memories, and memory making is the real business they are in.

Starting today, pay close attention to the lingo used by you and your fellow staffers in the hallways and conference rooms of your firm. What words are being used to describe customers and your firm's business-building processes? I've been part of corporate meetings for almost three decades, and in many industries, I'm sorry to report, not much has changed. I still hear leaders use terms like "conquest" to describe the auto dealer sales process and "census" to describe patients in a health care facility and "detail people" to describe customer-facing pharmaceutical representatives. Yikes! Like it or not, such language sends powerful, constant cues to employees, subtly confirming to them what their firms are mandating their jobs to truly be about. Want a different outcome? Start by paying careful attention to your business language. It communicates far more to employees than you may realize.

Stage 3: Turning Employees into Fierce Company Advocates

In preparing for a keynote for a global B2B manufacturer, I asked my executive sponsor why his troops (mainly engineers) should actually care about customer loyalty. He paused for what seemed like a very long moment and then replied, "To build true loyalty, you must make a real, noticeable difference for the customer. You go the extra mile to get results. And there's a huge personal satisfaction and pride that can come from that caliber of customer work."

So true. Building deep loyalty requires you to own your customers' problems. It moves you from the "Me Zone" to the "We Zone." You stick your neck out. You put your heart in it. Your customers' successes become your successes. And alas, their hard times become your hard times too. Hidden deep in every employee's soul is a yearning to make a real difference. To courageously serve a customer. To put some skin in the game. To make work life count for something. In a search-and-switch-prone world, companies that are loyalty leaders know this, and they constantly work to help, not hinder, their employees' natural affinity to make a difference for customers. But these savvy leaders know another truth as well: *showing* employees how their work makes a difference is one way to transform workers into fierce company advocates.

The guidelines examined in the previous two sections, of course, help build advocacy for your company. Likewise, the following guidelines are applicable to earlier stages, too. That said, here are seven factors that have particular relevance to building employee advocacy.

1. Measure the Right Things

We've all heard the mantra "measure what matters." To help build a culture of passionate-to-serve employees and grow them into company advocates, what should you measure?

Survey customers and staff. Bob Ulrich, CEO of Target Stores, recommends two essentials: regular team member and guest surveys. For example, he says, "We survey every single team member at all levels at least once a year. That gets potential problems surfaced early. The survey was a mindset changer for our management group, particularly store team leaders. . . . People don't want to work with low performers. . . . [The survey insights] gave managers the courage to say, 'I have to face this problem. It's not fair for our guests [and] not fair for my team members.'"[30]

In some firms, top executives perform client follow-up on poor survey scores. For example, Florida-based Protocol Integrated Marketing asks clients to rate the value of the service and the helpfulness of account managers on a 5-point scale. "If we get a rating of less than 4.0, I personally call to find out where we fell short," says CEO Charles Dall'Acqua. This direct line to the customer helps leaders work with staff to pinpoint and target the right areas for improvement.[31]

Drive staff engagement. Best Buy has been measuring employee engagement and store performance for years, but only recently has the retail giant begun to study how the two interrelate. When Best Buy connected the dots between employee engagement scores and store performance, the firm found that for every tenth of a point improvement in engagement, there was a $100,000 increase in a store's operating income. This information has led Best Buy to work toward a new system of measures. Says Joe Kalkman, VP of human resources at Best Buy, "Given the complexity of business today, single metrics are less effective."[32]

Take a recent twelve-month Towers Perrin study across fifty global companies that also points to the financial benefits of staff engagement. Firms with disengaged employees suffered significant decreases in operating income, whereas those with highly engaged employees enjoyed operating income increases of nearly 20 percent over the course of the twelve months. The study showed clearly that employees require three things for engagement: a rational understanding of their company's goals and values, an emotional attachment to the organization, and a willingness to go above and beyond their specific tasks.[33]

Need more convincing? Consider the case of the hospital parking attendant who, late one evening, encountered a couple whose child was about to undergo treatment. The couple was returning to their car after a consultation, grieving the illness of their daughter and feeling extremely anxious about her upcoming treatment. That's when they encountered the parking lot attendant.

The attendant greeted the couple and, seeing they were emotionally distraught, initiated a brief conversation.

The attendant assured them that the hospital provided great care and that he would be praying for their daughter's recovery. "I pray for all the kids who come here for treatment," the attendant reportedly shared. The child's surgery was a success, and on the hospital's post-treatment survey card, the father wrote that this brief, surprising encounter really helped him and his wife feel additional confidence about the hospital and the care their daughter would receive.

Ask the right survey questions. Many firms think that surveys (about engagement or any other topic) are a cinch to do. Truth is, questionnaire design requires real skill. It takes experience and know-how to design a survey that truly works. That's why I cringe whenever I hear a client talk about bringing a summer intern on board to spearhead a survey project. The old adage "garbage in, garbage out" is alive and well in designing research surveys.

It's critical that staff survey questions are designed in a way that does not bias the respondent. Take this question: "I am committed to doing quality work." Would any employee in his or her right mind not mark "completely agree" to that query? Yikes!

The good news is that more and more firms are getting smarter about the design of their staff engagement survey questions. For example, Long John Silver's and KFC ask employees to react to these statements, and are reaping great insights in return:

My restaurant is a great place to work.

People on my team help out, even if it is not their job.

I am told whether I am doing good work or not.

I understand the employee benefits that are available to me.[34]

Ask yourself these questions: When did your firm last update its employee questionnaire and survey plan? When's the last time the questionnaire was brutally evaluated on its ability to provide fresh insights about improving the employee experience or the employee's ability to serve customers well? A year ago or longer? Insights await. Get going!

2. Help Employees Find Meaning in Their Work

To put it mildly, Chip Conley knows a thing or two about turning employees into company advocates. This ace motivator, author, and founder of Joie de Vivre, a chain of seventeen boutique hotels in the San Francisco area, has seen firsthand the importance of helping employees on the front lines find meaning in their work. Says Conley, "We bring in small groups of housekeepers from different hotels and we ask them to talk about what would happen if they weren't there each day." Carpets wouldn't get vacuumed. Trash would pile up. Bathrooms would fill up with wet towels. Working with their answers, the housekeepers are asked to come up with alternative names for housekeeping. "The suggestions are always great: 'serenity keeper,' 'clutter busters,' 'peace-of-mind police.'"[35] This exercise, says Conley, never fails to give employees a very real sense of meaning of how the experience of the customer would not be the same without them. Likewise, this meaning helps satisfy what every human being desires: to make a difference.

Want to turn employees into company advocates? Help them find meaning in the work they do for your firm. Look for ways to sprinkle "meaning maker" reinforcement into the day-to-day activities of staff. From staff meeting discussions to newsletter articles to framed customer stories in staff break rooms, routinely remind employees why their contributions matter.

3. Be Congruent

When designing staff programs, think long and hard about staff buy-in and how to achieve it. Simply put, think *congruence:* what gets communicated to employees inside the organization must agree with the company's values and how employees internalize them.

One of my clients, a large U.S. utility company long recognized for stellar customer service, learned this very lesson when it began initiatives to enlarge the responsibilities of call center reps. The strategy was simple: train the service reps to sell additional services to customers already calling in for other reasons. But when the VP of marketing and customer service introduced the program specifics, he got strong, vocal pushback from the reps, who in effect said, "You're asking us to be telemarketers. That's not what we signed up for!" The VP quickly got the message and realized his mistake: in the company's zeal to leverage customer touch points for higher profits, a congruency problem emerged. The call center reps were extremely proud of the company's reputation for stellar customer service. But "selling" did not fit. The solution? The program was reframed as "enhanced service." Call center reps were trained in how to do a better job of satisfying customers by recognizing unmet needs and suggesting new services to address them. Results? Twelve-month revenue goals were achieved in nine short months. Lesson: think congruency when seeking staff buy-in.

4. Give Employees the Resources and Tools to Perform

To do their jobs, employees must have adequate resources. This sounds simple, and it's remarkable how many companies neglect the obvious. Here are just a few examples.

Adequate staffing. Few things demoralize staff and hamper employees' passion to serve more than chronic understaffing. Such conditions turn off customers and burn out the firm's existing talent. When Ken Thompson took the helm of Wachovia Corporation in 2000, customer service was in serious decline, and around 20 percent of customers were walking out the door every year.[36] Staff counts were thin, and many customer contact channels—phone, ATMs, online banking, kiosks—were in serious need of more manpower. Says Thompson, "The first thing we did was to dramatically increase our spending on staffing. We needed to be staffed appropriately so we could very quickly service customers through whatever channel they wanted to deal with us." Employees and customers responded to these additions, and beginning in 2002, Wachovia Corporation began its reign at the top of University of Michigan's American Customer Satisfaction Index.

Customer insight. How can firms help passionate-to-serve employees fight hard on behalf of the customer? By providing rich, revealing customer feedback information. A senior manager I know at a large insurance company lobbies hard with upper management to make processes more customer friendly. Describing how she routinely makes her case in management meetings, she shared, "When I go into meetings, there are all these people around the table that are way higher on the food chain than I am. I've learned to say, 'The data tell us this. . . . sixty thousand customers are saying XYZ.' You show these hard-core details on the customer comments and it blows their hair back."

Collaboration know-how. I can still remember this conversation as if it happened yesterday: I was interviewing a senior executive of a large telecom company on behalf of a supplier. (I was conducting a client loyalty study for the supplier, and this was my first in-depth interview with its major account.) Right off, the exec minced few words in describing the massive silo mentality and departmental fiefdoms he saw festering at the supplier. He reported, "The relations between sales and customer care, for example, are so toxic, I've learned not to comingle my contacts but instead manage my business department by department. Given their internal turf wars, I get far more accomplished on my own than having anyone on the inside try to work cross-functionally on my behalf." Just as he described, my staff interviews on-site at the supplier revealed crippling mistrust and competitiveness between departments. Staff seemed tentative and flatfooted, forward-thinking but frozen. Not surprisingly, top talent was departing.

Know this: it's next to impossible to grow passionate-to-serve employees when silo warfare runs rampant. There's a lot to know about breaking down corporate silos, and there are some great books to help you. Jeanne Bliss's *Chief Customer Officer* is one of my favorites.

One sure way to limit silo behavior inside a firm is to build cross-functional collaboration. In fact, show me a fierce company advocate and, chances are, that staffer is a collaborative employee as well. The two conditions typically go hand in hand. However, today's far-reaching work environments—peppered with virtual teams, global work sites, and diverse workers—can make collaboration tougher than ever. Here are some best practices from authors Lynda Gratton and Tamara Erickson, whose study of fifty-five teams across sixteen multinational companies uncovered helpful ways to boost collaboration:

- Human resources departments that teach employee collaboration skills, including relationship building, communication, conflict resolution, and so forth, can have a major impact on improving a firm's collaboration abilities.

- The more that senior executives model collaboration across a company, the more that subordinates will follow.

- Help employees build networks for collaboration. Managers should routinely coach employees on cross-functional relationship building and help employees build those bridges.

- To speed collaboration on any team, it's wise to have at least a few people who know each other. When all the team members are strangers, collaboration is slow and employee engagement is dampened.[37]

5. Give People Autonomy

Employees care about what they help create. Good thing, says retail giant Best Buy, which knows from experience that great merchandising decisions often originate at the store level, and that such autonomy helps drive employee engagement and customer satisfaction. For example, Best Buy store members at the Alma Road location in Mesa, Arizona, are free to display merchandise the way they think it will be most helpful to area customers. During a recent holiday season, staffers created a store first—prebundled packages of iPods and iTune gift cards, to appeal to "grab and go" busy shoppers.

But staff autonomy on seemingly minor things can matter too. Ask Theophilus McKinney, front desk operator at the San Francisco–based Hotel Carlton, who is allowed to wear his favorite funky shoes and to rearrange the reception phones in a way that makes them easier to answer. Fostering a spirit of employee autonomy has helped this boutique hotel's turnover rate remain at less than 10 percent, a significant reduction from the 50 percent staff turnover the hotel suffered in 2000–2002, before new, employee-centered management came on board.[38]

6. Come Through in the Hard Times

The most passionate company advocates are the people who know that their employers will stick by them when the going gets tough. There are hundreds of ways companies do this, of course. Here are three of my favorites.

Walk your talk. During the tumultuous post-9/11 period, most airlines responded to the precipitous drop in travel with deep, aggressive cost cutting that included employee layoffs and pay cuts. But Southwest Airlines was determined to operate through the crisis in ways that demonstrated the firm's commitment to valuing and empowering employees. Reports James Parker, then the airline's CEO, "We were very forthright in saying that we would protect the culture of our company and the jobs of our employees even if it meant we had to take some short-term loss of profitability."[39] As a result, Southwest transitioned out of the crisis with profitability and reputation intact. Concludes Parker, "It's fundamentally true that the way you treat people determines the way they're going to treat you back and the way they treat customers."

Demonstrate trust. Supporting employees in troubled times can help a firm boost company advocacy. When he lost his wife to ovarian cancer, Bob Hallman, senior VP and partner at Fleishman-Hillard International, felt deep support from his employer, and in return, his commitment to the firm grew stronger. Said Hallman, "The unspoken rule became 'work when you need to based on your own need to feel connected to something other than the tragedy you're living through.' There was never an insistence by anyone that I 'had to' do anything; there was tacit, unspoken acknowledgment that I was responsible and professional enough to ensure I handled my workplace responsibilities."[40] Commenting on his attitude about the firm three years later, Hallman said, "To this day, when I have tough days at work, I remind myself of how my company supported me. My loyalty to the company deepened immeasurably."

Plan ahead for employee crisis. When the 2007 California wildfires threatened the homes of area employees, the Hartford activated its BSAFE (read: be safe) employee hotline. Because a number of Hartford offices were closed due to smoke conditions, employees were directed to call the BSAFE number, report their status, and receive information on the numerous company resources available. For example, $500 cash advances were available for employees needing temporary housing, and outside-the-area travel was available through prearrangement with American Express Business Travel. Through it all, the Hartford stayed in close touch with affected employees through phone and the Web, advising them of local government announcements, office reopening schedules, and other needed information.

7. Nurture Your Alumni Network

When great employees leave, stay in touch! These folks are often ripe for returning to your firm later. And when they come back, they often return as your firm's staunchest company advocates.

This a unique talent retention strategy that Deloitte & Touche pursues rigorously and with great results. Consider Deloitte manager Katie Peterson, who left the firm after two years to get her MBA. She was rerecruited by Deloitte after eight years away. Peterson was happily employed elsewhere; she recalls, "I wasn't even looking for a job, but a recruiter at Deloitte who had been networking with others was directed to me. I had always held an affinity for Deloitte and missed it, so the opportunity was perfect."[41]

Peterson was a registered member of Deloitte's online alumni network, called AlumNet. The Web site features Deloitte-related news and job postings, organized into seven regions. Alums can post their resumes as well. Four years after its 2002 launch, the registered alums on the AlumNet site totaled seventy-five thousand.

Deloitte's internal recruiters rely on the site to help identify job candidates. Moreover, recruiters are provided annually with a list of people who left Deloitte offices in their region over the past two to three years. Says Peter DeMartin, recruiting director for Deloitte & Touche's southeast region, "We go through the list with our human resources managers and partners in various offices to identify those we might be interested in having return." In addition to their requiring less training, there's another big advantage to hiring ex-employees, says Deloitte's multiregional alumni coordinator, Karen Palvisak: "Our numbers show they also stay with the company longer when they come back the second time, because now they know what else is out there."

In 2003, Deloitte did a cost analysis associated with their alumni hiring program. At that time, 140 ex-employees had been rehired nationwide, with most of those sourcing through alumni relations rather than search firms. "It came out to saving about $3.8 million in search fees," reported DeMartin.

Moving On

Strategies for taming search-and-switch customers depend on one irreplaceable execution source: customer-driven staff members, at every level in the organization, who are passionate to serve. Employees are fundamental to your firm's ability to retain customers. Loyal staff who truly believe in your firm's mission naturally act as powerful firewalls around your customers, making it extremely difficult for competitors to infiltrate.

Although Google and other search technologies have changed many ways that businesses conduct business, some things remain the same. Your employees have always been and will always remain the face of your company. Whether your customers experience your staff through online interaction, on the phone, or in person, employees and their behavior will in large part determine how customers feel about your firm. Therefore, it is more important than ever that you learn how to turn your employees into passionate-to-serve advocates for your business.

For more help on how to how to find and grow passionate-to-serve employees, visit **www.loyaltysolutions.com/EmployeePlan.**

The next chapter, "Look for Tamers That Teach," gives you another strategy for your loyalty-building tool kit: finding and taking lessons from firms that are modeling important skills for succeeding in today's compulsion-to-compare marketplace. You will be able to see how four firms with very different challenges came up with very different ways to tame search and switch.

Taming Takeaways

- Acing the Worth-It Test; fostering strong, favorable brand perceptions; being and staying different; building customer trust—each of these loyalty strategies depends on one irreplaceable execution source: customer-driven staff members, at every level in the organization, who are passionate to serve.

- A number of employment trends are comingling to produce a power-punch outcome; in the coming decades,
  every firm, including yours, will have to fight harder
  and smarter to attract and keep top talent.

- Finding prospective hires who are predisposed to
  serve is an essential first step to growing passionate-
  to-serve employees. There is an aspect of service that
  is unteachable, and firms must tailor recruitment and
  selection strategies to reflect this reality.

- Employees have different needs at different stages of
  their careers. Employee policies and procedures that
  recognize and address changing needs will go a long
  way toward growing employee advocacy. It is helpful
  to dissect your employee strategies by employee stage
  (recruit, new hire, established employee) in order to
  identify opportunities and pitfalls.

- To grow employees into company advocates, you must
  help employees find and experience personal satisfaction in their work.

- Teaching employees the art and skill of collaboration
  with other employees is an often overlooked but essential strategy that should be addressed from the beginning of the new hire's employment.

- In today's marketplace, working at one firm for thirty years
  and collecting the gold watch are simply not how most
  employees want to manage their careers. That said, firms
  are smart to see former employees as potential re-hires (as
  well as referral sources). Smart firms are building alumni
  networks and finding ways to factor these ex-employees
  into the firm's recruitment initiatives.

Look for Tamers That Teach

Finding companies that I call *Tamers That Teach* from which you can learn successful customer loyalty strategies and techniques is the final fortify-your-firewall essential. Why? Because Tamers That Teach model valuable survival skills for these rough-and-tumble, search-and-switch times. What's more, they can offer you inspiration and hope when the going gets tough.

This chapter takes you inside four carefully chosen B2B and B2C firms that have leveraged important, yet different, skill sets aimed at taming the search-prone customer. Think of these firms as a beginning list of models for zeroing in on critical customer-keeping strategies. As you expand your search for Tamers That Teach, don't limit yourself to your own industry! Your best teachers, those that help shake up your business-as-usual thinking, often come from industries other than your own.

Cornell's True Value Hardware: Loyalty Program

In today's switch-prone marketplace, the right customer data are more important than ever in earning and keeping customer loyalty. After all, how can any firm effectively maintain and grow customer relationships without knowing customer identities?

What do you do when your member stores know **what** they are selling——and **where, when,** and **for how much**——but don't know to **whom** they are selling?

That's the quandary True Value Company, one of the world's largest member-owned wholesale hardware cooperatives, addressed head-on in 2003 by offering loyalty program capability to its more than five thousand coop retailers. Aptly named True Value Rewards, the program has helped redefine how member stores earn customer loyalty.

Take Cornell's True Value Hardware, owned by the Fix family, whose hardware expertise has served the Eastchester, New York, community (twenty miles north of New York City) since 1916. That's the year that, as a teenager, John Fix Sr. began working after school at the prominent hardware store, Cornell's. He eventually bought the company, which his offspring own and operate today.

Best Customers

When the True Value Rewards program became available, John Fix III led Cornell's adoption. Suddenly the store had a means to collect customer data through a red, white, and blue card attached to the customer's keychain; with this data, Cornell's could more precisely target and nurture customers. "It was a real eye-opener for us," says Fix. "We now have the sales data to understand who our best customers really are. It's made a difference on our sales floor. Now I can coach our paint clerk with, 'Mr. Smith, over there, is one of our top twenty customers, so do your best.'"[1]

With approximately twenty-three thousand customers signed on to the loyalty program (and around 65 percent of all store transactions captured through card usage), Cornell's works hard to make sure its highest-value customers stay rewarded. Years of retail experience have taught the firm that it's often fruitless to try to get lower-spending households to increase their purchases. Instead, the better strategy is to encourage top spenders to spend more. "We want our top customers to know we appreciate them," says Fix. "That's why we send our top hundred customers a Christmas letter of thanks and include a message that a gift is awaiting them at the register." How's it working? "We had almost a 50 percent redemption rate on that letter," Fix told me. "When customers came to the register, it was one more opportunity for our staff to thank these vital customers for their business."

There's more. On customers' birthdays, Cornell's sends $10 gift certificates to the top 15 percent of customers. "The birthday gift certificate always provides some fun rapport building," reports Fix. "For example, if a customer comes to the register with a toilet repair kit, our staffer often jokes, 'Do you really want *that* for your birthday?' and shares a good laugh with the customer."

Cornell's perceptively understands a loyalty program's two-prong business-building capability: yes, it helps reward best customers with savings, but, as important, the program enables staffers to acknowledge those customers and nurture relationships with them face-to-face. In today's world of faceless commerce, Cornell's staffers' ability to develop this special rapport is a priceless, loyalty-building advantage in a compulsion-to-compare marketplace.

Cross-Selling

Cornell's understands that the more customers buy across the store's various product lines, the less likely it is that they'll shop elsewhere. Most customers today are time starved. One-stop shopping matters.

Cornell's loyalty program data greatly enhance the store's cross-sell effectiveness. For example, rather than send the annual paint promotion to customers who are top paint buyers, the offer is targeted to top customers in the housewares department. Likewise, Cornell's has a rental store and promotes rental offers to its True Rewards members who are top buyers of the hardware store's power tools.

New Prospecting

The loyalty program data also are allowing Cornell's to prospect more precisely. In years past, the store would simply do a blanket mailing to all households with in a two-mile radius of the store. No more. Now Cornell's can overlay its customer data onto Google Maps and know with certainty the geographic penetration of its customers. "The data showed us that we have solid penetration at a three-mile radius. That knowledge has given us the confidence to extend our reach and target noncustomers in those outlying areas. This was not even possible a few years ago," says Fix.

Advertising Expenditures Down, Sales Up

One of the most telling signs of the loyalty program's value to Cornell's is the reduction in the store's advertising spending. Since the program's launch in 2004, Cornell's has reduced its advertising costs by 25 percent while enjoying annual sales increases. Most year-over-year increases have hovered around 4 to 5 percent, but in 2007 the store celebrated an 11 percent increase in sales over the prior year.

Favorable signs of customer commitment can also be seen by comparing the store's top 10 percent accounts in 2006 and 2007. Among 2006 customers, 82 percent remained top customers in 2007; the average sale grew from $30.74 to $32.36; and the average number of store visits per year grew from thirty-six in 2006 to forty in 2007.

Community Service

When Cornell's decided to sponsor its first-ever, in-store blood drive, True Rewards members were the target. "We mailed out an announcement letter offering a $10 rewards certificate for anyone contributing," said Fix. The blood center was thrilled, having never seen that much collected on a first-time drive—thirty-eight pints. The announcement had gone to the top 30 percent of Cornell's lawn and garden customers. Fix quipped, "We figured they were the most outdoorsy of our customers and therefore would be more apt to give blood."

Execution Smarts

Have you heard the old saying, "The devil is in the details"? Know this: smart, hands-on oversight is crucial to getting great returns from loyalty programs. Consider these additional execution tips from John Fix III:

- **Get the staff on board.** Prior to launching the program and then after the launch, hold store meetings, training, and on-the-job coaching so that the entire staff is educated and excited about the program.

- **Make loyalty central to all your promotions.** If you offer special prices and deals to nonmember customers, then you dilute the value in the minds of customers (and staff).

- **Adjust your advertising mix as appropriate.** At the start of the program, you're likely to continue a good portion of your existing advertising (general market direct mail, newspaper, radio, and so on). As more customers join the program, shift advertising to loyalty members and reduce mass media.

- **Highlight the program all over the store.** If your program has tiered pricing (that is, sale prices only with the card), make sure you have items on special in every department for maximum visibility. It's especially important to put some fast-moving items near the checkout. As an example, in the spring and fall, Cornell's puts lawn and leaf bags near the checkouts and prices them at $1.99 with a card, $2.99 without, making it easy for cashiers to sign up customers at the point of purchase.

- **Reward your staff.** Cornell's provides cash incentives to cashiers who exceed the store average for percentage of sales transactions through the loyalty card. For example, the store average for one two-week period was 60 percent. Clerks whose customer purchase transactions on the card exceeded 60 percent got cash bonuses based on an incremental formula. Cornell's offers these bonuses biweekly.

Perhaps the firm's most distinguishing trait as a Tamer model is simply its openness to new, ever-evolving methods for staying close to customers. When a firm is family owned, with over eight decades of history, it's often easy to get stuck in a "if it ain't broke, don't fix it" mentality. Instead, Cornell's seizes new customer-building opportunities whenever it finds them. Says Fix, "Our store has been mailing mass-market sales fliers since the 1960s. And we've done Yellow Pages and radio and TV. It began to feel so 'cookie-cutter.'... But with this melding of technology, we can now do things that weren't possible five years ago. We can analyze and control our customer data. The possibilities of who we reach and how are endless. I find it really invigorating."

PETCO: Social Commerce

To win budget support inside your firm for new loyalty-building tools, you need detailed proof that these programs can lift sales and influence customer behaviors. Here's how one firm built a solid business case for its social commerce initiatives.

Social commerce. You know the term. It's commonly defined as the act of harnessing the Internet's so-called wisdom of many to help a shopper find and buy products and services. "Social" denotes customer-to-customer interactions, such as users' rating of products and services online for other shoppers to read. "Commerce" is to remind us of an oft-forgotten truth: "Nothing happens until somebody sells something."[2]

Social commerce is proving to be an important online strategy for firms seeking to thrive in a world where customers enjoy near-perfect product information delivered through lightning-quick search tools. Two simple but critical factors are driving more and more firms to incorporate social commerce tools on their corporate Web sites. First, by their very definition, social commerce tools can help brands ace their shoppers' worth-it tests. That's because customer ratings and reviews lend important credibility to a brand. Second, the direct effects of social commerce on customer behavior are measurable through ROI-driven metrics, such as customer conversion, order value, and the like, that enable marketing and sales teams to win their CFO's blessing for budget allocation.

PETCO is one savvy firm that saw the light early and is reaping the benefits accordingly. The leading retailer of premium pet food, supplies, and services, PETCO operates over 850 stores in forty-nine states. In 2005, when many other firms were just waking up to Web 2.0 social media opportunities, PETCO sensed how buyer reviews and ratings could have leverage in driving purchase decisions, and began incorporating these social commerce features on its Web site. Working with hosted social commerce provider Bazaarvoice and search software maker Endeca, PETCO began promoting ratings and reviews to its online customers, inviting them to post their opinions. In return, shoppers could view the reviews other customers had written for guidance on purchasing decisions.

To its credit, PETCO didn't let the fear of negative customer reviews undermine the idea of inviting customers to post ratings and reviews. The company's instincts that the good from user-generated content outweighs the bad are more than confirmed nowadays. For example, Jupiter research found that 60 percent of online shoppers provide feedback about shopping experiences, and they are more likely to give feedback about a positive experience than a negative one.[3] But what if the review is negative? Not to worry. Explains Don Zeidler, director of marketing of the storied vendor W. Atlee Burpee Co.: "when customers see a mix of different ratings they are more apt to trust the review process. . . . As long as the reviews are not entirely and overwhelmingly negative—just nit picks that people decide they can live with (they usually are)—these negative reviews help customers pass through purchase paralysis."[4]

PETCO closely tracked online shopper behaviors, and over time, the positive influence of ratings and reviews was strongly confirmed.[5] Consider these findings:

Products without reviews had 20.4 percent higher return rates than those with reviews.

Products with fifty or more reviews had a return rate half of those with fewer than five reviews.

Products in the "Top Rated Products" category had a 49 percent higher conversion rate compared to the same products without reviews within their respective site categories.

Within the "Top Rated Products" category, customers spent 63 percent more compared to all browsers who progressed beyond the home page.

"Sort by Rating" drove 41 percent higher sales per unique visit, earning it the rank of number-one default sorting technique on PETCO.com.

Not a firm to rest on its laurels, PETCO continued to look for new ways to enrich customers' ability to share ratings and reviews. Next up? Enable customers to submit photos with their online reviews. Did this additional functionality increase PETCO community engagement? You bet. The company found a 5.6 percent incremental increase in customer conversion on top of any increase seen by products with reviews. In addition, the photos helped drive higher user-generated ratings. Photo reviews were found to have a 10.4 percent higher average rating compared to reviews without photos.

As the provider of the social commerce infrastructure on PETCO's Web site, Bazaarvoice has a keen eye for how ratings and reviews pass a client's worth-it test. Observes Sam Decker, marketing VP of Bazaarvoice,

Any feature you put on your site has a net present value [NVP]. In other words, the feature has a value to the firm's P&L. This value is the sum of the feature's impact over some time period, say two to three years. Some site features may have an opportunity to drive immediate benefit, but the impact declines over time. With ratings and reviews, the value is in the content, and the impact of this content grows over time. Early on, user-generated content allows you to identify and engage your influencers. But later on, you can further leverage user-generated content through e-mail, natural search, advertising, catalogs, etc., to attract even more buyers. So the feature's NPV is high.

And where's PETCO headed next with its social commerce strategy? Increased navigation capability. The retailer is looking to launch search capability on customer review content to enable a customer to (1) search reviews for words or phrases of interest, (2) navigate products using customer rating attributes, and (3) navigate products rated highly by "people like me."

Getting Started with Social Commerce

Want to harness the power of social commerce for your firm? Sam Decker offers these implementation steps:

1. **Start with user tasks.** Look at your Web site through the eyes of your users. As they come in contact with your company through your site, what are their purchasing obstacles? What information are they looking for? Do they need questions answered? Do they need support? Do they need help deciding between products?

2. **Explore how users can help users.** Once you've pinpointed key user tasks, consider how social interactions within and outside your site can help accomplish them. For example, if site visitors need help deciding between products, you can bring in ratings and reviews, voting mechanisms, and polling.

3. **Facilitate interactions.** Your job as a marketer is now to facilitate these interactions. As for any functionality, this requires a

mix of technology, moderation, and analytics. Your choices are either to build from scratch and manage yourself or to work with a hosted provider of these capabilities.

4. Participate and listen. Users who participate want to know that their voices are heard. Demonstrate that you're listening—for example, by responding to reviews posted. Show users how their comments and data are helping your firm become more customer centric.

5. Leverage and amplify. This is the most important step: leverage your word-of-mouth content to a wider audience. Examples include putting user ratings and reviews in your advertisements.

6. Measure. Profit and loss is the language of senior management. The good news is that social commerce effectiveness is very measurable. Use before-after, control group (A-B split testing) metrics to evaluate the effect of social commerce on site performance, e-mail, and product return rates, to name a few.

Verizon Wireless: Marketing Partnership

Want to maximize value for your customers? The cyberworld is rich with examples of an important best practice to help you do it: **partnerships.** But to forge strong partnerships with like-minded firms requires an innovative vision, the ability to find the win-win, and a commitment to execution excellence.

Just ask Verizon Wireless. Verizon combined marketing forces with an existing banking partner to increase online bill pay, which for Verizon Wireless served not only as a customer convenience but also as a defense against customer search and switch.

For years, Verizon Wireless had used Wachovia Treasury Services for assistance with customer bill processing. So when Verizon Wireless set out in 2007 to aggressively reduce its per-payment customer costs, the Charlotte-based bank was sought out as a valued adviser.

The Market Opportunity

Integral to Verizon Wireless's cost-cutting solutions was the need to migrate more of its customers from paper bill payment to online bill pay. Moreover, the ideal was to convert Verizon Wireless customers into e-bill payers who receive and pay their bills online. Consumer research suggested that Verizon's timing was perfect. A 2007 Javelin study found that 52 percent of consumers prefer to pay bills at their bank's Web site, compared to only 10 percent who indicated no interest in viewing and paying bills online.[6] The benefits consumers cited? Flexibility and control, easy setup of automatic payment, the streamlined process, and protection against fraud and identity theft.

Remember Chapter One's discussion on Gen Y buyers and the importance of that demographic to almost any firm's future growth? Check this out: the five-year (2007–2011) growth rate of online bill pay among Gen Y customers is projected to be an astounding 157 percent, according to Forrester Research. (The next highest growth rate is significantly lower: Gen X, at 42 percent.) What's more, Gen Y, representing 26 percent of U.S. households, will make up 36 percent of e-bill payers by 2011. The bottom line: Gen Y consumers are ripe for conversion to online bill pay.

Campaign Partnership

This is where the story turns. As Verizon Wireless's discussions with Wachovia progressed, a shift in the client-banker relationship began. The two firms identified a unique, mutually advantageous opportunity to become joint marketing partners: Wachovia would promote Verizon Wireless e-bills to its Wachovia.com customers, and in the same period, Verizon would promote Wachovia's online bill-pay services to Verizon Wireless customers. The objectives of the partnership were straightforward: (1) increase Verizon Wireless e-bill adoption (both receive and pay bills online), (2) increase adoption of Wachovia bill pay (pay bills online), and (3) test and evaluate various marketing channels.

Marketing messages were delivered concurrently to customers of both companies over a ninety-day campaign period as follows:

Wachovia customers who currently paid their Verizon Wireless bill online but had not signed up for Verizon's e-bill program were sent cobranded e-mail from Wachovia.

Wachovia online banking customers were targeted with a Verizon Wireless ad link on the right-hand side of their account screen. The link's landing page was also cobranded.

The welcome e-newsletter sent to Verizon Wireless customers linked to a cobranded splash page. (A splash page is an interlude page that is shown temporarily before the intended target page, usually for the purpose of airing an important announcement.)

All Verizon Wireless customers who logged into their account page were presented with an ad linked to a cobranded splash page.

Verizon Wireless customers who accessed the bill payment pages were presented with a banner that linked to the cobranded splash page.

Campaign Results

Verizon Wireless e-bill enrollment growth climbed to an impressive 6.5 percent during the period that both firms were jointly conducting the campaign. The average daily request for Verizon Wireless e-bills was ninety-five during the campaign, as opposed to seventy-two in the pre-campaign period. What's more, over half the customers who signed up for Verizon Wireless e-bill during the campaign period also requested e-bill for another vendor. This metric is perhaps the biggest endorsement of the campaign's effectiveness at growing customer use of e-bill.

Partnership Lessons

Is a marketing partnership in your future? The frontliners on the Verizon Wireless–Wachovia initiative offered this advice:

- Seek out marketing partners that can bring mutual strength to the partnership. Wachovia and Verizon Wireless both had very strong online customer reach, which made the cross-marketing to each other's customers effective and efficient for both partners.

- Choose a marketing partner that you are truly comfortable with promoting to your customers. In a joint marketing partnership, there is no escaping that your brand's good name will be associated with your marketing partner's brand. Choose wisely.

- When you approach a prospective marketing partner, ask for a confidentiality agreement. After all, the concept for a marketing partnership is valuable intellectual property that warrants protection.

Graniterock: Self-Leadership

When all is said and done, employees determine whether (or not) a firm will grow loyal customers in a search-and-switch world. Want your employees delivering maximum value for customers? Evolve into self-leadership and practice it religiously. The following Tamer case offers key insights.

A spirit of employee independence has filled the asphalt plant, quarries, construction sites, and offices of Watsonville, California–based Graniterock since 2001. The company culture is centered around an uncommon, highly evolved management style called self-leadership. Explains president and CEO Bruce Woolpert, "Some businesses have an approach that basically teaches dependency of employees on management. But we take a different approach with our 850 team members. Experience has taught us that independent people are the only ones who can really make a profound, important difference. It's the idea that 'my involvement matters' that makes people truly happy and fulfilled."[7]

Nine core corporate objectives—including customer satisfaction, product quality, safety, community involvement, and responsibility—guide the company's performance goals and operating objectives. To achieve those goals and objectives, Graniterock expects its team members to be self-leaders—owning their work, setting improvement goals, working to improve results, and owning responsibility for their job functions. The role of managers? To serve as self-leadership coaches, helping team members evolve as independent, value-making people who self-lead in their job functions.

"We operate on an open-door policy without lines of authority," Woolpert says. "Graniterock people with ideas talk to whoever they feel can be helpful or may have an interest in that suggestion. There's no expectation that management either directs or authorizes such changes. Each person is responsible for whatever improvement he wants to make, without having to get approval."

Graniterock's self-leadership philosophy produces a constant stream of team member–driven change across all the firm's departments. Here are three examples of how it all feeds into the firm's search-and-switch-taming success.

Shortened delivery times. Graniterock delivers ready-mix concrete to construction sites. Once they arrive, drivers must back the trucks into the job sites. The backup lights on the delivery trucks were once no better than the lights on the average car, which meant very poor visibility at night. This required drivers to get out of the truck to see where they were, get back in the truck, drive another few feet, get out of the truck . . . you get the picture. It was a slow, tedious, and sometimes treacherous process.

In many conventionally managed companies where change flows only from the top down, this set of circumstances would go unnoticed or at best be cast off as a "just grin and bear it" reality for drivers. But not at Graniterock. Practicing self-leadership, one driver saw the opportunity for a better solution and pursued it. He sought the help of a company mechanic, and together they reviewed various back-up lights in parts catalogs, ordered sample sets, installed them, and then, over several weeks, tested their effectiveness. Once the employees determined which lights worked best, the new lights were installed on all Graniterock trucks, helping improve the firm's delivery times and safety.

Continual improvement in delivery time performance has a long history at Graniterock. Explains Woolpert, "In our business, delivery times are crucial. Our customers measure their productivity by yards of concrete placed per hour, so our delays cost them money. When we began measuring delivery times in 1988, we found that only 68 percent of our deliveries were made within a half hour of the scheduled times. Since then we've taken steps to improve each year, most through a lot of little details—like upgrading the truck's back-up lights. All these small changes can add up to improved performance. Today our standard is 96.5 percent made within fifteen minutes of the scheduled time."

Check coding. Graniterock's office services department processes four hundred thousand pieces of mail and receives twenty-seven thousand checks annually. Matching the right check to the right account requires sleuth-like investigative skills at Graniterock. That's because many of the checks arrive without a copy of the invoice the customer is trying to pay. Others are handwritten and drawn on personal bank accounts with very similar company names (think ABC Construction and ABL Construction). In many companies, all these factors might combine to create record-keeping mayhem.

But of the twenty-seven thousand checks processed by Graniterock in 2007, only *eight* were miscoded! That's thanks to self-leadership in the two-person office services department, where check coding is pursued with Sherlock Holmes–like insight and determination. The team members have learned to recognize dozens of clues on just the checks and envelopes customers mail in.

This work is crucial to keeping the firm's revenues flowing. And accurate check coding is a critical customer relationship task as well. A sure way to destroy client goodwill is to send Payment Due notices to clients who have already paid, so matching the right check to the right account is imperative. Self-leadership in the office services department helps keeps the cash and customer satisfaction flowing smoothly.

Perfect product quality. Yes, you read that right: perfect quality. In September 2007, Graniterock became the first contractor in California history to receive a perfect score from the state Department of Transportation for a road paving job. To get this score requires *perfect* product and construction quality. Graniterock's material and workmanship had to meet an almost impossible standard: a zero statistical probability that neither the material nor the workmanship would fall outside the standard deviation guidelines specified by the California DOT. The probability that a contractor performs at this level of excellence is very low—so low that the department's quality inspectors checked and rechecked Graniterock's data as well as their own figures to be sure they weren't making a mistake.

How did Graniterock achieve such a feat? Paving crews from Graniterock's construction division came together with the firm's asphalt plant personnel to form a single team. In the past, the asphalt crew would produce the material, load it on a truck, and say "Done." In their minds, their job ownership related to *making* the material. But when these same team members converted to self-leadership, they saw their jobs as customer satisfaction. They realized they were in partnership with the construction division and that until that roadway was complete and customer quality was assessed, no one's job was done.

Getting Started with Self-Leadership

How does a firm jump-start self-leadership among its employees? *Don't*, advises Woolpert, who believes that Graniterock's ability to evolve to self-leadership in 2001 was possible because of the earlier years the firm had spent practicing the art of job ownership. Using the formula "Job ownership = doing the work + improving the work," Graniterock challenged employees to look for ways to perform their jobs better in addition to simply doing the task at hand. Once employees were comfortable practicing job ownership, self-leadership was a natural step up.

What distinguishes self-leadership from job ownership is the manager coaching element, observes Woolpert. Coaching team members to be self-leaders is a crucial management responsibility, and Graniterock is a living laboratory on how to do it well. Consider these Graniterock management principles for coaching self-leadership:

- Encourage problem solving by others; don't solve problems for others.

- Ask more questions and give fewer answers.

- Foster learning from mistakes, not fear of consequences.

- Share information; don't hoard it.

- Encourage creativity, not conformity.

- Encourage teamwork, not destructive competition.

- Foster independence, not dependence.

- Measure your success by the success of the people you manage.

- Seek to make yourself "irrelevant."

- Develop committed self-leaders, not compliant followers.

- Establish organizational structures that support self-leadership, such as self-managing teams.

- Listen more and talk less.

For almost a decade, Graniterock has earned a spot on *Fortune's* 100 Best Companies to Work For list, consistently ranking in the top 25 percent. The secret to the firm's unmatched track record of staff loyalty (and the customer loyalty that follows) can be found in Graniterock's fervent belief that job independence is a powerful motivator. "'I need to own something' is in the American worker's DNA," says Woolpert. "Our job as managers is to create an environment that taps and channels that energy to manage and control one's own work," he observes.

Moving On

To earn customer loyalty in a world where buyers relentlessly compare their vendor options, a firm must consistently deliver superb customer value that buyers recognize. To that end, it's the firms whose innovation and improvement ideas flow up the organization from employees and not simply down through management that will prevail. That's because in those firms, *everyone* rather than simply *someone* is constantly thinking about ways to be better. After all, the wisdom of the many beats that of the few every time. For more help on identifying Tamers That Teach, visit **www.loyaltysolutions.com/TamersThatTeach.**

Next up, how to move on *now* with the Ten-Day Starter Plan for taming the search-and-switch customer.

Taming Takeaways

- Be on the lookout for Tamers That Teach. These firms can provide valuable survival lessons in these rough-and-tumble, search-and-switch times. What's more, they can offer you inspiration and hope when the going gets tough. Don't limit your search to just your industry. And search out different role models for different functions in your company—for example, a Tamer role model for your information technology department, another for HR strategies, and so forth.

- One real value of a customer loyalty program is the customer purchase data it generates. Yet many firms don't harvest the data for insight. Instead, they simply treat their loyalty program as a way to offer discounts to frequent shoppers. In a search-prone world, this is a big mistake.

- Social commerce strategies and practices can be very powerful in taming search-and-switch tendencies. Interactions between customers—and the content those interactions create—help your prospective buyers (online and off) make smart purchase decisions. ROI measures suggest that social commerce tools are worth a closer look for a wide range of firms.

- Marketing partnerships can provide fresh Tamer opportunities. Choose a marketing partner you feel truly comfortable about promoting to your customers. In a joint marketing partnership, there is no escaping that your brand's good name will be associated with your marketing partner's brand. Choose wisely.

- Exploring the possibilities of self-leadership is well worth your time. Although this highly evolved management style is uncommon, and requires intensive groundwork to succeed, when your employees operate as self-leaders—owning their work, setting improvement goals, working to improve results, and owning responsibility for their job functions—your customers stay true to the truly remarkable performance that is unleashed.

Part IV

Move On Now!

9

Follow the Ten-Day Taming Plan

Few things in life are certain, especially when it comes to customers. But there are some realities you can count on. With every new day, your customers will have

Increasing choices

Easier ways to search for them

More efficient ways to compare and scrutinize

More offers of switching assistance from lurking vendors

A cyberworld brimming with more and more people ready to converse

Sound daunting? Sure it is. But reading this book has put you ahead of the game in one critically important way. You have begun the discovery journey toward taming your customers' search-and-switch tendencies. Starting with the fundamental weapon of knowing how to ace your buyer's worth-it test, you now have hundreds of guidelines and examples to draw from to craft a loyalty-building strategy and, by doing so, thrive on the compulsion-to-compare planet.

Now's the time to take the tools in this book and start to apply them. My Ten-Day Taming Plan for taming the Search-and-Switch Customer can help get you on your way.

One last bit of advice: throughout your learning journey, stay realistic. Your success in taming your customers' search-and-switch tendencies will be uneven at times. No doubt, you will have starts and stops along the way. (This book is filled with stories of firms that have lived through those frustrations too.) But there is much to gain from starting now. The truth is, customers need the value you can deliver, and they will reward you for it. So jump in!

Ten-Day Taming Plan for Taming the Search-and-Switch Customer

Week One

As the old saying goes, "Every journey starts with the first step." Here are your first three:

1. **Mobilize a Taming Team.** Recruit a cross-functional team of employees with decision-making clout. Select a team leader. Team members should be working hands-on for all remaining tasks outlined below. Assign Chapter Three, "Ace Your Buyer's Worth-It Test," as pre-meeting reading.

2. **Address this question: What customer relationships are worth taming?** For example, use account revenue, profit contribution, lifetime value, or some combination of measures to rank your accounts into three tiers (Tier One, Tier Two, Tier Three). If your firm has already conducted this account analysis, you're ahead of the game.

3. **Select accounts for a test program.** Choose a few accounts that are both high value and particularly vulnerable to competitive poaching. Develop "snapshots" of each account, keeping a keen eye on three categories of information:

   a. This is how we make money on this account (for example, product lines bought, product lines most profitable, untapped revenue potential, and so on).

b. These are the account stakeholders.

c. Here's what we know about each stakeholder's perceptions, likes, dislikes, and general outlooks about our brand.

Week Two

For each test program account, work through the following seven steps. (Use the snapshot information prepared in Week One for insight.)

1. Identify each stakeholder's key worth-it benefit(s).

2. Name each stakeholder's next best alternative. How does your brand stack up? What's your biggest vulnerability versus this competitor, and what's the plan for fixing it?

3. Expand each stakeholder's worth-it benefits list.

4. Brainstorm ways for stakeholders to experience the benefits identified in steps 1 and 3. Key question to ponder: What benefit(s) are you currently providing to these stakeholders that you aren't getting full credit for?

5. Devise a worth-it communication plan for each stakeholder.

6. Create a measurement plan. You need to decide how success will be measured: Higher sales? Improved account penetration? Higher product ratings? Improved margins? More corporate access? More referrals?

7. Devise an action plan: *Who* on the Taming Team is responsible for *what*? By *when*?

For more information on the Ten-Day Taming Plan and how to put it to work for your brand, visit **www.loyaltysolutions.com/ TenDayTamingPlan.**

Here's recap of my other Taming Too if you want more help:

- To ace your customer's Worth-It Test, visit **www .loyaltysolutions.com/WorthItTest**

- To leverage word-of-mouth, visit **www.loyaltysolutions. com/NineSpaceRule**

- To give your brand a compelling difference, visit **www .loyaltysolutions.com/BeingDifferent**

- To build customer trust, visit **www.loyaltysolutions .com/CustomerTrustPlan**

- To grow passionate-to-serve employees, visit **www. loyaltysolutions.com/EmployeePlan**

- To find role models that tame customer switching tendencies, visit **www.loyaltysolutions.com/TamersThatTeach**

It's a true honor and privilege to be in your world, thinking alongside you about your brand. I invite you to continue this learning journey with me at **www.loyaltysolutions.com.** No doubt, the ever-changing marketplace will give us much more to ponder together!

Notes

Chapter One

1. Clemons, E. K., Gao, G., and Hitt, L. M. "Consumer Informedness and Diverse Consumer Purchasing Behaviors," Sept. 8, 2006. http://digital .mit.edu/wise2006/papers/5A-2_ConsumerInformednessV2-2.pdf.

2. O'Reilly, B. "Profits from Polyester." *Fortune Small Business,* July 19, 2007. http://money.cnn.com/magazines/fsb/fsb_archive/2007/06/01/1 00051008/index.htm.

3. Biederman, I., and Vessel, E. "Perceptual Pleasures and the Brain." *American Scientist,* May-June 2006. www.condition.org/as65-6.htm.

4. Wailgum, T. "Your Customer Service Stinks." *Chief Information Officer,* Jan. 7, 2008. www.cio.com/article/print/169800.

5. Garlick, R., and Langley, K. "Reaching Gen Y on Both Sides of the Cash Register." *Retailing Issues Letter,* 2007, 18(2), 1–6.

6. Gallage, O. "I Thee Web." *Austin American Statesman,* Aug. 12, 2007, pp. J1, J9.

7. Gallage, 2007.

8. "International Shopping Spree Beckons Online." *Austin American Statesman,* Jan. 10, 2008, p. E1, E6.

9. "Cash Registers Are Ringing Online." *Business Week,* Mar. 5, 2007, p. 24.

10. Duff, M. "A Private Label Success Story." *DSN Retailing Today,* Dec. 19, 2005. http://findarticles.com/p/articles/mi.

11. "Demographics of Internet Users," July 22, 2008. www.pewinternet .org/trends/User_Demo_7.22.08.htm.

12. Rainie, L. *How the Internet Is Changing Consumer Behavior and Expectations.* Speech to a symposium of the Society of Consumer Affairs Professionals in Business, Washington, D.C., May 9, 2006. www.pewinternet.org/PPF/r/64/presentation_display.asp.

13. "Daily Internet Activities," July 22, 2008. www.pewinternet.org/ trends/Daily_Internet_Activities_7.22.08.htm.

14. "Online Ageism—Content and Advertising Miss an Important Target," Mar. 2008. www.burstmedia.com/research/current.asp.

15. Phillips, L. "B2B Marketing Online: Business Meets Social Media." *eMarketer,* 2008. www.emarketer.com/Reports/All/Emarketer-2000451 .aspx?src=report.

16. Phillips, 2008.

17. Phillips, 2008.

18. "Business to Business Survey." *Enquiro,* 2007. www.enquiroresearch .com.

19. "2008 B2B Search Marketing Strategy Guide: Advice from the Pros." Business.com, 2008.

20. "2008 B2B Search Marketing Strategy Guide," 2008.

21. "Word of Mouth the Most Powerful Selling Tool: Nielsen Global Survey." Nielsen press release, Oct. 1, 2007. www.nielsen.com/media/ 2007/pr.

22. Rainie, 2006.

23. Garlick and Langley, 2007.

24. "New Deloitte Study Shows Inflection Point for Consumer Products Industry: Companies Must Learn to Compete in a More Transparent Age." Deloitte press release, Oct. 1, 2007. www.deloitte.com/dtt/press_ release/0,1014,sid%253D2283%2526cid%253D173666,00.html.

25. Appleby, J. "WellPoint Doctors to Get Zagat Ratings." *USA Today,* Oct. 21, 2007. www.usatoday.com/money/industries/health/2007-10- 21-wellpoint-zagat_N.htm.

26. Miller, C. "What Would Hippocrates Do?" *Forbes*, Aug. 13, 2007, pp. 47, 49.

27. Miller, 2007.

28. Rainie, L. "Information Searches That Solve Problems," Dec. 30, 2007. www.pewinternet.org/PPF/c/1/topics.asp.

29. Kronholz, J., and Holmes, E. "Two Debates May Be Clinton's Last, Best Hope." *Wall Street Journal*, Feb. 21, 2008, p. A10.

Chapter Two

1. Callaghan, F. "What Readers Say: Loyal No More." *Forbes*, Oct. 29, 2007. www.Forbes.com/business/forbes/20071029/018.html.

2. All cites of Christina Nordman's ideas and research are from her doctoral dissertation, *Understanding Customer Loyalty and Disloyalty: The Effect of Loyalty-Supporting and -Repressing Factors*, Swedish School of Economics, Helsinki, Finland, 2004.

3. "Facebook Boom Could Change Look of Web, Social Sites." *Austin American Statesman*, Jan. 10, 2008, pp. D1–D2.

4. Locke, L. "The Future of Facebook." *Time*, July 17, 2007. www.time.com/time/business/article/0,8599,1644040,00.html.

5. Foust, D. "How Technology Delivers for UPS." *Business Week*, Mar. 5, 2007, p. 60.

6. "Not Exactly a Niche Market." *Insight* [publication of Hartford Life Insurance Company], Nov. 13, 2007.

7. McGregor, J. "Customer Service Champs." *Business Week*, Mar. 5, 2007, pp. 52–64.

8. Applebaum, M. "One Tough Customer." *Brandweek*, Mar. 19, 2007. www.brandweek.com/bw/esearch/article_display.jsp?vnu_content_id=1003559539.

9. McGregor, 2007, p. 58.

10. McGregor, 2007, p. 59.

11. McConnell, B., and Huba, J. *Citizen Marketers*. Chicago: Kaplan, 2007.

12. Roos, I., and Gustafsson, A. "Understanding Frequent Switching Patterns." *Journal of Service Research*, 2007, *10*(1), 93–108.

13. Greco, S. "The Merger That Ate My Customer," *Inc*. Oct. 15, 1998. www.inc.com/magazine/19981015/1109.

14. "Crisis Deepens for Northern Rock." *International Herald Tribune*, Sept. 17, 2007. www.iht.com/articles/2007/09/17/asia/17northern.php.

15. Pichnarcik, A. "It's Automated and Controlled," Oct. 2005. www.quirks.com.

16. McGregor, 2007, pp. 52, 53.

17. McGregor, 2007, p. 54.

Chapter Three

1. *2008 Miller Heiman Sales Best Practices Study Executive Summary*, http://store.millerheiman.com/kc/abstract.aspx?itemid=00000000000005B2.

2. Lauterborn, R. "The Behavioral Timeline," 1998. [Provided for marketing practicum courses, winter 2005, Penn State College of Business, University of North Carolina, Chapel Hill.]

3. Fripp, P. "Customer Retention and Loyalty: Find Out What Your Customers Want Before Your Competitors Do." www.Fripp.com/art.findout.html (accessed Oct. 2008). Fripp credits David Garfinkel, author of *The Money-Making Copywriting Course*, as the originator of the five questions listed in the chapter.

4. Fripp, 2008.

5. All quotes and data related to the Magnatag "Case in Point" box are from G. Bounds, "Taking the 'Common' out of Commodity." *Wall Street Journal*, June 26, 2007, pp. B1, B5.

6. Oliva, R. "Business-to-Business Marketing Overview." http://marketingpower.com/content (accessed Oct. 16, 2007).

7. Narayandas, D. "Building Loyalty in Business Markets." *Harvard Business Review*, Sept. 2005, pp. 131–139.

8. Copeland, M. "Start Last, Finish First." *Business 2.0*, Feb. 2, 2006. http://money.cnn.com/magazines/business2/business2_archives/2006.

9. Trottman, M. "Southwest's New Flight Plan: Win More Business Travelers." *Wall Street Journal*, Nov. 27, 2007, pp. B1–B2.

10. Brat, I. "How a Firm Got Smart to Fight Grime, Rivals." *Wall Street Journal*, Jan. 28, 2008, pp. B1, B3.

11. Bala, V., and Green, J. "Charge What Your Products Are Worth." *Harvard Business Review*, Sept. 2007, p. 22.

12. "Perspective" [quarterly publication produced by Research International Greater China], No. 23, 2007, p. 5. www.research-int.com.

13. All quotes related to the discussion of Elliott's Hardware are from M. Halkias, "Elliott's Hardware Thrives on Customer Service." *Dallas Morning News*, Sept. 2, 2007. www.dallasnews.com.

14. Hudson, K. "Turning Shopping Trips into Treasure Hunts." *Wall Street Journal*, Aug. 27, 2007, pp. B1, B3.

Chapter Four

1. All quotations of Dr. Gerald Zaltman are from A. C. Micu and J. T. Plummer, "On the Road to a New Effectiveness Model: Measuring Emotional Responses to Television Advertising." Report jointly sponsored by the American Association of Advertising Agencies and the AFT Task Force. Mar. 2007, p. 5.

2. Randall Ringer and Michael Thibodeau, telephone interview with the author, December 14, 2007.

3. "Twenty Deluxe Charmin Restrooms Open in Times Square in Time for Holiday Season & New York City's Thanksgiving Day Parade." Proctor & Gamble press release, Nov. 20, 2007.

4. "Charmin's Lesson on Being Photogenic," Dec. 14, 2007. http://brainsonfire.com/blog/2007/12/14/charmins-lesson-on-being-photogenic.

5. Griffin, J. "Leverage the Six Stages of Customer Loyalty: Attract Suspects and Convert Prospects." Customer Think, Sept. 4, 2007. www.customerthink.com/print/2141.

6. "Ten Questions: Richard Branson Will Now Take Your Questions." *Time*, Dec. 31, 2007, p. 12.

7. Hawkins, M. "Ratings and Reviews Increase Time Consumers Spend on Site." www.bazaarvoice.com/cs_rr_timeOnSite.html (accessed Sept. 12, 2008).

8. "Opinion Poll Shows 8 out of 10 US Shoppers Put More Trust in Brands That Offer Customer Reviews." Bazaarvoice press release, July 23, 2007. www.bazaarvoice.com/press072307.html.

9. "Online Consumer-Generated Reviews Have Significant Impact on Offline Purchase Behavior." comScore press release, Nov. 29, 2007. www.comscore.com/press/release.asp?press=1928.

10. Hawkins, M. "Customer Favorite Categories Drive Sales," Aug. 20, 2007. www.bazaarvoice.com/cs_rr_sort_customerFavorites.html.

11. Rockwell, L. "Making It to the Top of the List." *Austin American Statesman*, Feb. 17, 2008, pp. J1, J6.

12. Swensrud, K. "Marketing in the Google Era." Salesforce.com webinar, posted Feb. 28, 2007. www.bloglines.com/public/kswensrud.

13. "Search Engine User Behavior Study." *iProspect*, Apr. 2006, p. 4.

14. "All Things Aquarium." JumpFly case study, July 5, 2007. www.jumpfly.com/JumpFly_Case_Studies.pdf.

15. Shaw, C. "Engage Your Customers Emotionally to Create Advocates." Customer Think, Sept. 17, 2007. www.customerthink.com/print/2223.

16. Abboud, L. "Global Shippers Play Catch-up in Information Age." *Wall Street Journal*, Sept. 4, 2007, p. B2.

17. Zetlin, M. "Helping Customers Help Each Other Online," Oct. 2007. http://technology.inc.com/internet/articles/200710/community.html.

18. Zetlin, 2007.

19. Young, G. [Blog post]. www.customerthink.com, Jan. 7, 2008.

20. Johnson, C. Y. "Hurry Up, the Customer Has a Complaint." *Boston Globe*, July 7, 2008. www.boston.com/business/technology/articles/2008/07/07.

21. Gomes, L. "More Firms Create Own Social Networks." *Wall Street Journal*, Feb. 19, 2008, p. B3.

22. Stauss, B., Schmidt, M., and Achoeler, A. "Customer Frustration in Loyalty Programs." *International Journal of Service Industry Management*, 2005, 16(3), 229–252.

23. Peppers, D., and Rogers, M. "Tying Trust to Customer Value." *CRM News*, Feb. 9, 2005. http://searchcrm.techtarget.com/news/article.

24. Rubel, S. "Open Letter: A Lesson Learned Twittering." Apr. 17, 2007. www.micropersuasion.com/2007/04/open_letter_les.html.

25. Gogoi, P. "Wal-Mart's Jim and Laura: The Real Story." *Business Week*, Oct.9,2006.www.businessweek.com/bwdaily/dnflash/content/oct2006/db20061009_579137.htm.

26. Vogelstein, F. "Operation Channel 9." *Wired*, Mar. 2007. www.wired.com/wired/archive/15.04/wired40_microsoft.

27. Jarvis, J. "Poor Dell." *Buzz Machine Archive*, June 16, 2007. www.buzzmachine.com/2007/06/16/poor-dell.

28. Rockwell, 2008.

Chapter Five

1. Clemons, E. K. "Opening Statement: Resonance Marketing in the Age of the Truly Informed Consumer," Apr. 2007. http://cutter.com/meet-our-experts/clemonse.html.

2. Egan, J., and Rafferty, G. "Stuck in the Middle with You." In *Stealers Wheel*, A&M Records, 1972.

3. Peppers, D. *One-to-One Marketing*. Keynote address presented at the Inc. Customer Service Conference, New Orleans, Apr. l, 2000.

4. Clemons, 2007.

5. "How Companies Approach Innovation: A McKinsey Global Survey." *McKinsey Quarterly*, Oct. 2007. www.mcKinseyquarterly.com/article_print.aspx?L2=21&L3=35&ar=2069.

6. "Voices of Innovation: Steve Jobs." *Business Week*, Oct. 11, 2004. www.businessweek.com/print/magazine/content/04_41/b3903408.htm?chan=gl.

7. "Bang & Olufsen Research & Development," Sept. 7, 2007. www.beoworld.org/article_view.asp?id=28.

8. "Prestigious Technical Achievement Award Bestowed on Bang & Olufsen." Bang & Olufsen press release, Feb. 2, 2002. www.beoworld.org/article_view.asp?id=32.

9. Clemons, E. K., and Spitler, R. "The New Language of Consumer Behavior." *Financial Times*, Oct. 7, 2004, pp. 4–5.

10. Clemons and Spitler, 2004.

11. Borzo, J. "Nurses on Demand: ShiftWise Used the Nationwide Shortage of Skilled Caregivers to Create a Fast-Growing Business." *Fortune Small Business*, June 2007, pp. 88–89.

12. Kirby, J., and Stewart, T. A. "The Institutional Yes: How Amazon's CEO Leads Strategic Change in a Culture Obsessed with Today's Customer." *Harvard Business Review*, Oct. 2007. www.hbsp.harvard .edu/hbsp/hbr/articles/article.jsp?ml_action=get-article&articleID=R 0710C&ml_page=1&ml_subscriber=true.

13. Sloan, R. "Using the Power of PR: Sara Blakely & Spanx." StartUp Nation. www.startupnation.com/series/92/9035/power-pr-spanx.htm (accessed Sept. 12, 2008).

14. Covel, S. "A Dated Industry Gets a Modern Makeover." *Wall Street Journal*, Aug. 7, 2008, p. B9.

15. Perman, S. "How Failure Molded Spanx's Founder." *Business Week*, Nov. 21, 2007. www.businessweek.com/smallbiz/content/nov2007/ sb20071121_049670.htm.

16. Clemons, E. K., Spitler, R., and Barnett, S. "Finding the New Market Sweet Spots," Oct. 11, 2005, p. 9. http://opim.wharton.upenn.edu/ ~clemons/files/Find_New_Market.pdf.

17. Powers, D. "Underwater Music: Two Brothers Turned a Swimming Problem—and a Cheeky Way to Solve It—into a $3 Million Product Line." *Fortune Small Business*, June 2007, pp. 87–88.

18. Lalo Castillo, interview with the author, spring 2007.

19. Slywotzky, A. J. *Value Migration*. Boston: Harvard Business School Press, 1996, p. 4.

20. Worthen, B. "The IT Factor: Tech Staff's Bigger Role." *Wall Street Journal*, Dec. 4, 2007, p. B4.

21. Worthen, 2007.

22. Lukovitz, K. "Customer Loyalty Engagement Index Underscores Commoditization." *Marketing Daily*, Feb. 20, 2008. www.brandkeys .com/news/press/2.20.09.MarketingDaily.CLEI.pdf.

23. Adamy, J. "Starbucks Chairman Says Trouble May Be Brewing." *Wall Street Journal*, Feb. 24–25, 2007, pp. A4, A12.

24. Bruce Woolpert, telephone interview with the author, Mar. 2008.

25. Shein, E. "The Ultimate Test Drive: Why Companies Are Turning to Customers for Help with Design." *Chief Financial Officer*, Aug. 2007, pp. 54–61.

26. Mayer, M. *Learning from Mistakes*. Speech delivered to Stanford University's Entrepreneurship Corner, May 17, 2006. http://ecorner .stanford.edu/authorMaterialInfo.html?mid=1528.

27. Vranica, S. "Ad Houses Will Need to Be More Nimble." *Wall Street Journal*, Jan. 2, 2008, p. B3.

28. Fripp, P. "Customer Retention and Loyalty: Find Out What Your Customers Want Before Your Competitors Do." www.Fripp.com/art .findout.html (accessed Mar. 2008).

29. D'Aveni, R. A. "Mapping Your Competitive Position." *Harvard Business Review*, Nov. 2007, pp. 110–120.

30. Duncan, C., and others. "Raising Your Market IQ." *Wall Street Journal*, Dec. 1–2, p. R4.

31. Kim, W., and Mauborgue, R. "Value Innovation: The Strategic Logic of High Growth." *Harvard Business Review*, July-Aug. 2004, pp. 172–180.

32. Peng, T. "Funeral Homes Fight Profit Squeeze." *Wall Street Journal*, Oct. 15, 2007, p. A9.

33. Peng, 2007.

34. Ulwick, A. "Turn Customer Input into Innovation." *Harvard Business Review*, Jan. 2002, pp. 5–11.

35. Applebaum, M. "One Tough Customer." *Brandweek*, Mar. 19, 2007. www.brandweek.com/bw/esearch/article_display.jsp?vnu_content_ id=1003559539.

36. Morrison, S. "So Many, Many Words." *Wall Street Journal*, Jan. 28, 2008, p. R6.

37. Will She or Won't She?" *Economist*, Aug. 11, 2007, pp. 61–63.

38. All quotes related to the discussion of Nike are from Li Yuan, "To Sharpen Nike's Edge, CEO Taps Influencers." *Wall Street Journal*, Oct. 24, 2007, pp. A1, A18.

Chapter Six

1. Jones, R. "For the Company, It's as Good as Having a Direct Line into Your Wallet." http://www.guardian.co.uk/money/2008/mar/15/insurance.homeinsurance/print. *Guardian*, Mar. 15, 2008.

2. "Customer Affinity: The New Measure of Marketing." Research study published by the Chief Marketing Officers Council, Dec. 2007. Available for download at www.cmocouncil.org.

3. Mendonoca, L., and Miller, M. "Exploring Business's Social Contract: An Interview with Daniel Yankelovich." *McKinsey Quarterly*, May 2007, pp. 65–73.

4. Weckenmann, J. "CEO Efforts Key to Consumer Trust." *PR Week*, Jan. 14, 2008. www.prweekus.com/CEO-effects-key-to-consumer-trust/article/104033.

5. Nordman, C. *Understanding Customer Loyalty and Disloyalty: The Effect of Loyalty-Supporting and -Repressing Factors*. Doctoral dissertation, Swedish School of Economics, Helsinki, Finland, 2004, p. 43.

6. Lagace, M. "Your Customers: Use Them or Lose Them." *Harvard Working Knowledge*, July 19, 2004. http://hbswk.hbs.edu/tools.

7. Delaney, K. "Searching for Clients from Above." *Wall Street Journal*, July 31, 2007, pp. B1–B2.

8. "Pharma-Health Industry Practice." Nielsen BuzzMetrics. http://nielsenbuzzmetrics.com/pharma (accessed Sept. 13, 2008).

9. All quotations of Dennis Upah in the discussion of HealthCentral are from a telephone interview with the author, Mar. 2008.

10. A Dec. 2007 survey by iCrossing and Greenfield Online found that 72 percent of respondents use social media sites "all or some of the time" to educate themselves about specific medical conditions.

11. Kee, T. "Health Advertisers Should Think Social When It Comes to Online Media." *MediaPost*, Jan. 15, 2008. www.thehealthcentralnetwork.com/news.

12. Bannan, K. "Key Touch Point Metrics Trigger Custom E-Mails." *BtoB's E-Mail Marketing Insight Guide*, 2007, 92(12), 22.

13. Bannan, 2007.

14. Sloan, P. "Live Chat: Your New Online Salesperson." *Business 2.0,* Oct. 4, 2007. http://money.cnn.com/2007/10/03/technology/live_chat.

15. "Get Ready for Your Close-up." *Inc.,* Feb. 2008, p. 88.

16. "Readers and Owners Talk About Branding." *Wall Street Journal,* July 16, 2007, p. B3.

17. Hymowitz, C. "CEOs Are Spending More Quality Time with Their Customers." *Wall Street Journal,* May 14, 2007, p. B2.

18. Hymowitz, 2007.

19. "Opinion Poll Shows 8 out of 10 US Shoppers Put More Trust in Brands That Offer Customer Reviews." Bazaarvoice press release, July 23, 2007. www.bazaarvoice.com/press072307.html.

20. Resnick, R., Zeckhauser, R., Swanson, J., and Lockwood, K. "The Value of Reputation on eBay: A Controlled Experiment." *Experimental Economics,* 2006, 9(2), 79–101.

21. Mangalindan, M. "eBay Makes a Bid to Lure Lapsed Buyers." *Wall Street Journal,* Oct. 12, 2007, p. B2.

22. Mangalindan, 2007.

23. McElhaw, M. "You Who? Trust in Web 2.0." Webcredible, June 2007. www.webcredible.co.uk/user-firenldy-resources/web-credibility/web20-trust.shtml.

24. "The Good Consumer." *Economist,* Jan. 18, 2008, p. 16.

25. "The Good Consumer," 2008.

26. Buckingham, M., and Coffman, C. *First, Break All the Rules.* New York: Simon & Schuster, 1999.

27. "Chief Humanizing Officer." *Economist,* Feb. 10, 2005. www.economist.com/displaystory.cfm?story_id=3644293.

28. All quotes and information in the remaining discussion of Lenn Pryor and Channel 9 are from Fred Vogelstein, "Operation Channel 9," *Wired,* Mar. 2007. www.wired.com/wired/archive/15.04/wired40_microsoft.

29. Kelly Cook, director of customer relationship management, Continental Airlines, telephone interview with the author, spring 2006.

30. Nolan, H. "A Matter of Trust." *PR Week*, Sept. 3, 2007. www.prweekus.com/A-matter-of-trust/article/57641.

31. Yardley, W. "When Wildfires Threaten, Wealthy Get Extra Shield." *New York Times*, Aug. 28, 2007. http:topics.nytimes.com.

32. Weinberg, A. "Focusing on the Customer: An Interview with the Head of Merrill Lynch's Operations and IT. *McKinsey Quarterly* [premium content], June 2007. www.mckinseyquarterly.com/article_print.aspx?L2=13&L3=13&ar=2021.

33. Jacqueline Rosse, account management, Siebel Systems, interview with the author, Oct. 2005. (Coloplast is a Siebel client; Rosse is assigned to the Coloplast account.)

34. Bell quoted in Cardis, P. "Homebuilder Customer Loyalty Begins with Trust." *Professional Builder*, Oct. 1, 2007. www.housingzone.com.

35. "Do Customer Loyalty Programs Help Retailers?" *Forbes*, Apr. 11, 2007. www.Forbes.com/2007/04/10amr-corp-starbucks-ent-sales-cx_kw_0410whartonloyal.

36. "Do Customer Loyalty Programs Help Retailers?" 2007.

37. "Influence: Exploring Perspective in Private Customer Communities." Communispace white paper, 2007. www.communispace.com/research/abstract/?Type=Social%20Networking%20Landscape&Id=18.

38. Brennan, R. "Here Comes the Fansumer." *Digital Ministry*, Dec. 12, 2007. www.digitalministry.com.

39. Ahuja, V. "Building Loyalty the Southwest Way: Let Your Customers Drive the Discussion." Customer Think, Jan. 28, 2008. www.customerthink.com/print/2939.

Chapter Seven

1. The photograph was posted by Ben McConnell at www.churchofthecustomer.com/blog/2006/02/a_different_typ.html, on Feb. 9, 2006. McConnell linked to the photo's original posting at www/beyondrobson.com.

2. Gaudin, S. "Ex-UBS Systems Admin Sentenced to 97 Months in Jail." *Information Week*, Dec. 13, 2006. www.informationweek.com/shared/printableArticleSre.jhtml?articleID=196603888.

3. Mayer, M. *Learning from Mistakes*. Speech delivered to Stanford University's Entrepreneurship Corner, May 17, 2006. http://ecorner .stanford.edu/authorMaterialInfo.html?mid=1528.

4. "The Battle for Brainpower." *Economist*, Oct. 7–13, 2006, pp. 3–24.

5. "The Battle for Brainpower," 2006.

6. "One Tough Customer." *Brandweek*, Mar. 19, 2007. www.brandweek .com/bw/esearch/article_display.jsp?vnu_content_id=1003559539.

7. "Innovating the Customer Experience." Knowledge@W.P. Carey, Feb.13,2008.http://knowledge.wpcarey.asu.edu/article.cfm?articleid= 1557.

8. "Master of the Universe." *Economist*, Oct. 7–13, 2006, pp. 19–20.

9. Covel, S. "Startup Lures Talent with Creative Pitch." *Wall Street Journal*, June 4, 2007, p. B4.

10. Covel, 2007.

11. Needleman, S. "Need a New Situation? Check the Internet." *Wall Street Journal*, Feb. 12, 2008, p. B6.

12. "Aronson & Company Gives Away $2,500 Professional Makeover." Aronson press release, Aug. 29, 2007. www.aronsoncompany.com/ NewsEvents/pr_detail.asp?PR_ID=207.

13. Stephen White, director of marketing and sales, Aronson & Company, telephone interview with the author, Feb. 2008.

14. Hira, N. "You Raised Them, Now Manage Them." *Fortune*, May 28, 2007, pp. 38–46.

15. "The Battle for Brainpower," 2006.

16. "The Batter for Brainpower," 2006.

17. Hira, 2007.

18. Hira, 2007.

19. "The Battle for Brainpower," 2006.

20. "The Battle for Brainpower," 2006.

21. Needleman, S. "Demand Rises for Talent-Management Software." *Wall Street Journal*, Jan. 15, 2008, p. B8.

22. Greene, M. V. "Education, Recognition Keep Container Store Employees Engaged and Fulfilled." *Stores*, Nov. 2007. www.stores .org/Current_Issue/2007/11/Edit12.asp.

23. "Glazed Over in a Good Way." *Chief Financial Officer*, July 22, 2007, p. 80.

24. "The Battle for Brainpower," 2006.

25. Hira, 2007.

26. Coffey, B. "The Leadership Quotient." *Executive Travel*, May-June 2007, pp. 43–48.

27. Coffey, 2007.

28. "Readers, Experts Talk About Employee Retention." *Wall Street Journal*, Dec. 3, 2007, p. B7.

29. "Lifestyle Makeover: Alex Brennan-Martin." *Executive Travel*, Mar.-Apr. 2007, p. 44.

30. "Employing Excellence." *Chief Executive*, Jan.-Feb. 2008, p. 44.

31. "Employing Excellence," 2008.

32. Leibs, S. "Measuring Up." *Chief Financial Officer*, June 2007, pp. 63–66.

33. "Involved Workforce Highly Correlated with Better Business Results." *B2B*, July 16, 2007, p. 14.

34. White, E. "How Surveying Workers Can Pay Off." *Wall Street Journal*, June 18, 2007, p. B3.

35. Hofman, M. "The Idea That Saved My Company." *Inc.*, Oct. 2007, pp. 43–44.

36. "Getting Customer Service Back on Track." *Wall Street Journal*, Dec. 1–2, 2007, p. R2.

37. Gratton, L., and Erickson, T. "Ways to Build Collaborative Teams." *Harvard Business Review*, Nov. 2007, pp. 101–108.

38. Dvorak, P. "Hotelier Finds Happiness Keeps Staff Checked In." *Wall Street Journal*, Dec. 17, 2007, p. B3.

39. Pellet, J. "CEO Chronicles." *Chief Executive*, Jan.-Feb. 2008, p. 8.

40. Mr. Hallman's quote was published in the *New York Times* on January 14, 2007; Charles H. Green posted it on his book blog, Trust Matters, following his blog entry "Faking Sincerity: The Case of Loyalty," Jan. 12, 2007. http://trustedadvisor.com/blog/76/Faking-Sincerity--The-Case-of-Loyalty.

41. All quotes and data related to the discussion of Deloitte & Touche are from Eilene Zimmerman, "The Boom in Boomerangs." *Workforce Management Online*, Jan. 2006. www.workforce.com/section/06/feature/24/25/79/index_printer.html.

Chapter Eight

1. All quotes and data related to the discussion of Cornell's True Value Hardware are from an interview the author conducted with John Fix III, Feb. 2008.

2. Motley, A. "Bob Moore's Great Quotes from Great Leaders." http://toptalentcoach.com/Great%20Quotes.htm#S.

3. "Jupiter: Consumer-Created Content Altering Online Business." Marketing Vox archives, Aug. 2006. www.marketingvox.com/Jupiter_consumercreated_content_altering_online_business.

4. Decker, S. "Negative Reviews Do Not Hurt a Product." Bazaarblog, Aug. 1, 2006. www.bazaarblog.com/2006/08/01/negative-reviews-do-not-hurt-a-product (accessed Mar. 31, 2008).

5. The data cited in the discussion of PETCO are from three Bazaarvoice case studies written by Matt Hawkins: "Reviews Reduce Product Returns 20%," www.bazaarvoice.com/cs_rr_returns_petco.html; "Social Navigation Drives 49% Increase in Sales at PETCO.com," www.bazaarvoice.com/cs_rr_sort_Petco.html; and "Photo Reviews Drive Conversion, Enhance Customer Experience," www.bazaarvoice.com/cs_rr_photoReviews_petco.html." (Web sites accessed Oct. 2008.) Other information is from an interview the author conducted with Sam Decker, chief marketing officer of Bazaarvoice, Mar. 2008.

6. All quotes and company data related to the discussion of the Verizon Wireless–Wachovia partnership are from telephone interviews the

author conducted with Mike Rossi, senior VP of Wachovia Treasury Services, Mar. 2007, and Tammy Buck, Wachovia's VP for online services marketing, Mar. 2008; and from *Maximizing Opportunities— Electronic Payments and Billing,* a presentation by Tammy Buck and Howard Forman of Wachovia to industry colleagues, Oct. 23, 2007.

7. All quotes and data related to the discussion of Graniterock are from an interview the author conducted with Bruce Woolpert, CEO of Graniterock, Mar. 2008.

Acknowledgments

It truly takes a village to write a book, and I have been blessed with many contributors. A big thank-you is owed to Bernadette Walter, "saleswoman extraordinaire" at Jossey-Bass, to whom I first raised this book concept and who in turn found willing listeners. And to my talented editors, Karen Murphy, Byron Schneider, Leslie Stephen, and Michele Jones, who helped me bring my best ideas to life (while wisely coaching me away from the bad ones). What a privilege to count ace book promoter Barbara Henricks as both my friend and my book publicist. To Cheryl Rae for her tireless dedication and "always ready" attitude and design skills, to Kristen Friend for her promotion creativity, and to Margaret Sheridan, Carol Parenzan Smalley, and Judy Barrett for their valuable manuscript feedback and suggestions.

Getting access to great business stories is critical to my book writing, and many doors were opened for me. Heartfelt thanks go out to Margaret Sheridan, Ann Pincelli, Bruce Woolpert, Bob Gutermuth, Dennis Upah, Eleanor Chote, Dr. Linda Golden, Jennifer Malone, Harris Pappas, Chris Pappas, Rick Black, Kathy Smith-Willman, Sam Decker, Chris Daverse, Britt Jenkins, Wayne Craig, Suzanne Christopher, Jamie Rhodes, Zachary Hall, John Fix III, and Honi Puetz.

I thank Jeanne Bliss, Pat McMahan, Karen Post, Lisa Webb, Joene Grissom, Jim Bearden, Sarita Toma, Bill Fitzpatrick,

Suzanna Sugarman, Peggy Sheehan, and my Seekers classmates for always staying close and ready to lend an ear.

To family members who gave me strong roots: Mildred Griffin, Vent Griffin, Ada Marsh, Marsha Griffin Alexander, and all who came before them—and blazed the trail—I owe enormous thanks.

And last, but most important, I thank my husband and best friend, Mack Nunn. How did this girl get so lucky?

—J. G.

About the Author

Jill Griffin's clients call her The Loyalty Maker for good reason. Since 1988, she has led the Austin-based Griffin Group, helping firms around the globe build fiercely loyal customers. Clients served include Microsoft, Dell, Toyota, Marriott, Hewlett-Packard, Wells Fargo, and Western Union.

Jill's book *Customer Loyalty: How to Earn It, How to Keep It* was named to Harvard Business School's Working Knowledge list and has been published in six languages. Her coauthored book (with Michael Lowenstein), *Customer Winback,* earned Soundview Executive Book Summaries' Best Books Award.

Since 2003, Jill has served on the board of directors for restaurant chain Luby's Incorporated, a New York Stock Exchange company with 129 locations and over seven thousand employees. She has served on the marketing faculty at the University of Texas (UT) McCombs School of Business. Her books have been adopted as textbooks for MBA and undergraduate customer management courses taught at UT and other universities. Jill is a magna cum laude graduate, Distinguished Alumna recipient, and member of the board of advisers of the University of South Carolina Moore School of Business, from which she holds her MBA. An in-demand speaker, Jill keynotes conferences world-wide.

Subject Index